DICTIONARY
OF
GEMS AND GEMOLOGY

DICTIONARY
OF
GEMS AND GEMOLOGY

including

Ornamental, Decorative and
Curio Stones
(excluding diamonds)

A glossary of over 4000 English and foreign words,
terms and abbreviations that may be encountered in
English literature or in the gem, jewelry or art trades.

BY

ROBERT M. SHIPLEY
*Founder, Gemological Institute of America
and American Gem Society*

ASSISTED BY

The late ANNA McCONNELL BECKLEY
*Research Librarian, Gemological
Institute of America*

The late EDWARD WIGGLESWORTH, Ph.D., C.G.
Past President, Gemological Institute of America

AND

ROBERT M. SHIPLEY, JR.
*Formerly Director of Laboratories,
Gemological Institute of America*

Sixth Edition

Revised and Updated by the Staff of the
GEMOLOGICAL INSTITUTE OF AMERICA
1660 Stewart Street
Santa Monica, California 90404

PREFACE TO SECOND EDITION

Toward fulfillment of our purpose of meriting the acceptance of this **Dictionary** as an international reference source for the gemological profession, criticism of the first edition was invited from a number of outstanding gemologists, mineralogists and jewelers. As a result, errors of varying importance have been corrected and many definitions clarified.

Credit for revision is due principally to the coöperation of the following authorities: B. W. Anderson, FGA, Director of the Precious Stone Laboratory, London Chamber of Commerce; Dr. Sydney H. Ball, author of important reports and articles on diamonds and colored stones; Dr. Edward Gübelin, CG, FGA, internationally known gemologist and founder of the Swiss Gemmological Association; Dr. Edward H. Kraus, coauthor of *Mineralogy* and *Gems & Gem Materials;* Dr. G. F. Herbert Smith, author of *Gemstones* and president of the Gemmological Association of Great Britain; Dr. L. J. Spencer, translator of Bauer's *Precious Stones* and secretary of the Mineralogical Society of Great Britain; and A. Espositer, lapidary of New York City. George H. Marcher, CG, lapidary and authority on the gemstones of the western United States, contributed invaluable criticisms and suggestions.

To these men we are especially grateful for their generous assistance toward what we hope will be only the first of many improved editions of the *Dictionary* in future years.

PREFACE TO FIFTH EDITION

Since the last edition of the Dictionary of Gems and Gemology was printed in 1948, the most important gemological developments have occurred in the production of synthetic gem materials. These and other pertinent data have been incorporated in this later edition.

Further elaboration has been made in the introductory section entitled *The Use of the Book*. Much of the value to be obtained from this dictionary will be lost unless that section is studied and the instructions followed.

Robert M. Shipley

June 1, 1951

PREFACE TO SIXTH EDITION

Through five editions, the *Dictionary of Gems & Gemology* was written in the major part and edited in the remainder by Robert M. Shipley, GIA's founder. This edition has been revised and updated by the Institute staff.

Shipley, a jeweler of long experience, after taking courses in gemstones and gem identification in Europe, first taught gemology to jewelers in classes offered in the Extension Division of the University of Southern California. This effort was the forerunner of today's GIA.

He wrote GIA's original mail courses in fundamental and advanced gemology, diamonds, jewelry and silverware, and against overwhelming odds directed the early growth of an unique institution. As in the educational development, instrumentation, periodical and book-publishing activities, and the development of regional study groups, he won the aid and support of dedicated jewelers and outstanding authorities, plus jewelers' associations and trade publications, through his utter dedication to a dream — one he has seen realized in a remarkably productive life.

In the ensuing years, Shipley wrote several books, revised and expanded the courses, and helped to accumulate the necessary reserve to build the initial structure that housed GIA's permanent home in Los Angeles.

Robert M. Shipley retired in 1952, after launching the Institute and directing its activities for 21 years.

The GIA staff

January 1, 1971

THE USE OF THE BOOK

In determining the format of this book the compiler's principal
purpose was to produce a compact, all-inclusive reference
book that for the layman or the beginning student would
(1) be a pocket-sized volume, (2) contain a definition of
every unusual word or term used in any of its definitions,
and (3) contain all essential gemological information in
such form that it will create a demand that it be revised
and expanded frequently by the present compiler and his
successors in future years. To accomplish this principal
purpose, certain departures from conventional practice
have been made:

Titles in quotation marks mean that the name or term is incorrect or misleading, as evidenced by the definition. For example: "African jade" is an incorrect term for green
grossularite, as stated in the "African jade" definition.

Names or terms in bold type, whether in the body of the definition or at the end of it, mean that the reader should refer
to the entry for that name, to be sure that the full meaning
of the first definition is clear. Although the reader may
find no information that is new to him under the second
definition, even advanced students of gemology are advised
to follow this practice to assure accuracy.

The physical properties of varieties of gemstones are not included under the definition of the variety, unless such
properties are especially distinctive from those of the entire gem mineral species under which the properties are,
of course, listed.

All abbreviations used are defined in their alphabetic order.

All descriptive terms, such as those used in the nomenclature
of mineralogy, color, etc., are defined.

Such terms as *oriental amethyst, Colombian emerald, ruby
spinel* and others are listed but once as such. They are not
again listed under *amethyst, oriental; emerald, Colombian;
spinel, ruby* — as is the common practice.

Accent marks. A primary accent (') indicates the syllable of the word that receives the greatest emphasis; a secondary accent (") indicates that that receives secondary emphasis.

The dictionary's use as a gemological directory. An effort has been made to include the names, descriptions and addresses of organizations, museums, laboratories and periodicals that are especially concerned with gems.

Gemological titles are described.

The Dictionary of Gems & Gemology is primarily concerned with colored stones, pearls and their substitutes.

Diamonds are the subject of a companion dictionary by the same publisher, entitled THE DIAMOND DICTIONARY.

"Every other author may aspire to praise; the lexicographer can only hope to escape reproach."
— DR. SAMUEL JOHNSON

DICTIONARY

OF

GEMS AND GEMOLOGY

A

A or **A.U.** Abbreviation for Angström unit, as, 7900 A.

abalone (ab"a-lo'nee). The mollusc Haliotis, also known as an ormer or ear-shell. From Pacific waters of California, Mexico, Japan, N. Z., and other countries. See also **Haliotis**.

abalone pearl. A colored pearl from the **abalone**. Usually **a** blister pearl although a **true pearl** is found occasionally, especially in Mexico and California. Usually of pronounced green, pale green or pink hues.

abas. Persian weight for pearls. About 2.66 troy grains.

aberration (ab"er-ae'shun). The failure of a lens or mirror to bring the light rays to the same focus. When aberration is due to the form of the lens or mirror it is called *spherical aberration*. When due to the different refrangibility of light of different colors, it is called *chromatic aberration*. When present in magnifiers it often causes inaccurate decisions as to flawlessness or color of gems.

abrade. To wear away by friction; to produce abrasion. **See abrasive.**

abrasive (ab-rae'siv). A substance such as emery (powdered co-

rundum) used to wear away another substance by friction. Carborundum, diamond powder and other abrasives are used in **fashioning** gemstones.

absorption. (a) White light is a combination (blending) of those hues of the **spectrum** which are seen in the rainbow. The **hue** of a gemstone is due to the absorption of certain portions of white light in its passage through the gemstone. The remainder of the light which is not absorbed in the gemstone combines or blends to produce the hue seen. This process is called *selective absorption*. See also **selective reflection.** (b) The exact portions of white light which are absorbed by a gemstone or other substance may be determined by means of the spectroscope forming a band of colors known as an *absorption spectrum*. (c) Dark zones crossing the spectrum represent the portions of the light absorbed and are known as *absorption bands* or *absorption lines*. See **Fraunhofer lines.**

absorption bands. See **absorption.**

absorption lines. Same as **absorption bands.**

absorption spectrum (plural, spectra). See **absorption.**

1

accarbaar. Southeastern Asiatic name for black coral. See **akabar.**

accidental pearl. Genuine natural pearl as distinguished from (artificially induced) **cultured pearl.** A term not used in the trade as it is of questionable meaning.

acentela (Span.). Rock crystal.

acetylene tetrabromide. A **heavy liquid** used for specific-gravity determinations. Density, 2.964 at 20°C.; formula, $C_2H_2Br_4$. It may be reduced to lower figures by diluting with toluene or alcohol.

Achat (German). Agate.

achates. Ancient name for agate.

achirite. Same as **dioptase.**

achroite (ak'roe-ite). Colorless tourmaline.

achromatic. Free from hue. See **achromatic color; achromatic loupe.**

achromatic color. White, black, or any tone of neutral gray, i.e., gray containing no tinge of any **hue.** See **chromatic color.**

achromatic loupe. Any **loupe** containing an **achromatic lens.**

achromatic triplet. Loupe corrected for chromatic **aberration.** See **loupe.**

acicular. Needlelike.

aciform. Needle shaped.

acroita (Span.). Colorless tourmaline.

acrylic resin. A highly transparent synthetic resin. It is used widely in scientific and optical instruments and makes excellent imitations of sapphire, amethyst, emerald, ruby, topaz and garnet. Luster, vitreous; hardness, 2; fracture, uneven; specific gravity, approximately 1.18; and refractive index, 1.485 to 1.50. It is better

known to the British under the name **Perspex,** and to Americans as **Lucite.**

actinolite. A green calcium-magesium-iron amphibole of which **nephrite** and an **asbestos** are usually considered to be varieties (Dana; Kraus and Hunt). Occurs as fibers in prase, and as **macroscopic** inclusions in **sagenitic quartz** and other gemstones. S.G. 3.0-3.2. R.I. 1.61/1.64.

acute. Sharply pointed.

adamantine spar. A name for silky brown corundum. Same as **seal sapphire.** Now more generally applied to dull opaque corundum from India, ground for use as polishing agent.

adductor muscle. A muscle passing across from one valve of a **bivalve** to the other, for the purpose of closing the shell.

"Adelaide ruby." Blood-red **pyrope** (garnet) from South Africa.

adularescence (ad"-u-lar-es'-sence). An optical phenomenon applied to **feldspar** (usually, **orthoclase moonstone,** or **adularia)** that exhibits a floating, billowy, white or bluish light effect in certain directions as the stone is turned. It is caused by diffused light reflection from parallel intergrowths of **albite** feldspar, which has a slightly different refractive index from the main mass of orthoclase.

adularia (ad"ue-la'ria). A transparent to translucent, colorless to milky, gem variety of **orthoclase,** principally from Ceylon. Same as **precious moonstone.** See **orthoclase.**

aetites. Same as eagle stone

Afghanistan lapis. Fine blue, best quality **lapis lazuli** from Badakshan district, of Afghanistan, or

2

from just over the border in Russia. Better known in the trade as **Russian lapis.**

Afghanistan ruby. Ruby formerly mined near Kabul and also in Badakshan (Schlossmacher).

"African emerald." Deceiving name for green fluor; also for green tourmaline. See **African emerald.**

African emerald. Emerald from the Transvaal. It is usually yellowish green, flawed, and lacks the rich chrome green of fine Colombian stones. The caliber-size Sandawana emeralds, although from Rhodesia, are not usually called African emeralds.

"African jade." Green **grossularite.** Same as **"Transvaal jade."**

African nephrite. Same as **Transvaal nephrite.**

African pearl. True pearl found in small quantities on east coast of Africa between Zanzibar and Inhambane.

African tourmaline. (1) Trade term sometimes applied to all yellowish-green to bluish-green tourmaline whether or not from Africa. Same as **Transvaal tourmaline.** (2) A term sometimes used especially for fine, almost emerald-green, tourmaline from S. W. Africa.

africita (Span.). Black tourmaline.

Ag. Abbr. for the element silver.

agalmatolite or **pagodite.** Names applied to certain varieties of **pinite** (muscovite), pyrophyllite (pencil stone), and **steatite.** From all of these the Chinese fashion small images, miniature pagodas and other objects, which are generally sold as soapstone in North America. Soft (H. 1-3;

S.G. 2.7-2.9), compact, greenish, yellowish, brownish or grayish. An **ornamental stone.**

agaphite. A vitreous variety of **Persian turquoise.**

agata musgo (Port. and Span.). **Moss agate.**

agate (agg'-it). One of the many varieties of **chalcedony** (cryptocrystalline quartz). Best known in its curved, banded form, it also occurs in straight, parallel bands **(onyx)** and in a translucent form with dendritic inclusions **(moss agate).** It is found in virtually all colors, usually of low intensity, and translucent to semitransparent. Most gray-banded agate is dyed to improve its color. See **onyx, moss agate.**

agate jasper. Mixture of jasper and chalcedony. Same as **jaspagate.**

agate opal. See **opal agate.**

agate shell. Same as agate snail, a large land snail of no gemological interest.

agate ware. A variety of **Wedgwood** colored and marked to resemble agate.

agatiferous. Producing or containing **agate.**

agatine. Like, or pertaining to, **agate.**

agatize. To change into, or cause to resemble an **agate.**

agatized wood. A variety of **silicified wood** which resembles any variety of agate.

aggregate. Cluster or group. See **crystalline aggregate.**

Ago Bay. Historically and currently, the world center for Japanese cultured-pearl farming in Mie Prefecture, Honshu, Japan.

A. G. S. American Gem Society.

3

Agstein (German). Jet.

ahkan. Burmese name for bed rock, usually limestone, below the **byon.**

Ahlamah. The ninth stone in the breastplate of the High Priest. Generally accepted to have been an amethyst. Engraved with the name Dan.

Ahrens prism. A modification of the Nicol prism.

aigue-marine (French). Aquamarine.

ajkaite. A fossil resin.

à jour (a-zhoor) (French). Literally, allowing light to penetrate. Used to describe the method of setting a gem in any mounting which permits a view of its pavilion.

akabar. A name used for black coral in Indian Ocean region. See **accarbaar.**

akori. A porous coral which, previous to beginning of 18th Century was fished and fashioned and prized by the negroes of West African coast. Red, blue or violet. Has also been fished in Samoa; probably still used as gem by natives. The name has more recently been applied to substitutes such as rock, glass, and pearl with little nacre.

Al. Abbr. for the element aluminum.

"Alabandine ruby" (al″ a-ban′-din). Originally, almandine garnet from ancient Alabanda, Asia Minor. Now sometimes applied to violetish-red spinel.

alabaster. A translucent to semi-transparent massive form of gypsum. Usually snow-white in color. Easily carved. $CaSO_4.2H_2O$; H. 1½-2; S. G. 2.3. Calcite is also sometimes in-correctly called alabaster. See **Egyptian alabaster; oriental alabaster.**

alajites (Mexican). Altered **rhodonite** (Dwight).

alalite (al′a-lite). A mineral. Same as **diopside.**

alaqueca (Span.). Bloodstone.

albandine (al′ban-din). Same as almandine.

albite. A transparent to translucent, colorless, gray, reddish, greenish, bluish or yellowish species of the **plagioclase** series of the **feldspar** group, of which **albite moonstone, sunstone** and **aventurine feldspar** are varieties. Chemical composition, sodium-aluminum silicate $(NaAlSi_3O_8)$; crystal system, triclinic; hardness, 6 to 6½; specific gravity, 2.65; refractive index, 1.532-1.542; birefringence, .011; dispersion, .012.

albite moonstone. A variety of **albite feldspar** that exhibits a silvery, or pale-blue **adularescence.** Sources: Penn., N.Y. and Ontario, Canada.

alejandrita (Span.). Alexandrite.

"Alencon diamond." Rock crystal.

Aleppo stone. Eye agate.

alexanderite. A misspelling of alexandrite which has been used deceivingly for alexandrite-like synthetic sapphire or synthetic spinel.

Alexandrian turquoise. A trade term for **Egyptian turquoise.**

Alexandria shell. Mother-of-pearl.

"alexandrine." Incorrect name for **alexandrite-like sapphire;** also for so-called **"synthetic alexandrite."**

alexandrine sapphire or **alexandrite-like sapphire.** A sapphire; blue in daylight, changing to violet, purple or reddish under most artificial light. So named because **alexandrite** also changes color under similar conditions.

"alexandrite." Alexandrite - like synthetic spinel or synthetic sapphire. See **alexandrite.**

alexandrite (al"eg-zan'drite). A variety of **chrysoberyl,** emerald green in daylight, red to violet by ordinary artificial light. From Russia; Ceylon.

alexandrite cat's-eye. A chatoyant variety of alexandrite.

alexandrite-like tourmaline. Same as **chameleonite.**

Algerian coral. Trade term for coral of inferior quality from the Mediterranean Sea. More specifically only that from the coast of Algeria.

alladinite. A casein resin used as a mould material for many common objects.

allanite. A mineral which may very occasionally be cut as a gemstone (Eppler). Interesting only to gem collectors. Semitranslucent to opaque, reddish brown to pitch black with semimetallic luster. Mono. H. 5.5-6; S.G. 3.0-4.2; R.I. varies from 1.64 to 1.80. H. (Ca,Fe)$_2$(Al, Ce)$_3$Si$_3$O$_{13}$. From Saxony, N. Y., N. J., and a few other sources. Same as **orthite.**

allochromatic stone. A mineral that in its purest state would be colorless or white, but is often colored by submicroscopic impurities or inclusions of other minerals. Most gemstones are allochromatic. See **idiochromatic.**

allotrope. One of the forms assumed by an allotropic substance; e.g., diamond and graphite are allotropes of carbon.

allotropy, allotropism. The capac-

ity of existing in two or more conditions that are distinguished by differences in properties. Thus carbon occurs in the cubic system as diamond, in the hexagonal system as graphite, and in amorphous forms as charcoal.

alloy. An intimate combination of (1) two or more metallic elements, as bronze, which is an alloy of copper and silver, or (2) two or more metallic and nonmetallic elements, the principal one of which is a metal, as steel, which is an alloy composed principally of iron. An alloy, like a metal, is a **crystalline aggregate.** See **solid gold.**

alluvial. Pertaining to the action of rivers, or to unconsolidated material such as soil, sand and gravel which has been washed from one place and deposited in another. Such a **secondary deposit** is known as an **alluvial deposit** whether found in a still active river bed or one now covered by soil. See **detritus.**

alluvial deposit. An unconsolidated or loose deposit, such as gravel, sand, etc., deposited by rivers. (Wigglesworth).

alluvial fan. An outspread sloping deposit of boulders, gravel, and sand left by streams where they spread from a gorge upon a plain, or an open valley bottom.

alluvial stone. A mineral that has been transported and deposited by water. See **alluvial deposit.**

almandine (al'man-deen). (1) Gemologically, a red to purple to black species of garnet. Gem qualities transparent and usually purplish red. Fe$_3$Al$_2$(SiO$_4$)$_3$. Iso. H. 7½; S.G. 3.9-4.2; R.I., 1.76-1.81. Bi. none. Disp. 0.024. From many countries, including

Alaska, which produces few of gem use. **Almandite** is the mineralogical name. Purple variety of spinel is, rarely, called almandine, but more correctly. **almandine spinel.** (2) As an adjective a color designation meaning purplish-red or purple-red, as in **almandine spinel.**

almandine sapphire. Reddish purple sapphire.

almandine spinel. Reddish purple to purplish red spinel.

"almandite." This term has been deceivingly used as a trade name for synthetic almandine spinel. See **almandite.**

almandite (al′man-dite). Mineralogical name for almandine garnet. See **almandine.**

"almaz" (Russian, or Slavic). An uncut diamond.

almond stone. Almandine garnet.

almashite. A green or black variety of **Rumanian amber.** From Alamash Valley, Moldavia, Rumania.

alomite. Trade name for the fine blue **sodalite** quarried at Bancroft, Ontario, Canada, used as an ornamental stone. Also called princess blue.

aloxite. Proprietary name for a form of fused crystalline alumina, or artificial corundum.

alpha quartz. Quartz which has formed at less than 573°C. in veins, geodes and large pegmatites (Dana). Includes most of the quartz cut as gems. Atomic structure varies as temperature increases to this point when there is a distinct and permanent change to **beta quartz.** Wild states that most fired amethysts change in color from 200° or 300° up to about 573°

when they change to **topaz quartz.** Other authorities with less practical experience in heat treatment differ.

alpha zircon. A mineralogical name for any zircon with properties about S. G. 4.7; R. I. 1.92/1.98. Strongly birefringent, 0.059. Almost no other type is used in jewelry. See **zircon, beta zircon, gamma zircon.**

alshedite. Sphene.

altered stone. Any stone of which the appearance, especially the color, has been changed by any artificial means, whatsoever. Such change may be either external or internal. See **treated stone, coated stone, heated stone, stained stone.**

alumina. Aluminum oxide, the composition of colorless corundum. Synthetic ruby and sapphire is manufactured from powdered alumina.

alundum. A trade name for artificial corundum.

amaryl. A trade name for green synthetic sapphire.

amatista (Spanish). Amethyst.

amatista mosquito (Span.). Same as **mosquito amethyst.**

amatrice. Trade name for concretions of variscite (sometimes containing wardite), occurring in gray, reddish or brownish matrix of crystalline quartz (or chalcedony quartz or both), which may also contain inclusions of variscite or wardite or both. H. 5-7. See **amatrix.**

amatrix (abbreviation of American matrix). Same as **amatrice** which is the preferred American spelling.

amause. Same as **strass.**

amazonite (am'a-zon-ite). Bright green laminated variety of **microcline**. Used more as an ornamental stone than as a gemstone. Opaque. H. 6-6½ ; S.G. 2.5; R.I 1.52/1.53. From Russia, Virginia, Pike's Peak, Colo., and other sources. Same as **amazonstone**. Also see **feldspar**.

"Amazon jade." Amazonite.

amazonstone. The earlier and still popular name for **amazonite**. Also written *Amazon stone*.

amber. (1) A transparent to translucent **fossil resin** (a hydrocarbon). It was exuded from certain pine trees, particularly *Pinis Succinefere*, which flourished in Oligocene times more than 20 million years ago. It is usually yellowish or brownish but may also be red, orange, black, whitish, greenish, bluish or violetish or be stained various colors. Sometimes, amber contains the remains of insects or plants. **Pressed,** or **reconstructed,** amber is made by melting small fragments of the material and compressing it into blocks by hydraulic pressure. Crystallographic character, amorphous; hardness, 2 to 2½; specific gravity, 1.05 to 1.10; refractive index, 1.539 to 1.545 (usually, 1.54). Sources: southern shores of the Baltic Sea in Poland; shores of East Germany; Sicily; Mediterranean Sea off Sicily; Upper Burma; and Rumania. See **true amber, block amber, burmite, rumanite, simetite, succinite.** (2) A color designation meaning the color of orangy-yellow amber, as in **amber glass** and **amber opal.**

amber colophany. Same as **amber pitch.**

amber drop. Term describing a shape in which amber occurs.

amber forest. A fossil forest from which amber has been formed.

ambergris (am'ber-grees). A waxy substance found floating in tropical seas; a morbid secretion in the sperm whale, whence it is all believed to come. Valued in perfumery. Not used in jewelry. Often popularly confused with **amber.**

amberine. A local trade name of a yellowish green **chalcedony** from Death Valley, California (English).

amber lac. Same as **amber varnish.** Amber pitch powdered and dissolved in turpentine or linseed oil.

amberoid. A name for pressed amber.

amber, oil of. A reddish brown distillation of amber.

amber opal. Brownish-yellow variety stained by iron oxide.

amber pitch. The residue resulting from the distillation of oil of amber.

amber tear. Term describing a shape in which amber occurs.

amber varnish. Same as **amber lac.**

ambery. Amber-like.

ambra (Italian). Amber.

ambre (French). Amber.

ambre jaune (Fr., yellow amber). Amber in contrast to *amber gris* (Fr., grey amber). See **ambergris.**

ambrite (am'brite). A fossil resin occurring in large masses in New Zealand.

ambroid. Same as **amberoid.**

American Gem & Mineral Suppliers' Association. Founded in 1950, the Association consists of retailers, wholesalers, manufacturers, importers or publishers in the gem, mineral, lapidary and allied fields. The organization sponsors educational programs in the earth sciences, and provides exhibits and speakers for mineral, gem and lapidary societies. Scripts and colored slides are loaned to members without charge. Headquarters: P.O. Box 274, Costa Mesa, California 92627.

American Gem Society. A professional society of jewelers numbering approximately 1000 firms and 2500 individuals in the United States and Canada. Purpose: to promote high standards of business ethics and encourage gemological education among its members, in order to further the growth of the fine-jewelry business. The Society awards the titles of Registered Jeweler and Certified Gemologist to qualified members and member firms. Established 1934. Headquarters: 3142 Wilshire Blvd., Los Angeles, California 90005. See **Registered Jeweler, Certified Gemologist.**

American green jade. A Chinese trade name (Mei Kuo Lu) for a poor variety of light green jade, which because of its cheapness, became very popular with American tourists and exporters in China. The name was unheard of before World War I.

American jade. (1) Nephrite from Wyo. (2) A misnomer for **californite.**

American jet. Jet from Colorado and Utah. Former takes high polish but latter is full of cracks. Inferior to **Whitby jet.**

American pearl. A term often used to refer to fresh-water pearl of North America.

"American ruby." Red garnet.

American Stone Importers' Association, Inc. An association of firms that import genuine and synthetic stones to the United States. The principal function of the ASIA is to correct and improve conditions in the industry. Its purposes are to see that tariff laws are equitable; that nomenclature of stones is correct, both from an academic and commercial standpoint; that smuggling is eliminated; that any deceptive practices of merchants are exposed; that the industry knows that there are three classes of stones: genuine, synthetic and imitation; that the industry, both here and abroad, be kept aware of the organization's existence through advertising activities; and that any matter pertaining to stones be referred to the Association. The ASIA is strictly a trade group and does not indulge in any business enterprises. It co-operates with the United States Government and other governments whenever requested. Headquarters: 15 W. 47th St., New York City 10036.

American turquoise. Turquoise from the southwestern states of U.S.A. Usually pale blue or bluish green to greenish blue. Also known as **"Mexican turquoise."**

amethyst. (1) A pale violet to a deep purple transparent variety of crystalline **quartz** used as a gemstone. February birthstone. From Siberia, Brazil, Uruguay and other sources. See **Ahlamah.** (2) A color designation, same as **amethystine.**

amethystine. A color designation meaning violet to purplish, used as in amethystine glass, amethystine sapphire, and others.

amethystine quartz. Quartz of an amethyst color not necessarily in crystals or solidly colored or transparent.

amethystine sapphire. Violet to purplish sapphire.

amethyst point. Hexagonal amethyst crystal from an amygdaloidal geode. Usually possesses only the six (or sometimes three) termination crystal faces and usually graduated as to color with best color at point or apex and often colorless at base See **burnt amethyst.**

amethyst quartz. A term used loosely in the jewelry trade to designate badly flawed cabochon amethysts, especially those cut from **amethystine quartz.**

amorphous (a-mor'fus). A word meaning "without form" applied to minerals or **gem materials** that have no definite or orderly arrangement of atoms or **crystal structure** and hence no external **crystal form.** Sometimes incorrectly applied to **crystalline** minerals that lack external crystal form.

amphibole (am'fi-bole). A group of ferro-magnesium silicate minerals. This group of minerals is usually classified by German mineralogists as hornblende. See also **smaragdite.**

ampullar pearl. Any pearl such as a **true pearl** formed in the ampulla or epidermis of the mollusc, as distinguished from **cyst pearl** and **muscle pearl.**

amulet. A charm, or talisman, worn on the person to prevent disease or misfortune. Gems are so worn and may have been before man used them as adornment.

amygdaloid (a-mig'da-loid). An igneous rock having gas vesicles filled with secondary minerals.

amygdaloidal geode. (a-mig"da-loi'-dal). A geode which has formed in an **amygdaloid.** See also **geode.**

amygdule (a-mig'dule). A spheroidal aggregate of secondary minerals formed in a cavity of igneous rocks.

anaglyph (an'a-glif). Same as **cameo.**

Anakie sapphire. See **Queensland sapphire.**

analyzer. A polarizer placed above the objective in a polarizing microscope. In any polariscope the polarizer nearest the observer. See **polariscope.**

anatase (an'-ah-tace). A rare, transparent to opaque, dark-brown, reddish-brown, red, yellowish, bluish or black mineral species. The transparent brown or brownish-red material is sometimes cut for serious collectors. Chemical composition, titanium dioxide (TiO_2); crystal system, tetragonal (polymorphous with rutile and brookite); hardness, $5\frac{1}{2}$ to 6; specific gravity, 3.82 to 3.95; refractive index, 2.493-2.554; birefringence, .061. Sources: France, Brazil, Switzerland, Russia, Austria, Colorado and other localities. It is also known as **octahedrite,** because of its usual octahedral habit.

anatasia (Span.). Anatase.

anatherie. Same as **anitari.**

"Ancona ruby." A reddish or brownish quartz, colored by iron.

"andalusite." Incorrect trade name (rare) for brown tourmaline. See **andalusite.**

andalusite (an"-dah-loo'-site). A transparent to opaque, brownish-green, brownish-red, yellow-green, yellow-brown, green, gray or brown mineral species, the opaque variety of which is **chiastolite**, or **macle**. In transparent gem quality, it is prized for its very strong and attractive pleochroism: brownish-green in one direction and brownish red at 90°. Chemical composition, aluminum silicate (Al_2SiO_4—trimorphous (same chemical composition) with kyanite and sillimanite); crystal system, orthorhombic; hardness, 7 to $7\frac{1}{2}$ (chiastolite, $3\frac{1}{2}$ to $4\frac{1}{2}$); specific gravity, 3.16 to 3.20; refractive index, 1.634-1.643; birefringence, .007 to .013; dispersion, .016. Sources of transparent material: Brazil and Ceylon. See **chiastolite, viridine.**

andradite (and'-rah-dite). A transparent to opaque, green, yellowish-green, yellow, gray-green or black species of the **garnet** group, the varieties of which are **demantoid, topazolite** and **melanite**. Because of its intense green to yellowish-green color, coupled with its dispersion, brilliancy and luster, demantoid is the most desirable member of the garnet group, although it is very rarely found in sizes that will produce cut stones of more than a few carats. Chemical composition, calcium-iron silicate ($Ca_3Fe_2(SiO_4)_3$); crystal system, isometric; hardness, $6\frac{1}{2}$ to 7; specific gravity, 3.81 to 3.87; refractive index, 1.856 to 1.895 (usually, 1.875); birefringence, none; dispersion, .057. Garnet is the birthstone for January, and it is correct to use andradite or any other member of the garnet group for this purpose.

angel stone. A hard and highly silicified layer of clay or sandstone found just above the opal level in the Australian opal diggings. It often contains cracks filled with precious opal.

angle of incidence. The angle, which a ray of light, falling upon the surface of an object, makes with the perpendicular to that surface.

angle of polarization. That angle whose tangent is the index of refraction of a reflecting substance. (Dana.)

angle of reflection. The angle which a reflected ray of light, on leaving the exterior or interior surface of an object, such as a transparent stone or crystal, makes with the **normal** to that surface.

angle of refraction. The angle which a refracted ray of light, upon leaving the surface of an object, makes with the **normal** to that surface.

angle of total reflection. Same as **critical angle.**

Ångstrom unit. A unit used in spectroscopy for measurements below infra-red in the electromagnetic spectrum, which includes the visible spectrum. One ten-millionth of a millimeter.

anhydrous. Not containing hydrogen or water in its composition.

ani. Ceylon trade grade for pearls of fine luster, almost perfectly spherical in shape.

anisometric. Not **isometric.**

anisotropic (an-ei"so-trop'ik or troep'ik). Doubly refractive, affecting light differently as it passes along lines of different direction. See **refraction, isotropic; double refraction.**

anitarı or **anatherie pearl.** Ceylon trade name for slightly lower quality of pearl than **ani.**

anomalous. Abnormal.

anomalous double refraction. Double refraction in a normally **singly refractive** substance. Caused by internal strain. Seen by irregular extinction when substance is observed between crossed **Nicols,** as in synthetic spinel and sometimes in garnet. See **polariscope.**

anorthic system. Same as **triclinic system.**

anorthite. A basic plagioclase feldspar.

antelope jade. A descriptive term applied by Chinese to a particular color of jade.

Antero aquamarine. See **Colorado aquamarine.**

anthrax (Greek). Ruby, garnet, or other red stone.

antigorite. A brownish green **serpentine** resembling jade in appearance. H. 2.5; S.G. 2.4.

"Antilles pearl." Not a pearl but mother-of-pearl of a sea snail.

anygyi. Burmese term for second-water rubies.

anyum. Burmese term applied to first quality two-carat rubies.

Apache tears. Rounded, pebblelike, solid cores of unaltered **obsidian** that have weathered out of the decomposed obsidian flows (perlite) of the American West. They are usually translucent, a light- to dark-gray to gray-brown color, and average about one inch in diameter. Outstanding localities are Maricopa and Pinal Counties, Arizona.

apatite (a'pa-tite). A transparent green, blue, violet, purple, pink, yellow, or colorless gem mineral; except blue or green, is of light tone only. Also grey or brown, non-gem varieties. Hex. $Ca_5(F, Cl) (PO_4)_3$, H. 5; S.G. 3.2; R.I. 1.63/1.63-1.64/1.65; Bi. 0.002-0.005. Ceylon, Burma, Bohemia, Mexico, Maine, and other sources.

aphrizite. A rarely used name for black tourmaline from Norway.

aphroseline (Greek) Adularia.

aplanachromatic lens. A lens free from both chromatic **aberration** and **spherical aberration.** See **achromatic lens; aplanatic lens.**

aplanachromatic loupe. A loupe containing an **aplanachromatic lens.**

aplanatic lens (ap"la-nat'ik). A lens free from spherical aberration. See **aberration; apochromatic lens.**

aplanatic loupe. A loupe containing an **aplanatic lens.**

aplanatic triplet. An aplanatic lens composed of three portions cemented together to eliminate spherical aberration. A more popular name for this is the term *triple aplanat.*

apple jade. A descriptive term applied by Chinese to a particular color of jade.

appraisal. The estimation or fixing of a money value on anything, such as a gemstone. Differs from **valuation** and **evaluation.**

apricotine. Trade name for yellowish-red, apricot-colored quartz pebbles from near Cape May, New Jersey, used as gemstones. (English). Other authorities mention colors from red to reddish yellow, which would be close to orange in color and nearer the predominant color of apricot.

apya. Burmese term applied to

fine-quality flat rough rubies.

apyrite. A little - used name for peach-bloom colored tourmaline.

aquagem. Trade name for a light blue synthetic spinel (i.e.) a synthetic aquamarine spinel.

aquamarine (ak-wa-ma-reen'). (1) The pale or light green-blue to blue variety of beryl. H. 8; S.G. 2.68-2.75; R.I. 1.57/1.58-1.58/-1.59. From Brazil principally; also Madagascar, Russia, Ceylon and California. (2) A color designation meaning light blue to light bluish green as in **aquamarine glass; aquamarine tourmaline,** etc.

"aquamarine chrysolite." Greenish-yellow beryl.

"aquamarine emerald." Trade name for a genuine beryl or aquamarine triplet. See **"emerald triplet."**

aquamarine glass. A term loosely used for any light blue or greenish blue glass, regardless of its chemical composition or physical properties.

aquamarine sapphire. Pale blue sapphire.

aquamarine topaz. Greenish blue topaz.

aquamarine tourmaline. Pale greenish blue, sometimes pale blue, tourmaline.

aquamarine triplet. A genuine triplet which is used to imitate an emerald, and often incorrectly called an **"emerald triplet."** It consists of two portions of aquamarine with a cemented layer of green coloring matter between them.

aqueous. Of, pertaining to, or partly consisting of water.

aragonite (ar'-a-gon-ite). A mineral of chemical composition identical with **calcite** but differing from it as to crystal system, specific gravity, etc. Not a gemstone but is the principal constituent of the **pearl.** Ortho. $CaCO_3$. H. 3.5-4; S.G. 2.85-3.15; R.I. 1.53/1.68. Bi. 0.155.

arborescent (ar"bo-res'ent). Treelike in appearance.

arciscuro. Italian trade term for very dark red coral. Same as **carbonetto.**

arendalite. Dark green epidote from Norway.

argillaceous (ar" ji-lae' shus). Consisting of or containing clay.

Arizona peridot. Peridot from Arizona, usually found in small sizes and light tones.

"Arizona ruby." Deep red pyrope (garnet) from Arizona and Utah.

"Arizona spinel." Deep-red pyrope (garnet) from Arizona and Utah. Same as **"Arizona ruby."**

Arkansas pearl. Fresh-water pearl from rivers in Arkansas, once a larger producer of pearls than any other state.

Arkansas stone. Not a gem. An oil or hone stone.

arlequines (Mexican). Precious opals.

Armenian stone. (1) Lapis lazuli. (2) An old name for azurite.

artificial ivory. See **ivory, artificial.**

artificial stone. A stone which is either an **imitation stone** or a **synthetic stone.**

artificial or **simulated pearl.** Same as **imitation pearl.**

Aru, Aroe, or **Aroo pearl. Fine pearl** from the Aru Islands south of Dutch New Guinea. Less silvery white than **Australian pearl.**

As. Abbr. for the element arsenic.

asah. Burmese term for third-water rubies.

asbestos or **asbestus.** A name for fibrous varieties of actinolite, tremolite, and other amphiboles, and for chrysotile, which is a variety of serpentine which possesses unusual heat - resisting properties (Kraus and Hunt). Only actinolite of differing varieties is of gemological interest. See·also **blue asbestos.**

aschentrecker or **aschentrekker.** A Dutch name for tourmaline given it when first imported to Holland from Ceylon. Meaning "ash drawer," it referred to its capacity for attracting ashes as it cooled. See **pyroelectricity.**

aschtrekker. See **aschentrekker.**

ash drawers. Early name applied to tourmaline because of its electrical property.

asparagus stone. Transparent yellowish green **apatite.**

assembled cameos. Cameos made of two or more portions cemented together. See **assembled stone; composite stone.**

assembled stone. The term introduced by Shipley in 1931 for any stone constructed of two or more parts of gem materials whether they be genuine, imitation or both. An alternate term **composite stone** was later suggested by Webster of London. See **doublet; foil back; triplet.**

asteria (as-te′ria). Any gemstone which, when cut cabochon in the correct crystallographic direction, displays a rayed figure (a star) by either reflected or transmitted light. See **diasteria; epiasteria; star.**

asteriated (as-te′ri-ate″ed). Like a star—with rays diverging from a center.

asteriated beryl. A variety of beryl which in thin sections exhibits **diasterism.** As yet of no gemological importance.

asteriated stone. (Asteriated ruby, sapphire, etc.) Stone exhibiting a star by either reflected or transmitted light. See also **star stone.**

asterism. The optical phenomenon of a rayed figure possessed by an **asteria.** See **diasterism; epiasterism.**

asterite (French). Star quartz.

astrumite. A trade name for greygreen Tibet **stone.**

athaibouk. Burmese term applied to ¾ carat rubies.

"Atlas ore." Malachite.

"Atlas pearls." White satin-spar.

Atlas spar. Same as **satin-spar.**

Atlas stone. Same as **satin-spar.**

atom. When ordinarily used in mineralogy, or gemology, refers to the smallest particle of an element which exists either alone or in combination with similar particles of the same or a different element. See also **molecule.**

atomic plane. Any one of the layers into which **atoms** form themselves in an orderly pattern during the growth of a **crystal.**

atomic structure. The arrangement of atoms in a substance. See **amorphous; crystal structure.**

attached crystal. One which is attached to the mother rock, usually **singly terminated.**

Au. Abbr. for the element gold.

Aurora Borealis. A trademarked name for glass that has been coated with an extremely thin, iridescent layer of some compound, usually a fluoride, sputtered on in a vacuum to create a colorful effect.

Australian emerald. Usually light green beryl, rarely sufficiently dark to be classed as emerald in the American trade. Principally from 9 miles NE of Emmaville, New South Wales, where a few of fine color have been found. From Poonah, West Australia, and a few other localities. Mostly pale (green beryl), and badly flawed.

Australian jasper. Jasper speckled with red and light grey flecks

Australian opal. Any opal from Australia, but the term is often restricted to mean only the black opal. Usually fashioned in flat, polished slabs with beveled or perpendicular sides, instead of in cabochons. Smith lists S.G. as 2.12. See **black opal; light opal.**

Australian pearl. (1) A trade grade including silvery white **fine pearl** from both (a) the *Meleagrina margaritifera* which is found in the waters north of Australia and yields **Thursday Island pearl,** and (b) the *Meleagrina maxima* of the northwest coast of Australia, which yields most of the **Broome pearl.** All these pearls are much whiter and have less orient than **Celebes pearl, Manila pearl** and others from Australasia. (2) As a geographical classification, any pearl from any Australian waters, including the yellowish **Shark's Bay pearl.**

"Australian ruby." Misnomer for red garnet.

Australian sapphires. Sapphires from Australia, most of which are olive green or bluish green. The blue variety is usually very dark greenish or blackish. *As a trade term,* very dark blue or blackish sapphires.

Australian zircon. Genuine zircon from Australia including (a) brown, red or yellow varieties from near Anakie, in Queensland, which are especially sensitive to light or heat, the light yellow becoming blue by heat: (b) hyacinth from Campbell Island and (c) colorless and dark red zircon from New South Wales. See also **Tasmanian zircon.**

australite. A local name for **tektite** from New South Wales, Western, Victoria and South Australia and Tasmania. Some of the specimens have a characteristic button shape, complete with a flange around the edge.

Austrian emerald. An emerald whose occurrence and inclusions are similar to **Russian emerald.** Usually cloudy to almost opaque, and of dark emerald green, or light green color, which is sometimes irregularly distributed. Rarely of gem quality. From near Salzburg, Austria.

autoclave. A metal container, built to withstand high temperatures and pressures, used for the manufacture of synthetic minerals.

Avanturine (German). Aventurine.

aventurescence. Word used to describe the metallic spangled effect seen, in reflected light, in aventurine and aventurine feldspar. A sort of **schiller** but more scintillating.

aventurine (ah-ven'-chu-rin). (1) Translucent, grayish, greenish, brown or yellowish **quartzite** (a massive granular kind of quartz) that exhibits bright or strongly colored reflections **(aventurescence)** from inclusions of tiny platelets or flakes of another mineral. Fuchsite, a chromium mica, produces a greenish spangled effect (the most commonly encountered kind); mica, a silvery brassy or golden glitter; and hematite or goethite, reddish metallic reflections. Sources: India, Russia, Brazil, Spain and Chile. (2) Aventurescence in **albite feldspar** caused by inclusions of hematite or goethite, as above. Sources: California, Norway and Russia.

aventurine feldspar. See **sunstone.**

aventurine glass. Same as **goldstone.**

Avicula. The genus of salt-water bivalves allied to and in some cases including the principal pearl-bearing molluscs. See **Aviculidae; Meleagrina.**

Aviculidae (av"i-kue'li-de). The family of **bivalves** which include among others the principal pearl bearing molluscs. Same as **Pteriidae.**

axe stone. Nephrite.

axes. (Plural of axis). See **crystallographic axes.**

axial angle (optic). See **optic axial angle.**

axinite (ak'-sin-ite). A rare, transparent to translucent, purplish-brown, brownish-red, brownish-yellow, brownish-gray, bluish-gray, grayish-violet, violetish-blue or light-gray mineral species, usually occurring in low-intensity colors, and occasionally cut for collectors.

Chemical composition, a complex hydrous calcium-aluminum borosilicate $(CaFe)_7Al_4B_2(SiO_4)_8)$; crystal system, monoclinic; hardness, $6\frac{1}{2}$ to 7; specific gravity, 3.27 to 3.30; refractive index, 1.678-1.688; birefringence, .010. Sources: France, Nevada, California, England, Baja California, Mexico, and elsewhere.

axis. See **crystallographic axes.**

azabache (Mexican) . Jet.

azorite. A little used synonym for zircon.

Aztec Eagle Opal. Same as **El Aguila Azteca Opal.**

Aztec stone. A name for greenish smithsonite; also for green turquoise. See also **chalchihuitl.**

azurchalcedony. Same as **chrysocolla quartz** or **azurlite.**

azure. Lapis lazuli (Standard).

azure malachite. Same as **azurmalachite.**

azure quartz. Same as **sapphire quartz.**

azure spar. Lazulite.

azure stone. Same as (1) **lapis lazuli;** (2) **azurite.**

"**azurite.**" Trade term for sky-blue **smithsonite.** See **azurite.**

azurite (azh'-u-rite). A semitransparent to opaque, intense, darkblue to violetish-blue mineral species, used more for ornamental objects than as a gemstone. An important ore of copper, it is often intimately associated with malachite, when it is called **azurmalachite.** Chemical composition, copper carbonate $(Cu_3(OH)_2(CO_3)_2)$; crystal system, monoclinic (commonly massive and fibrous; transparent crystals rare); hardness, $3\frac{1}{2}$ to 4; specific gravity, 3.75 to

15

3.89 (porous material as low as 3.25) ; refractive index, 1.730-1.838; birefringence, .110. Sources: Russia, France, England, the Congo, South-West Africa, Arizona, New Mexico and elsewhere.

azurlite or **azurchalcedony** (azh'-ure-lite, a'zhure-lite).Chalcedony colored blue by chrysocolla, from Arizona, used as a gemstone. See **chrysocolla quartz.**

azurmalachite. Intergrowth of azurite and malachite, in compact form is cut and polished as an **ornamental stone.** When botryoidal it is sometimes fashioned as gem stones of beauty, but it lacks durability.

B

B. Abbr. for the element boron.

Ba. Abbr. for the element barium.

Babel quartz. A variety of rock crystal so named for its fanciful resemblance to the successive tiers of the Tower of Babel.

Babylonian quartz. Same as **Babel quartz.**

bacalite. A variety of amber said to be from Baja California, Mexico (English).

back (of a gemstone). The pavilion.

bacon stone (obsolete). A variety of **steatite.**

Badakshan lapis. Lapis lazuli from SE of Faisabad, Badakshan district, Afghanistan. Deep violetish blue; also green. Also deep violetish blue lapis from near Khorog, in Russian Badakshan.

"Baffa diamond." Rock crystal.

baffle. A baffle plate. A plate in an optical instrument which checks, deflects or otherwise controls light in a desired manner, as in the **Diamondscope,** in which it checks any direct rays which might pass from the source through a stone to the eye, directing them to a reflector which redirects them into the stone from the side.

bague (bag') (French). A ring.

baguette (ba-get'). French word meaning *a rod.* A style of **step cut** for small gems, rectangular in outline. Often called cushion cut by dealers in the colored stone trade.

Bahia (ba-ee'a). A gem-bearing state or territory in Brazil. Also a name for diamonds from this territory.

Bahia amethyst. Amethyst from Bahia, generally of lighter violet tone than Uraguay amethyst but more often reddish and smoky in appearance.

Bahia emerald. Light slightly yellowish green beryl from Bahia. See **Brazilian emerald.**

bakelite. A resinoid or plastic made of phenol (carbolic acid) and formaldehyde. Used as a substitute for amber. Can be dyed various colors. S.G. 1.25-1.28; R.I. 1.54-1.70 (usually 1.62-1.66).

balance. A scale, such as used to determine S.G. or to weigh gems.

balas. (1) Same as "balas ruby." (2) A term listed by Pough as being used in Brazil for a gem fragment of tourmaline from which the non-gem layers have been removed.

"balas ruby" (bal'as). Rose-red spinel. Differs in color from ruby spinel.

"balias ruby." Same as "balas ruby."

ball jasper. Jasper which occurs in spherical masses.

ball pearl. Name given to round pearl by pearlers at the inland fisheries of the United States.

Baltic amber. (1) In the jewelry trade, a name usually confined to **succinite,** which is found on shores of all countries on the Baltic Sea. (2) According to some authorities succinite and gedanite, which are the only Baltic fossil resins often seen in the trade. (3) **Succinite, gedanite, glessite, beckerite, krantzite and stantienite,** (Schlossmacher).

Baltimorite. Picrolite from Maryland.

banco (pl. bancos). The series of benches each about one meter in height, cut from hillsides in emerald mines of Colombia

banded agate. Agate with colors usually disposed in parallel bands, which are more or less wavy. Most agate in the trade is dyed and bands are of differing tones due to their varying ability to absorb dye. See **agate; onyx; chalcedonyx; chalcedony onyx.**

banded jasper. Jasper banded like agate, frequently in distinct colors.

banded obsidian. Obsidian with differently colored irregular bands.

Barbara beryl. Term applied to beryl from near Barbara in northeastern Transvaal, a source of African emerald.

Bareketh or **Bereketh.** Third stone in Breastplate of High Priest. Often translated as emerald, but probably amazonite. Engraved with the name of Levi.

barite (bare'-ite; bay'-rite). A transparent to semi-transparent, colorless, white, gray, pale-yellow, brown, reddish, greenish or blue mineral species. Chemical composition, barium sulphate ($BaSO_4$); crystal system, orthorhombic (also massive); hardness, 3 to $3\frac{1}{2}$; specific gravity, 4.30 to 4.60; refractive index, 1.636-1.648; birefringence, .012. Cut infrequently for collectors. A brown stalagmitic variety, with a concentric structure at right angles to the length of the stalagmite, has been fashioned as an ornamental stone. Some massive material has a slight chatoyancy. Sources: widespread.

barium glass. Glass of unusually high S.G. and high R.I. used rarely in the manufacture of imitation stones.

baroque. In the jewelry field, baroque means *irregular in shape;* e.g., baroque pearls, tumble-polished gem materials.

baroque pearl (ba-roke'). Any pearl of very irregular form, including slug pearl. See also **oriental baroque.**

barrok or **barock pearl.** Baroque pearl.

basal. Parallel to the basal pinacoid of a crystal; a direction perpendicular to the principal axis of a **prism.**

basalt (ba-solt' or bas'olt). A basic igneous rock, dark and compact.

basanite (baz'a-nite). (1) Lydian stone, or touchstone. Velvety black quartz used for testing the color of the streak of metals. Not a gemstone. (Kraus) (2) Black jasper (Dana; Eppler).

base. (1) The portion of a cut stone which is below the girdle; the pavilion. (2) The basal plane of a crystal. (3) Same as **base price.**

base price (of pearls). The price of a single pearl is computed by squaring its weight in grains and multiplying the result by the base rate. This scheme of establishing the price of a pearl takes into consideration the fact that small pearls are many times more common than large ones and that their value therefore increases as the square of their weight. For example: The price of a pearl weighing 8.64 grains, the base rate of which is $11, is $821.15. (This is computed as follows: $8.64 \times 8.64 = 74.65$. The latter (when multiplied by the unit of money in any country) is known as the "once." Multiplying 74.65 by $11 base = $821.15, which is the price of an 8.64 grain pearl at $11 base.) If there are two pearls of approximately equal size, weighing 10 grains with a base rate of $9 they are figured as follows: $10 \div 2 = 5$ grains. 5×10 grains = 50 (once). $50 \times \$9 = \$450$. Expressed as a formula: the average size, times the total weight, times the base rate = the price of a group of pearls.

basic igneous rocks. Those low in silica; heavy and generally dark-colored.

baskets. Brass sieves used in Ceylon for separating pearls of different sizes. See **peddi.**

bas-relief (bah-re-leef'). Extending but slightly from the background, as the figures (designs) in most **cameos.** The same as **low relief.**

bastard amber. Cloudy amber.

bastard emerald. Peridot.

"bastard jet." A soft variety of Canadian jet.

bastard quartz. A miner's term for white glassy quartz found unassociated with other minerals.

bastite. A light green bronzite, altered more or less completely to **serpentine.** H. 3.5; S.G. 2.5-2.7. Also called schiller spar.

bati xaga. Term meaning arrow obsidian used by Pomo Indians of California for obsidian which was not as hard as **dupa xaga** (S. H. Ball).

Baumstein (German). Tree stone. Same as **mocha stone.** See **Moosstein.**

"Bavarian cat's-eye." Quartz cat's-eye, from Hof and other locations in Bavaria which produce only a few stones of fine quality. Other qualities usually sold as "Hungarian cat's-eye." Quartz cat's-eye from Harz Mountains in north of Germany is sometimes sold as Bavarian cat's-eye.

bayate. A local name for a brown ferruginous variety of jasper from Cuba.

Bazaruto pearl. True pearl from Bazaruto Islands near Zanzibar. See **African pearl.**

bdellium. (dell'i-um). A substance mentioned in Genesis (II. 12). Variously translated by different authorities to be pearl, a red stone, a resin, or no stone at all but manna.

Be. Abbr. for the element beryllium.

bead. The bead usually is essentially spherical, with or without facets, but is distinguished by the fact that it always has a hole drilled through the center.

beccarite. An olive-green **alpha zircon** from Ceylon. S.G. 4.7; R.I. 1.93/1.98. Biaxial positive.

beckerite. A **fossil resin.**

"beckite." Same as **beekite.**

beef · blood ruby. Term used in England for a subdivision of Burma rubies. Darker tone of red than pigeon's blood. See **pigeon blood ruby.**

beekite. Silicified coral. See especially **coral agate.**

Beilby layer. The mirror-like surface layer, on all well-polished stones other than diamond, which seems to be caused by a fusion of tiny surface projections on the stone during the polishing operation. In corundum and quartz this layer is crystalline; in zircon and spinel it is amorphous and "pits" more easily than other stones (Smith).

belgite. Same as **willemite.**

bell pearl. Bell- or pear-shaped pearl.

belomorite. A variety of moonstone from near the White Sea (Russia).

"Bengal amethyst." Purple sapphire.

benitoite (be-nee'toe-ite). A transparent pale blue to deep blue colored gem species found only in San Benito County, Calif. In color resembles the sapphire, but is easily distinguished because of inferior hardness and distinctly different dichroic colors. Hex. BaTiSi₃O₉. H. 6-6½; S.G. 3.6; R.I. 1.76/1.80. Bi. 0.047. Disp. 0.039-0.046 (very high.) Discovered 1907.

Berekketh. See **Barekketh.**

berigem. (Copyrighted name). Chrysolite-colored synthetic spinel.

berilo (Span.); **berilo** or **berilio** (Port.); **berillo** (Ital.). Beryl.

berilo verdemar (Span.). **Aquamarine.**

berkeyite. A transparent variety of lazulite from Brazil.

Berman balance. A sensitive torsion spring balance made by Roller-Smith Co. for rapidly and accurately determining the S.G. of stones weighing less than 2 carats. See **specific gravity.**

Bernstein (bearn' shtine). German name for amber.

beryl (bare'-il). A transparent to translucent mineral species, the gem varieties of which are **emerald, aquamarine, morganite, heliodor** and **goshenite.** Chemical composition, beryllium-aluminum silicate (Be₃Al₂(SiO₃)₆); crystal system, hexagonal; hardness, 7½ to 8; specific gravity, 2.67 to 2.84; refractive index 1.565/1.570-1.592/1.599; birefringence, .005 to .009: dispersion, .014.

beryl cat's-eye. Beryl with a **cat's-eye** effect. Extremely rare.

beryl glass. Same as beryllium glass, or fused beryl. Includes emerald glass colored with chrome oxide, and a blue glass used for imitation gems. H. 6½; S.G. 2.44; R.I. 1.51-1.52 (Anderson).

berylite (copyrighted name). Rose-colored synthetic spinel of same color as balas ruby.

berylline. Like a beryl (Webster).

beryllium. An element (metallic). A principal constituent of beryl. See also **beryllium glass.**

beryllium glass. Consisting either of same chemical composition as that of the mineral beryl, or so closely approaching it as to be analysis proof, but not crystalline. See **beryl glass.**

beryllonite (bare-ill'-oh-nite). A very rare, transparent, colorless to light-yellow mineral species. Chemical composition, sodium-beryllium phosphate (NaBePO₄); crystal system, monoclinic (with pseudo-orthorhombic symmetry); hardness, 5½ to 6; specific gravity, 2.83-2.87; refractive index, 1.552-1.562; birefringence, .010; dispersion, .010. It is very seldom used as a gemstone, having only its rarity to recommend it. Sources: the Stoneham and Newry regions, Oxford Co., Maine.

beryloscope. A color filter, same as the **emerald glass.**

beryl triplet. Correct name for a genuine triplet made from two portions of greenish or colorless beryl with a cemented layer of green coloring matter between them. Often incorrectly called **emerald triplet.**

beta quartz. Quartz that has formed at high temperatures (573° to 870° C.), as in graphic granite, granite pegmatites and porphyries. It has a lower refractive index and birefringence than **alpha quartz.**

beta zircon. Mineralogical name for any zircon with properties intermediate between alpha and gamma zircons. In the heat process used to change zircon colors the properties are converted into those of alpha zircon. See **zircon, alpha zircon, gamma zircon.**

betel nut jade. A descriptive term applied by the Chinese to a particular color quality of jade.

bevel cut. A term applied to any style of cutting with a very large table, joined to the girdle by one or sometimes two bevels, and a pavilion which may be step cut, brilliant cut or any other style. Used mostly for opaque stones, and often intaglios. Bevel cut shapes include: round, square, cushion, rectangular, ob-

long, oval, pendeloque, navette, heart, d i a m o n d, horseshoe, shield, pentagon, and hexagon shapes. The style is used predominantly for less valuable gems. Also known as **table cut.**

bezel. (1) That portion of a brilliant-cut gemstone above the girdle; same as **crown.** (2) More specifically, the sloping kite-shaped facets between the girdle and the table. (3) Still more specifically, only a small part of that sloping surface just above the girdle; the co-called **setting edge.**

bezel facets. The eight facets on the crown of a round brilliant cut gem, the upper points of which join the table and the lower points, the girdle. If the stone is a cushion-shaped brilliant, four of these bezel facets are called corner facets.

bezil. Same as **bezel.**

Bi. Abbr. used in this book for **birefringence.** See also **D.R.**

bianco. Italian trade-name for white precious **coral.** The word means *white.*

biaxsal or **biaxial** (bie-ak′sal or bie-ak′si-al). Having two **optic axes** and, therefore, two optic directions, a property possessed by crystals of the orthorhombic, monoclinic and triclinic systems only, all of which are anisotropic. See **biaxial stone.**

biaxial stone. Stone having two directions of single refraction. See **biaxial.**

"bicycle tires." Brilliant-cut diamonds with girdles which are too thick.

bijouterie (bee″zhoot-ree′) (Fr.) General term applied to all jewelry in which metal work is most important. See also **joaillerie**.

bike. Same as **boke**.

billitonite. Moldavite (tektite) from Billiton Island, Dutch East Indies.

bion. An alterate spelling of **byon**.

bird's-eye quartz. Jasper containing minute spherulites of usually colorless quartz.

birds'-eyes. Term applied by American fishermen to pearls which have slight imperfection on the best surface.

birefringence (bi-re-fring'-enz). The strength, or measure, of double refraction, the amount being measured by the difference between the refractive indices of the ordinary and extraordinary rays in uniaxial stones and between the alpha and gamma rays in biaxial stones. This difference is expressed by numerals (e.g., .006 for danburite), the R.I. of the alpha ray being 1.630 and of the gamma ray, 1.636. **Synthetic rutile** has the highest birefringence (.287) of any gem material.

Birne (German). Same as **boule**.

birthstones. In 1952, the Jewelry Industry Council sponsored the following list, which was subsequently accepted and approved by the American Gem Society, the American Stone Importers' Association and the National Retail Jewelers' Association (at that time the American National Retail Jewelers' Association and the National Jewelers' Association). It will be noted that the major changes consisted of adding alexandrite as a choice for June and replacing lapis-lazuli with zircon for December: January, garnet; February, amethyst; March, aquamarine or bloodstone; April, diamond; May, emerald; June, pearl, moonstone or alexandrite; July, ruby; August, peridot or sardonyx; September, sapphire; October, opal or pink tourmaline; November, topaz or citrine; December, turquois or zircon.

Biseau cutting. Same as **bevel cut**.

bishop's stone. Amethyst.

bivalve (bie'valv). A mollusc having two shells. See **univalve**.

Biwa pearl. A cultured fresh-water pearl grown at Lake Biwa, Shiga Province, Honshu, Japan, the largest fresh-water lake in Japan and the center of the fresh-water pearl-farming industry in that country. Some of the pearls are grown with nuclei and others with only mantle tissue, to initiate the formation of the pearl sac. The nonnucleated product is typically white, baroque in shape, has an attractive luster, and is about 3 x 6 millimeters in size. The hosts are the fresh-water mussels *Hyriopsis Schlegeli* and *Cristaria Plicata*.

bizel. Same as **bezel**.

black amber or stantientite. A fossil resin of rare occurrence.

black andradite garnet. Melanite.

black and white onyx. Onyx with alternate black and white bands, from which many cameos are cut. The black bands are sometimes produced (permanently) by artificial process.

black chalcedony. Correct designation for most of the so-called "black onyx."

black coral. A corallike, black to dark-brown horny substance *(An-*

22

tipathes Spiralis), distinct from precious coral. It is used in beads, bracelets, art objects, etc., and is highly regarded by the natives of the East Indian Islands. Hardness, 2½ to 3; specific gravity, 1.37. Sources: Malaya, Red Sea, Bermuda, Hawaii and the Mediterranean. It is also called **king's coral** and **akabar.**

black garnet. Melanite (andradite garnet).

"black onyx." Incorrect name for black single colored agate or chalcedony which is usually colored artificially. Properly called **black chalcedony.** See **onyx.**

black opal. Opal of black or other very dark color exhibiting play of color. Fine specimens from Australia are most desirable of opals. See **Australian opal.**

black pearl. A trade name which in the narrowest usage refers to a black or almost black pearl, or sometimes to a grey pearl; but in its broadest sense refers to a brown or a dark blue, blue-green, or green pearl with a pronounced metallic sheen.

"Black Prince's Ruby." A famous red spinel in the British Imperial State Crown, once thought to be a ruby. Still uncut. Length almost 2 inches, or 5 cm. Weight unrecorded.

black sapphire. The black (or very dark tones of brown, purple, green or blue) variety of sapphire, popular only if asteriated. See **sapphire.**

black seed pearl. Very small blackish pearl from the *Pinna* mollusc. See **seed pearl.**

Black Star of Queensland. This stone, found in 1948 in Australia's Anakie sapphire field, Queensland, is the largest asteriated corundum of any color ever reported. Weighing 1165 carats in the rough, it weighed 733 carats after cutting and measured 2¾₁₆ x 2⁷⁄₃₂ x 1½₃₂ inches. It has a fine star, is oval in shape, and is about the size of a hen's egg. The stone was presented to the Smithsonian Institution, Washington, D.C. (where it is on display) by Kazanjian Bros., Los Angeles gem dealers.

bladed. A mineralogical term used to describe the long, flat, knife-bladelike habit of some minerals. Examples: kyanite and some coarse jadeite.

bleached pearl. Pearl which has been lightened in color. See **over-bleached pearl.**

blebby. Containing bubbles, cavities or vesicles.

blende. Same as **sphalerite.**

blended pearls. Pearls blended in a necklace according to close similarity of hue, tone and intensity of color. See **matched pearls.**

blister pearl. Pearly concretion attached to the shell and therefore not **true pearl.** Flattened, irregular and sometimes contains clay, water, etc., and occasionally a true pearl. See **true pearl.**

block amber. Natural amber, as it has been found; as distinguished from pressed **amber.**

blood agate. (1) Flesh-red, pink, or salmon-colored agate from Utah. (2) **Hemachate.**

blood coral. Name sometimes applied to intense red coral.

blood ironstone. Hematite.

blood jasper. Bloodstone.

bloodstone. Same as **heliotrope,** an

23

impure variety of chalcedony. Also an ancient name for **hematite**. See **plasma**.

"blue alexandrite." Incorrect name for alexandrite-like sapphire.

blue asbestos. Same as **crocidolite**.

bluebacks. Shell of a variety of **Haliotis**.

blue chalcedony. See **"sapphirine."**

blue chrysoprase. Chalcedony colored by inclusions of chrysocolla. Same as **chrysocolla quartz, azurlite and azurchalcedony**.

blue coral. A variety of **akori**.

blue earth. A greenish sand in which succinite occurs in East Prussia.

blue-gray. In **color nomenclature system** of North American gemology, a color midway between vivid blue and **neutral gray**.

blue-green. In **color nomenclature system** of North American gemology the hue midway between blue and green. Same as **greenblue**.

blue jasper. See **"Swiss lapis."**

blue john. The massive, crystalline variety of **fluorite**, often having curved bands of bluish violet to purple and a reddish to colorless background. It is used principally for carved decorative objects. The primary source is Treak Cliff, near Castleton, Kinderscout, Derbyshire, England.

"blue malachite." Incorrect name for **azurite**.

"blue moonstone." Bluish chalcedony. See **blue moonstone**.

blue moonstone. Term frequent'y applied to fine quality piecious moonstone of bluish tinge; also incorrectly applied to chalcedony artificially colored blue.

"blue onyx." Incorrect name for single colored blue agate or chalcedony which is dyed blue.

blue opal. Precious **Australian opal** from Queensland, with bluish body color.

blue pearl. Dark-colored pearl of opaque slate-blue color sometimes caused by a layer of conchiolin near the surface. Also may be caused by a center of mud or silt, although recent investigation indicates that the color is usually caused by various impurities in the **aragonite** (or calcite). See **pearl**.

blue point pearl. Pearl from a fresh-water mussel *(Quadrula undulata)* known as blue-point or three ridge mussel, which was largest North American producer of pearl.

blue schorl. (1) The earliest name for octahedrite. (2) Blue tourmaline.

blue spar. Lazulite.

"blue talc." A misnomer for **kyanite**.

blue-violet. In **color nomenclature system** of North American gemology the hue midway between blue and violet. Same as **violetblue**.

blue white. (1) A term most often used, except in the jewelry trade, to mean a color more white than blue. (2) In the North American jewelry trade, a term once used for a **color grade** of diamond, which, to experts, appeared (a) more bluish than yellowish in diffused daylight free from bluish reflections, or (b) colorless when examined by **transmitted light**. Now widely used for any diamond color grade between (a) that grade which appears colorless in transmitted light, and (b) any grade with a yellowish tinge which is not apparent to the average inexperienced purchaser.

blue zircon. Zircon which, by heating, has been changed from a naturally occurring color, usually grayish or brownish, to some hues or tones of blue. No natural occurrence of zircon of any pronounced blue color has ever been authenticated, although it was once reliably reported that very pale blue, almost white, zircon had been found in Ceylon.

bluish gray. In **color nomenclature system** of North American gemology, a color midway between blue-gray and neutral gray.

bluish green. In North American gemology the **hue** midway between green and blue-green, and hence more green than blue.

bluish violet. In North American gemology the hue midway between violet and blue - violet. More violet than blue.

bluish white. In North American gemology, a color which is whiter than **blue white.**

boart. Same as **bort.**

borco de fogo (Brazilian). Crystals of green tourmaline with pink centers.

body appearance (of a stone). The optical effect produced by internal structure, such as laminations or numerous small and widely distributed inclusions or fractures. Often called **sheen** in translucent to opaque stones.

"Bohemian chrysolite." Moldavite.

Bohemian garnet. A term used loosely for any intense, dark-red **garnet** or, more specifically but less often, for this quality of **pyrope**

garnet found in Bohemia (Czechoslovakia). At the turn of the century, small Bohemian garnets were used to make large quantities of low-karat-gold jewelry.

Bohemian glass. A potash lime glass made in Czechoslovakia. Used to make cheap imitation stones but principally for table ware.

"Bohemian ruby." Red, or rose quartz. Although ruby does occur in Bohemia, it is not suitable for fashioning into gems.

"Bohemian topaz." (1) Citrine or **topaz quartz.** (2) Yellow fluorite.

boke. A pale quince-colored coral from Japan.

Boley gauge. A Vernier slide **gauge.**

bolivarite. Probably **variscite** from Spain.

Bolivian jasper. A red **jasper** from Bolivia, So. America.

Bombay pearl. Usually a **cream rosé pearl** but may be any **Persian Gulf pearl, Red Sea pearl,** or other **pearl** which is commonly marketed through Bombay, on west coast of India.

bonamite (boe'na-mite). A jeweler's trade name for an applegreen **smithsonite,** resembling chrysoprase in color, from Kelly, New Mexico. Named "bonamite" by Goodfriend Brothers, N. Y. from the French *bon ami* meaning "good friend." Now rarely seen.

bone. The hard material that comprises the skeletons of mammalian animals. It is sometimes used as a substitute for **ivory,** carvings being made particularly from the long bones of oxen and the mandibles of large whales. Hardness, 2¾; specific gravity, 1.94 to 2.10; refractive index, 1.54 to 1.56.

bone amber or **bony amber.** A variety of amber more opaque than cloudy amber and resembling bone or ivory in appearance. White to brown. Takes an inferior polish. Same as **osseous amber.**

"bone turquoise." Fossilized bone or teeth naturally stained blue. A substitute for turquoise for which artificially stained bone or teeth are in turn often substituted.

boort. See **bort.**

"borax." (1) Inferior jewelry merchandise. (2) The stores that sell merchandise at unfairly high prices or by unethical methods. (3) The methods used by such stores.

Borazon. A trademarked name for an extremely durable, heat-resistant, nongem-quality synthetic material (chemically, boron nitride) that was first produced by the General Electric Co. in 1957. It may be black, brown, dark red, yellow, white or gray and is approximately equal to diamond in hardness. Also, its atomic structure and specific gravity are similar to those of diamond.

borosilicate glass. An unusually hard glass used for imitation stones, especially aquamarines.

H. 5½ to almost 7. S.G. 2.3-2.4; R. I. 1.47-1.51.

botch. A worthless opal.

botryoidal (bot-ri-oi'dal). In mineralogy, closely united spherical masses resembling a bunch of grapes.

bottle stone. (1) Moldavite. (2) An old name for chrysolite. (3) A little-used term for any mineral which can be melted directly into glass.

bottom (of a gemstone.) The **pavilion.**

boulder opal. Term used by miners for nodules of siliceous ironstone of concretionary origin containing precious opal and occurring in the opal-bearing sandstone and clay of Queensland, Australia.

boule (bool). French, meaning a ball. A pear- or carrot-shaped mass of alumina that forms during the production of synthetics.

bouquet agate. Translucent milky to grayish **chalcedony** containing bright inclusions of several hues arranged in the form of the spreading sprays in a bouquet. Presidio Co., Texas, is noted for this agate variety. See **agate.**

bourguignon pearls. An obsolete name for wax-filled imitation pearls.

bouton (boo'ton). French term for button pearl.

bowenite. A translucent, massive, fine-grained, greenish-white to yellowish-green variety of **serpentine** that resembles nephrite jade in appearance and sometimes is sold as such, when it is known by the popular misnomer of "Korean jade." Hardness, 5 to 5½; specific gravity, 2.50 to 2.80; refractive index, 1.55-1.57. Sources: China, New Zealand, Afghanistan, India and R.I.

"bowenite jade." Same as **bowenite.**

Braganza Topaz. A colorless topaz of 1680 c. of unusual beauty and clarity in Portuguese crown. Has been erroneously known as the Braganza Diamond.

Braunschweiger clear amber. German trade grade of amber; medium color quality; dark yellow. See **clear amber.**

Brazilian amethyst. (1) Any amethyst from Brazil. Principally from (a) Brejinha Mine, Bahia, (deep velvety purple); and (b) Rio Grande do Sul (violet to purple to bluish violet). Also from Minas Geraes and Espirito Santo Goyaz, and Diamantina. (2) As a trade grade in U.S.A., purple to brownish purple, sometimes with patchy or streaky color.

"Brazilian aquamarine." Greenish topaz. See **Brazilian aquamarine.**

Brazilian aquamarine. Aquamarine from various gem-bearing districts of Minas Geraes, Brazil. Many of very large size, but until the discovery of the process of heat treatment to improve color, were not as fine blue as **Madagascar aquamarine.**

Brazilian cat's-eye. Chrysoberyl cat's-eye from the state of Minas Geraes, Brazil. Inferior to Ceylon cat's-eye.

Brazilian chrysoberyl. Chrysoberyl from near Minas Novas. Often of large size and finest greenish yellow color.

"Brazilian chrysolite." Same as **chrysolite chrysoberyl.**

Brazilian-cut brilliant. A cushion-shaped brilliant, with eight additional facets around the culet, making 66 facets. Term has also been used synonymously with **old mine cut.**

"Brazilian emerald." Green tourmaline. See **Brazilian emerald.**

Brazilian emerald. Light yellowish green beryl from Bahia and Minas Geraes. That from Bahia and most from the other sources is probably too light to be gemologically classed as emerald. S. G. 2.67-2.72.

brazilianite. A rare, transparent to translucent, yellowish-green to greenish-yellow mineral species, seldom used as a gemstone. Chemical composition, hydrous sodium-aluminum phosphate $NaAl_3(OH)_4(PO_4)_2$; crystal system, monoclinic; hardness, $\frac{1}{2}$; specific gravity, 2.94 to 2.98; refractive index, 1.602-1.621; birefringence, .019; dispersion, .014. Sources: Brazil and New Hampshire.

"Brazilian onyx." An incorrect trade term for onyx marble of superior color, from Argentina.

"Brazilian pebble." Rock crystal (quartz).

"Brazilian peridot." Light yellowish-green tourmaline.

"Brazilian ruby." Rose-red or pink topaz, either naturally or artificially colored. See **pink topaz.**

"Brazilian sapphire." Light-blue or greenish topaz. Also, blue tourmaline.

Brazilian topaz. True yellowish topaz. Same as **precious topaz.**

break facets. The triangular facets which adjoin the girdle of a brilliant cut; the 16 above are called top break facets and the 16 below, the bottom break facets.

Breastplate of the High Priest. Hebrew "hoshen," exact meaning of which is obscure, but the directions for making the Breastplate are sufficiently clear in Ex. XXVIII, 13-30 and XXXIX, 8-21. A species of pouch adorned with precious stones. Worn by the High Priest when he presented, in the Holy Place, the names of the Children of Israel.

breccia. A rock in which angular fragments have been naturally embedded or cemented. See **conglomerate.**

brecciated. Containing angular fragments naturally embedded or cemented in the stone.

brecciated agate. Agate that has been broken into irregular fragments and recemented by silica solutions.

brecciated jasper. A reconstituted form of jasper in which the patterns appear as mosaics. Occurrences are widely distributed, but a particularly interesting brown-and-yellow variety occurs near San Miguel, San Luis Obispo Co., California, and on the beaches north of Ventura, Ventura Co., California. It is particularly suitable for bookends and spheres. See **jasper.**

Briggs Scale. A table of comparative tenacity or toughness of gemstones, compiled from original experiments by Henry E. Briggs, the author of *An Encyclopedia of Gems.*

brilliancy. (of a gemstone.) The amount of light reaching the eye as a result of (1) reflections from the internal surface of facets (called total internal reflection); and (2) reflections from the external surfaces of the table and other facets of a gemstone. See **total reflection, luster, scintillation.**

brilliant. (1) Most correctly, a brilliant cut diamond. (2) Less correctly, any brilliant cut gemstone, especially a colorless glass imitation. See **single cut, Swiss cut, full-cut brilliant, standard brilliant.**

brilliant cut. The most popular cut for most stones; with round girdle outline and usually 58 facets, sometimes less and often more. See **full cut brilliant, single cut.**

Brinnell hardness. A hardness test for minerals or similar substances accomplished by measuring the comparative depth to which a hard steel point or ball penetrates the substance.

briolette (bre-oh-let'). A pear- or drop-shaped stone with a circular cross section, entirely covered with triangular facets. This form of cutting is very rarely encountered.

British amber. A term which has been used for amber washed ashore on beaches of England, probably from Baltic Sea. Clear or cloudy, yellow or greenish yellow and rarely wine color.

brittle. Mineralogical term meaning not flexible, ductile, i.e., that a stone will crumble under a knife or hammer, but not necessarily that it is fragile.

"brittle amber." Gedanite.

broker. One who buys and sells. In the jewelry trade one who buys from, and sells to, both the trade and the public, although a' few brokers sell only to the trade.

bromoform. A heavy liquid, S.G. 2.90. Gems of higher S.G. will sink, those of lower S.G. float in it.

broncita (Span.). Bronzite.

bronze pearls. The variety of so-called black pearls with bronze-like color and sheen.

bronzite. A variety of **enstatite.**

"bronzite cat's-eye." Bronzite with a chatoyant effect.

brookite. A mineral fashioned rarely as a gem even for collectors. Same composition as **rutile.** Ortho. TiO_2; H. 5.5-6; S.G. 3.9-4.1; R.I. 2.58/2.74. Urals, Mass., N.Y. and other sources.

Broome pearl. Australian pearl marketed through Broome, Western Australia.

brown. In **color nomenclature system** of North American gemology a range of colors which includes **red-brown, orange-brown, yellow-brown, reddish brown, orangy brown** and **yellowish brown.**

"brown hematite." Limonite.

"brown hyacinth." Vesuvianite.

brownish orange, brownish red, brownish yellow. In North American gemology, colors which, respectively, are lower in **intensity** and darker in **tone** than orange, red or yellow, but not as dull or dark as **orange-brown, red-brown, yellow-brown.**

brown-orange, brown-red, brown-yellow. In **color nomenclature system** of North American gemology colors which, respectively, are approximately midway between (a) vivid orange, red or yellow and (b) the **tone** and **intensity** of brown which is almost black. Same as **orange-brown, red-brown, yellow-brown.**

bruciato. Italian trade name for dark brown to blackish coral, discolored by having lain on bottom of sea. Lowest quality of

precious **coral.** The word means *burnt.*

bubbles. Globules of air or gas or globular vacuums such as in synthetic or imitation stones. In the trade, inclusions of small crystals of similar or different minerals are, erroneously, also called bubbles.

buckhorn pearl. A **fresh-water pearl** which rarely occurs in spherical form in the Mississippi Valley mussel *Tritigonia verrucosa,* popularly known as the "buckhorn clam."

buffed top. A term used for any stone which is faceted below the girdle, with a slightly convex surface above the girdle produced by polishing on a buff instead of a metal lap.

buff stick. A piece of stick covered with leather or velvet and charged with emery or other powder used in polishing.

buff-top. Same as **buffed top.**

bulb opal. Menilite opal.

bullhead pearl. A fresh-water pearl from the North American mussels *Pleurobema oesopus* popularly known as the "bullhead clam."

bull's-eye. Labradorite with a dark sheen.

Burma jade. Same as **Burmese jade.**

Burma moonstone. M o o n s t o n e (feldspar) from Burma, which during recent years has included fine **blue moonstone.**

Burma ruby (or Burmese ruby). Trade term for the finest colored rubies whether or not from Burma, where most of them are mined.

Burma sapphire. Term often used

in America for fine royal blue sapphire whether or not from Burma. Same as **oriental sapphire.**

Burmese jade or **Burmese jadeite.** Finest known jadeite. From mines in Mogaung, subdivision of Myitkyina district, Upper Burma. The term Burma jade is commonly used in the Orient to distinguish it from any and all varieties of nephrite (jade). Same as **soda-jadeite.**

Burmese spinel. Red spinel and flame spinel found in perfect octahedra and fine gem quality in alluvial deposits near Mogok in upper Burma, in association with rubies which are usually water worn.

burmite. Amber found in Burma. Generally pale yellow, but reddish and dark brown specimens are also known. Slightly harder than **Baltic amber.** See also **Chinese amber.**

burnt amethyst. Term applied to artificially colored yellow transparent quartz **(topaz quartz)** which, unlike poorly colored yellowish quartz **(citrine),** is largely produced by heating natural amethyst of brownish hue. See **"burnt stone."**

burnt cairngorm. Term applied to that **topaz quartz** which has been changed from the color of cairngorm **(smoky quartz)** to topaz color. See also **burnt amethyst; burnt stone.**

burnt coral. Dark brown or blackish coral discolored by having lain at bottom of sea. Same as **bruciato.**

burnt stone. A stone such as topaz, aquamarine, etc., the color of which has been changed by burning or heating. See **blue zircon; topaz quartz, heated stone.**

burnt topaz. Genuine topaz which has been altered in color to **pink topaz.**

bustamite. Greenish to reddish grey rhodonite.

butterfly pearl. A pearl from the Mississippi Valley mussel *Plagiola securis* popularly known as the "butterfly clam." One of the finest of **fresh-water pearls**
This clam was abundant only in **Illinois and Ohio Rivers (Cattelle). More recent reports of pearl production make no mention of the continued finding of pearls in this mussel.**

button onyx or **button opal.** Names for an **opal agate** with alternating bands of black chalcedony and common opal.

button pearl. Dome-shaped pearl with one surface almost plane.

byon or **byone.** Burmese name for the **alluvial deposits** in which rubies are found.

bytownite. A transparent to translucent, white, gray, green, yellow or colorless plagioclase feldspar, usually occurring as massive material. Occasionally used as a gem material.

byssus (bis′sus). The threads secreted by glands in the foot of certain shellfish, for attachment to hard bodies or to one another.

C

c Abbr. used in this book for carat.

C. Abbr. for (1) the element carbon, and (2) **centigrade**.

Ca. Abbr. for the element calcium.

cabinet stone. An especially fine specimen of a gem or mineral; a collector's item.

cabochon. An unfaceted cut stone of domed or convex form, or the style of cutting itself. The top is unfaceted and smoothly polished; the back or base, usually flat, or slightly convex, and unpolished. The height of the domed top is varied to accomplish various desired effects. With convex top and flat base it is called a *simple* or *single cabochon*; with convex top and base, a *double cabochon*. All asterias, cat's-eyes, and girasols, most moonstones, opals and turquoise, are cut cabochon (or s p h e r i c a l), as well as many translucent or semitransparent jades and other gem minerals. Less desirable specimens of various gem varieties are also sometimes cut cabochon. The girdle outline may be oval, round, square or any other shape. The backs of almost all transparent or semi-transparent cabochons are polished. See **hollowed cabochon; lentil; tallow top; shell.**

cabocle. A compact rolled pebble resembling red jasper, supposed to be hydrous aluminum-calcium phosphate. Found in the diamond-producing sands of Bahia, Brazil

cabra stone. Fluorite.

cabujon (Span.). Cabochon.

cachalong (kash'oe-long) or **cacholong.** A pale bluish white, opaque or feebly translucent, porcelain-like variety of **common opal.** Highly regarded in the Orient, but of little gemological interest in the Occident, although, banded with chalcedony, it has been cut as cameos.

caesium. A metallic element.

cairngorm. Same as **smoky quartz.** A Scottish name. It has also been loosely used for any variety of quartz, and even for a style of large brooch in which quartz gems are set. From Scotland and other sources.

calamine. European name for both a carbonate of zinc and a silicate of zinc. The former is classified in U.S.A. and England as **smithsonite;** the latter (a non-gem mineral) as calamine or **hemimorphite.**

calcareous. In mineralogy, composed of, containing, or in the nature of calcite. In general, consisting of or containing calcium carbonate ($CaCO_3$).

calcédoine (Fr.). Chalcedony.

calcedonia (Span. and Port.). Chalcedony.

calcedonia veteada (Span.). Cacholong.

calcedony. A corrupt and little-used spelling for **chalcedony.**

calcite (kal'-site). A very common, transparent to semitranslucent mineral species, occurring in a wide variety of colors and patterns in both massive form (fibrous, fine to coarse granular and stalactitic) and a tremendous variety of crystal habits (more than 700 are

31

known). Varieties include **Iceland spar, satin spar, marble** and **travertine.** Calcite is difficult to facet because of its softness and perfect, easily developed, three-dimensional cleavage. The massive forms are popular for cabochons and ornamental and decorative articles. Chemical composition, calcium carbonate ($CaCO_3$); crystal system, hexagonal; hardness, 3; specific gravity, 2.71; refractive index, 1.486-1.658; birefringence, .172. Sources: widespread.

calcite satin spar. See **satin spar.**

calcium-aluminum garnet. Same as **grossularite.**

calcium-chromium garnet. Same as **uvarovite.**

calcium glass. See **crown glass.**

calcium-iron garnet. Same as **andradite.**

calcomalachite. Mixture of malachite and calcite, and also, often, gypsum. An ornamental stone often sold as malachite.

calibre cut (kal'i-bray or kal'i-ber). (1) Stones of square, rectangular keystone or other shape, cut for setting in ring shanks, band rings, bracelets, etc. Usually very small and set **pave'** in lines or masses to improve the design or enhance the beauty of a jewel.

"California cat's-eye." Compact fibrous serpentine, exhibiting an indistinct light line or **chatoyant effect,** and occasionally a fine **cat's-eye.**

"California hyacinth." Hessonite.

"California iris." Kunzite (spodumene).

"California jade". Californite.

"California lapis." Misnomer for blue **dumortierite quartz.**

"California moonstone." White or whitish **chalcedony.** A misnomer.

California morganite. Morganite from California; some of fine color but more often of salmon pink color.

"California onyx." A European name for "Mexican onyx."

California pearl. Term often used overseas, for **La Paz pearl,** from Baja (Lower) California, Mexico.

"California ruby". Garnet.

"California tiger eye." Same as "California cat's-eye."

California topaz. Topaz from Mesa Grande and Ramona districts of Southern California. Usually pale blue to almost colorless, but occasionally as fine in color as any blue topaz.

"California turquoise." Variscite.

California turquoise. Term sometimes used overseas to mean **any** turquoise from California or other southwestern states of U.S.A.

californite. The massive, translucent to opaque, yellowish-green to dark-green variety of **idocrase,** usually mottled with white or light gray. It is often used as a substitute for poor-quality jade. Principal source: Fresno, Siskiyou and Tulare Counties, California.

caliper. A device for measuring the dimensions of an object, usually with movable jaws which hold or contact an object. When equipped with means for accurate measurement of small units, is called a **micrometer caliper** or simply a **micrometer.**

callaica, callaina, callais, callainite. Ancient names still sometimes used for turquoise.

32

callainite. Translucent, yellowish to bluish green aluminum phosphate **mineral** found in a Celtic grave in Brittany. Indicated by Dana and Bauer to be closely related to variscite.

callaite. See **calaite.**

calliper. See **caliper.**

calmazul. Same as **chrysocarmen.**

calorescence. The phenomenon of glowing when a substance is stimulated by the heat rays which lie beyond the red end of the visible spectrum. Same as **thermoluminescence.**

camafeo (Span.). Cameo.

Cambay stone. Carnelian.

cameo doublet. A doublet in which the top is molded or carved glass and the back is chalcedony. Some are composed of two pieces of glass, and the carnelian color is produced by the cement that joins the two pieces. *Intaglio doublets* are made in the same way.

cameos. Cameos are generally, but not always, fashioned from substances composed of two or more differently colored layers. *Genuine cameos* contain a design which has been produced by cutting away portions of the upper layer or layers (or of the upper surface, in singly colored substances). If cut from genuine gem materials, it is advisable to describe such cameos as *stone cameos;* if from shell, as *shell cameos;* if from coral, as *coral cameos,* etc. If cut from synthetic stones, they should be described as *synthetic stone cameos.* Cameos are also molded or pressed, and when so constructed should be described as *molded* or *pressed.* Cameos which are made of two or more separate pieces joined together should be described as *assembled cameos* when one or more parts are genuine, and *imitation cameos* when made of glass or composition. (Definition jointly prepared and adopted by Nat'l. Better Business Bureau, and the American Gem Society). See **shell cameo; stone cameo.**

cameo ware. Same as **jasper ware.**

Campeche pearl. Pearl from Gulf of Campeche. In the trade more often called **Venezuela pearl.**

camphor jade. A variety of white translucent jadeite resembling crystallized camphor in appearance.

Canadian jet. Jet which came from Pictou, Pictou Co., Nova Scotia. Softer than **Whitby jet.** (Kunz)

Canadian Jewellers' Association. The Canadian Jewellers' Association, which includes retailers, wholesalers and manufacturers, was organized in 1918. Its primary function is that of intervention with the government at any level on behalf of the industry. A monthly bulletin keeps members informed on matters in any way related to the trade. A group health- and life-insurance plan is offered. The CJA conducts the National Jewellery-Week Program and various meetings across the country among jewelers, including an annual convention. The Canadian Jewellers' Institute, a subsidiary of the Association, conducts the Retail Jewellers' Training Course, the course in Introductory Gemology, a library service, and an examination for qualified watchmakers that leads to a certificate. Headquarters: 800 Bay Street, Toronto, Ontario, Canada.

canary beryl. Greenish - yellow beryl.

canary stone. Yellow carnelian.

cancrinite (kan'-kri-nite). A rare transparent to translucent, white, gray, yellow, orange, blue, green, reddish or pale-violet mineral species. Chemical composition, a complex sodium - carbonate aluminosilicate; crystal system, hexagonal (crystals rare; usually massive); hardness, 5 to 6; specific gravity, 2.42 to 2.52; refractive index, 1.50 to 1.52. Bright orange to lemon-yellow masses associated with sodalite have been cut as cabochons and beads; transparent material suitable for faceting tiny stones is very rarely encountered. Sources: Quebec, Russia, Transylvania, Norway and Maine.

cand or **cann.** (Cornish). Same as **blue-john.**

candite. Blue spinel.

candling. A method of gaining an indication of the nature of pearls in a strand. A circular opening smaller than the diameter of the pearls to be examined is cut in an opaque light shield. The shield is placed over an intense light, and each pearl is rotated over the circular opening. Most cultured pearls with relatively thin nacreous coatings will reveal a striped effect as they are rotated, caused by unequal transmission of light through the flat mother-of-pearl layers in the large nucleus. If the majority of pearls in a strand show the striped effect, it is likely that they are cultured.

"Candy spinel." Same as **"Kandy spinel."**

cannel coal. Compact, often dull black coal. Sometimes substituted for jet.

Canton jade. Any jadeite or nephrite from Canton, one of China's three largest jade markets.

canutillos. Term used in Colombia for fine emeralds suitable for gems.

"Cape chrysolite". Green prehnite from South Africa.

"Cape emerald." Incorrect name for prehnite.

carat (kar'at). A unit of weight for diamonds, other gems and pearls. The carat formerly varied somewhat in different countries, but the metric carat of 0.200 grams or 200 milligrams was adopted in the United States in 1913, and is now standard in the principal countries of the world. Sometimes spelled *karat* but in U. S. A. *karat* refers only to the fineness of **solid gold.** See also **grain.**

carato (Ital.). Carat.

carbon dioxide test. Same as **dry ice test.**

carbonetto. Italian trade term for very dark red coral. Same as **ariscuro.**

Carborundum. A trade-marked name for an artificial abrasive, crystallized carbide of silicon (SiC.) discovered in 1891. Between 9 and 10 in hardness on **Mohs scale,** it is powdered and used in grinding gemstones other than diamonds.

carbuncle. Name used in ancient and middle ages for any cabochon-cut red stone, especially red garnet, and gemologically confined to the latter. See **Karfunkel.**

Carlotta pearl. An 86-gr. oval shaped pearl which seems to have been once pawned by Empress Carlotta of Mexico.

carnelian (kar-neel-yan'). Red, orange-red, brownish red, or brownish orange, translucent to semitranslucent variety of **chalcedony.** Sometimes. yellow or brownish yellow. Grades into more brownish intensities of these colors which are called **sard.** See **carnelian onyx.**

carnelian agate. Banded agate similar to **carnelian onyx** in coloring except bands are not straight and parallel.

carnelian onyx. Onyx with alternating bands of white **chalcedony** and **carnelian.** The term is also used in a broader sense for any true onyx, one or more of the alternating bands of which are carnelian colors.

carneol (obsolete). Carnelian.

carré (French). Square cut.

carving. That branch of the lapidary art devoted to the working of gem materials into articles of ornament and utility (vases, statues, etc.).

casein. An amorphous plastic made from the albumen of milk by treating milk with acid. Sometimes colored to imitate amber, agate, malachite, tortoise shell, ivory and other decorative materials. S.G. 1.3-1.4; R.I. 1.55-1.56.

Cashmere sapphire; also **Kashmir** or **Kashmere.** (1) Any sapphire from Kashmir, a native state of northwest India. (2) A trade grade of blue sapphire applied to stones of the velvety cornflower color (violetish blue) of the most desirable sapphires from Kashmir.

cassiterite (kah-sit'-er-ite). A transparent to opaque, dark reddish-brown, light-yellow, gray, black or colorless mineral species. It is rarely fashioned but is prized by collectors, because of the high brilliancy and dispersion of fashioned specimens. Cassiterite is the principal ore of tin. Chemical composition, tin oxide (SnO_2); crystal system, tetragonal; hardness, 6 to 7; specific gravity, 6.95; refractive index, 1.996-2.09; birefringence, .097; dispersion, .071. Sources: Bolivia, Mexico, Malaya, Saxony and elsewhere.

"cave pearl." A calcium-carbonate concretion (massive **calcite),** formed in limestone caves by the agency of water.

catalin. An amorphous plastic similar to **bakelite.**

"Catalina sardonyx". (kat'a-lee'-na). Catalinite.

catalinite. Beach pebbles from Santa Catalina Island, California.

cateye. A word used, apparently in error, for **cat's-eye.**

cathode. The negative terminal of an electrical source.

cathode rays (kath'ode). Rays projected from the cathode of a vacuum tube in which an electric discharge takes place. By impinging on solids the cathode rays generate Röntgen rays or X rays.

cat sapphire. Same as **lynx sapphire.**

cat's-eye. (1) Term most properly applied only to cymophane, the

chrysoberyl cat's - eye. (2) Term applied to any gemstone which, when cut cabochon, exhibits under a single, strong **point source,** a sharp, well-defined light band, line or streak of white light across the dome of stone, which moves as the stone is turned about. This phenomenon which resembles in shape the slit pupil of the eye of a cat is caused by reflection of light from included fibers (crystals) or long parallel cavities or tubes. Few mineral species produce well-defined cat's-eyes, and as the unmodified term is used only for **cymophane,** the varieties of those species which do are known as alexandrite cat's-eye, tourmaline cat's-eye, scapolite cat's-eye, or cordierite cat's-eye, several varieties of quartz cat's-eye, etc. Many other gemstones exhibit a broader or less well-defined light line, but these are more properly said to have a cat's-eye effect or a **chatoyant effect.** See also **girasol.** "New Guinea cat's-eye." (3) A name incorrectly used for so-called "shell cat's-eye."

"cat's-eye enstatite." Enstatite with a **chatoyant effect.**

cat's-eye opal. Same as **opal cat's-eye.**

"cat's-eye resin." See **dammar.**

cat's-eye ruby. See **ruby cat's-eye.**

cat's-eye sapphire. See **sapphire cat's-eye.**

"cat's quartz." Same as **quartz cat's-eye.**

catty. A Siamese measure of weight by which rough zircons are sold; 1-1/3 pounds averdupois.

cave pearl. A concretion with a pearly luster formed in limestone caves by the agency of water.

Ce. Abbr. for the element cerium.

cedarite. A fossil resin resembling amber. From bed of Saskatchewan River, Canada.

Celebes pearl. Pearl from the Celebes Archipelago. In quality, better than **Australian pearl** but inferior to **Bombay pearl** or **Madras pearl.**

celestial opal. A name for **precious opal.**

celestial stone. Turquoise.

cellon. A non-inflammable celluloid. An amber imitation. S.G. 1.26; R.I. 1.48. (Anderson)

cellular. Full of small openings; sponge-like.

celluloid. A plastic produced from a cellulose base of two varieties, sometimes used for imitations of amber, ivory, tortoise shell, etc. The newer noninflammable cellulose acetate variety, or safety celluloid, has S.G.1.3-1.8; R.I. 1.49-1.50. The old inflammable cellulose nitrate variety has approximately same properties.

cellulose acetate. A transparent to opaque plastic that finds wide application for various jewelry articles and gemstones. It is extremely tough, has a resinous luster, a hardness of 1½, an uneven fracture, a specific gravity of 1.27 to 1.37, and a refractive index of 1.46 to 1.50.

centigrade thermometer. A thermometer, on the scale of which the distance between the two standard points, the freezing point and boiling point of water, is divided into one hundred equal parts or degrees.

cer-agate. Yellow chalcedony. See **carnelian.**

cerannite (French).Nephrite.

cerkonier. Jargoon from Ceylon.

Cerkonier (German). Colorless zircon.

Certified Gemologist. A title awarded by the American Gem Society to qualified jeweler - members. To qualify, a person must study colored stones and their identification and diamond grading and appraising. Also, he must prove his proficiency with several written examinations, a diamond-grading examination, and pass a 20-stone identification examination without error. This is the AGS's most advanced title. See **American Gem Society, Registered Jeweler.**

cerulene. (1) Trade name for a variety of **calcite** colored green and blue by **malachite** and **azurite.** From near Bimbowrie, So. Australia and other sources. An ornamental stone. (2) Less correctly, blue **satin spar.**

ceylanite. Same as **ceylonite.**

Ceylon alexandrite. The unusually transparent **alexandrite** which occurs in Ceylon in large sizes, often of 20 or more **carats** in weight, after cutting.

Ceylon or **Ceylonese cat's-eye.** Chrysoberyl cat's-eye.

Ceylon chrysoberyl. Chrysoberyl from Ceylon, the principal source of that gemstone. Most of it yields **cat's-eye** or stones with **chatoyant effect,** and if dark green exhibits more or less the changeable color quality of **alexandrite.**

"Ceylon or Ceylonese chrysolite." Yellowish green to greenish yellow **tourmaline.**

Ceylon cut. A trade term for a stone of almost any faceted style that has been fashioned unsymmetrically to preserve as much of the original weight as possible.

Ceylon garnet. Almandite from Ceylon.

"Ceylon hyacinth." Hessonite garnet.

ceylonite. Dark, almost black, especially greenish black spinel. Sometimes cut for mourning jewelry.

Ceylon moonstone. Historically, the most important source of **orthoclase** moonstone. It usually has whitish adularescence; less often, bluish.

"Ceylon opal." Misnomer for moonstone (feldspar).

Ceylon pearl. (1) A pearl from the salt-water mollusc *Pinctada Vulgaris,* from the Gulf of Mannar, between India and Ceylon. It is noted for its beautiful silvery-white color, spherical shape and lovely luster. (2) As an American trade grade, a white pearl with a blue, violet or green orient. See **Pinctada.**

"Ceylon peridot." Honey-yellow or yellowish green tourmaline.

Ceylon ruby. Mineralogically, a ruby from Ceylon. However, being lighter red and more transparent than fine ruby, is often classed as pink sapphire. Also an incorrect name for **almandite.**

DICTIONARY OF GEMS AND GEMOLOGY

Ceylon, Ceylonese or **Singhalese zircon.** (1) Any zircon from Ceylon. (2) More especially, a fine red, cloudy zircon.

C.G. Abbr. for **Certified Gemologist,** a title of the **American Gem Society.**

chalcedony (kal-sed'-o-ny). (1) The cryptocrystalline subspecies of quartz as distinguished from **crystalline quartz.** Massive semitransparent to translucent, white, gray, black and light tones or low intensities of all hues, many of which are known by variety names. Such names are in general use in the trade of U. S. A. except for the blue variety. (2) By popular usage in some portions of the trade of U.S.A., a word used to describe only the light blue variety of the subspecies just described.

"chalcedony moonstone." The white, or almost colorless chalcedony. Gathered from beaches in various parts of world, especially in California, it has been widely sold as **moonstone.** It lacks adularescence of genuine moonstone. Same as **"California moonstone."** See **quartz.**

chalcedony onyx or **chalcedonyx.** Chalcedony w i t h alternating stripes of grey and white.

"chalcedony patches." White blemishes in rubies.

chalchihuitl, chalchihuite, chalchiguite, chalchuite, chalchuites, or **chalchuhuites.** A Mexican name for jade, turquoise, smithsonite, or any greenish stone of similar appearance; more specifically green turquoise, although Kunz distinguishes jade as the precious stones of Chalchihuitl. The words are sometimes applied to any stone which can be carved,

regardless of species or color.

chalcocite or **chalcosite** (copper glance). Lead-grey metallic mineral sometimes used in cheap jewelry. H. 2½-3; S.G. 5.5-5.8.

chalk jade. A descriptive term applied by Chinese to a specific color quality of jade.

chameleonite. Name proposed for a rare variety of tourmaline, olive green in daylight, changing to brownish red in most artificial light.

chameleon stone. Hydrophane.

changeant (Fr.). Labradorite.

change of color. (1) An alternate name for **labradorescence.** (2) Any stone that shows a difference in color from daylight to artificial light, caused by selective absorption; e.g., **alexandrite.**

chank pearl. A pearl similar in appearance to **conch pearl,** pink, devoid of nacreous luster and therefore not a **true pearl.** From the *Turginella scolymus* gastropod.

channel setting. The style of setting stones, with edges almost touching, in a channel that is usually a straight line. See **paved** or **pave'.**

C h a n t a b u n r u b y. Marketed through city of Chantabun (Siam) and mined in the district of the same name, or Krat, southwest of that district. See **Siam ruby.**

Charlemagne's Talisman. See **Talisman of Charlemagne.**

Charles II Pearl. A pearl found in 1691, presumably in the Americas, and presented to Charles II. Almost equal in weight to **La Peregrina;** the two were worn in earrings by the

Queens of Spain.

Charles II Sapphire. Same as **Stuart Sapphire.**

Chatham-Created Emerald. A trademarked name for a flux-fusion synthetic emerald manufactured by Carroll Chatham of San Francisco, California. See **synthetic emerald.**

chaton (Fr.). (1) Bezel of a ring. (2) Same as **chaton foil.**

chaton foil. (1) an **imitation foilback** or **imitation lacquerback.** (2) more specifically, a **colored** imitation foilback.

chatoyancy (sha-toy'an-see, or Fr., sha'twa-yan-sy). The phenomenon of a movable white light band in either a **cat's-eye** or a stone with a **chatoyant effect.**

chatoyant. Possessing chatoyancy.

cheky (Turkish). Unit of weight, 320 grams.

Chelsea filter. See **color filter.**

chemawinite. A pale yellow to dark brown fossil resin related to succinite. S. G. 1.055. From near mouth of N. Saskatchewan River, Canada.

chemical formula. Indicates the composition of the substance. For example, Al_2O_3 indicates that each molecule of the substance is composed of two atoms of aluminum and three atoms of oxygen; other formulas have similar meanings.

cherry opal. A reddish translucent opal from Mexico.

cherry pearl. (1) Pearl of pronounced pink of the hue of any variety of cherry; (2) pearl approximately the size of a cherry (very rare).

chert. An opaque, fine-grained, compact variety of **cryptocrystalline quartz.** Long used by primitive peoples for making arrowheads, spearheads, knives and other useful objects, chert is occasionally cut and polished by amateur lapidaries. Source: widespread.

chessylite (ches'i-lite). Same as **azurite.**

chestnut jade. A descriptive term applied by Chinese to a specific color quality of jade.

chevee (shev-vae). A flat gem with a smooth concave depression. If a raised figure is in the depression it is a **cuvette,** although the two terms are often used interchangeably in the North American trade.

chevvü. (1) A Ceylonese weight. Same as **chow.** (2) Ceylonese term used for pearls of superior quality including **ani, anitári, masaku,** and **kaiyéral.** See **vadivu; kuruval.**

chiastolite (kei-as toe-lite). A variety of andalusite containing black carbonaceous inclusions. These usually have a definite arrangement resembling a cross. A curio stone. H. 3-7½.

chicken bone jade. Chinese descriptive term for the disintegrated texture and the yellowish discoloration of white jade which has been burned or buried. See **tomb jade.**

chicot pearl. Same as **blister pearl.**

Chi Ku Pai jade. Same as **chicken bone jade.**

Chilean lapis. Pale to light blue lapis lazuli containing veins of white matrix; often tinged or spotted green and prominently veined with white or gray.

chimaltizatl. Aztec word for selenite

China or **Chinese pearl.** (1) A pearl with two drilled holes for fastening to a mounting by a peg and a screw. (2) Pearl from China; usually fresh-water, rarely **oriental pearl.**

China opal. Common opal resembling white porcelain.

Chinese amber. Sometimes correctly applied to amber mined in Burma and marketed in China, but more often applied incorrectly to pressed **Baltic amber** and often to **bakelite** or other amber colored plastics.

"Chinese cat's-eye." Same as **"shell cat's-eye."**

Chinese jade. Term correctly applied to jadeite.

"Chinese tourmaline." Tourmaline from California and other non-Chinese sources fashioned as gems or art objects in China.

"Chinese turquoise." A name rarely used for a mixture of soapstone, calcite and quartz, dyed blue.

Ch'iung Yü. Chinese name for a valuable type of red jade.

Chivor emeralds. Emeralds from the ancient Chivor mine. Used as a trade term, Chivor refers to a more bluish, less velvety and usually less intensely colored emerald than Muzo emeralds. See **Somondoco emeralds.**

chlorastrolite (klor-ast'-row-lite). An opaque, mottled, light- and dark-green mineral (a variety of **pumpellyte**) with a radial fibrous structure that occurs in grains or small nodules within the main mass. When the structure consists of parallel fibers, a silky luster is imparted. Cabochons cut from the material resemble a miniature tortoise shell. Chemical composition, a hydrated calcium-aluminum silicate; hardness, 5 to 6; specific gravity, 3.10 to 3.50; refractive index, about 1.66. Source: Lake Superior region, particularly Isle Royale.

chloromelanite (kloe'roe - mel'anite). A gem mineral usually classed as a dark-green, nearly black variety of **jadeite**; rarely is it classed as a separate species.

chloropal. A name for two different stones of no gemological interest. (1) A green opal-like hydrous silicate of iron (Dana). (2) A greenish common opal from Silesia.

chlorophane. A variety of fluorite which yields a green fluorescence when heated.

chlorospinel. A green spinel.

chlor-utahlite. Same as **utahlite.**

choker. A necklace commonly measuring between 14 and 15 inches.

chondrodite. Dark red garnet-like stone found near Putnam, New York. Mono. H. 6-6½ ; S.G. 3.1-3.2; R.I. 1.59/1.64. Also yellow (and orange-red). Eppler mentions as similar to peridot.

chorlo (Span.). Tourmaline.

chow. Indian pearl unit. See **tank.**

chromatic (kroe-mat'ik). Of or pertaining to color or colors.

chromatic aberration. See **aberration.**

chromatic color. A hue, as distinguished from white, black or any tone of gray. The opposite of **achromatic color.**

chrome. Same as **chromium.**

chrome diopside. An intense, dark-green, chromium-bearing variety of **diopside.** Occasionally used as a gem material.

chrome idocrase. An emerald-green, chromium-bearing variety of **idocrase.** Occasionally used as a gem material.

chrome mica. Fuchsite.

chromepidote or **tawmawite.** A chrome epidote from Mt. Tawmaw, source of Burma jadeite.

chrome spinel. A translucent to opaque, dark-green, chromium-bearing variety of spinel. Intermediate in composition between spinel and chromite.

chrome tourmaline. Green tourmaline with a color reminiscent of emerald. Color caused by a small amount of chromium.

chrome-vesuvian. Same as chrome idocrase.

chromite. An opaque iron-black to brownish black mineral, very occasionally cut as a gemstone for collectors. Resembles jet in color but has higher metallic luster. Iso. $FeCr_2O_4$. H. 5.5; S.G. 4.3-4.6; (4.1-4.9 Dana). From Turkey, So. Rhodesia, Pa., Md., and other states and nations.

chromium. A metallic element. Gemologically important as coloring agent of emeralds and rubies.

chromium garnet. Uvarovite.

chrysoberyl (kris'oe'bare'l or bar'-il). One of the hardest and most important gem minerals, of which **alexandrite** and **cymophane** are varieties. Also green-ish yellow to bluish green and yellowish brown varieties. Ortho. $BeAl_2O_4$. H. 8.5. S.G. 3.5-3.8; R.I. 1.74/1.75-1.75/1.76. Bi. 0.009; Disp. 0.015. From Ceylon, Urals, Brazil, and China.

chrysoberyl cat's-eye. See **cymophane.**

"chrysoberyllus." A confusing name, rarely applied to greenish yellow beryl.

chrysocarmen. Reported to be a red or brown copper-bearing ornamental stone from Mexico containing light and dark blue as well as numerous green spots of, perhaps, azurite and malachite.

chrysocolla (kris"-oh-kol'-lah). A soft, opaque, cryptocrystalline, vivid-blue to greenish-blue mineral. As an inclusion, it is the coloring matter in **chrysocolla chalcedony.** Chemical composition, a hydrous silicate of copper ($CuSiO_3.2H_2O$); hardness, 2 to 4; specific gravity, 2.00 to 2.20; refractive index, 1.46-1.57. Sources: Nevada, Arizona, the Congo, Chile and Russia. See **chrysocolla quartz.**

chrysocolla opal. A light-blue to greenish-blue translucent to semi-translucent **common opal** colored by the copper mineral **chrysocolla.**

chrysocolla quartz. A translucent chalcedony colored by **chrysocolla.** Same as **azurlite.**

chrysodor. A trade name for a green and white stone with markings like marble.

chrysojasper. Jasper colored with chrysocolla.

chrysolite (kris'oe-lite). (1) A mineral species more generally known as olivine by geologists and peridot by gemologists. (2)

In **gemology** the almost color-less to yellow to yellowish green variety cf that mineral species. See **olivine; peridot.** (3) As a qualifying adjective, as in the term **chrysolite chrysoberyl. chrysolite beryl,** etc. refers to **hues** between pale or light greenish yellow to pale or light yellowish green.

chrysolite áquamarine. Same as **chrysolite beryl.**

chrysolite beryl. Light yellowish green to light yellow-green beryl.

"chrysolite cat's-eye." Chrysoberyl cat's-eye.

chrysolite chrysoberyl. Light green-ish yellow to light yellow-green chrysoberyl.

chrysolite sapphire. Light greenish yellow to light yellow-green sap-phire.

chrysolite spinel. Light greenish yellow to light yellowish green spinel.

chrysolite topaz. Greenish yellow to pale yellowish green topaz. Same as **"Saxon or Saxony topaz."**

chrysopal. Translucent apple-green common opal colored by nickel. From Silesia. See **prase opal.**

"chrysophrase." A misleading word proposed for green-dyed chal-cedony, to replace the trade misnomer **"green onyx."** Obvi-ously used by those who mis-spelled **chrysoprase** or proposed by those who intended to imply that green-dyed chalcedony was chrysoprase.

chrysoprase (kris'-oh-prase). Semi-transparent to semitranslucent, light to medium yellowish green **chalcedony,** the most desirable and valuable variety of cryptocrystal-line quartz. The distinctive color is caused by finely disseminated in-clusions of nickel silicate. Sources : Australia, Calif. and elsewhere.

"chrysoprase colored onyx." Term which although formerly recom-mended by National Better Business Bureaus for green-dyed chalcedony, is neverthe-less incorrect as it is not onyx. Same as **"green onyx."**

chrysoprase matrix. Chrysoprase with noticeable white or brown inclusions.

chrysoprasus. Ancient spelling of chrysoprase.

chrysoquartz. Green aventurine quartz.

chrysotile. A variety of fibrous serpentine popularly known as asbestos.

chunam. (1) Ceylonese term for a shell-lime powder to which **tul** is sometimes ground for use as an ingredient of a food. (2) Also used to mean various other calcareous substances. (3) A unit of weight for gold.

Ch'uti. A Chinese term meaning "out of the earth." Applied to jade of various colors stained with oxides of all colors result-ing from long reburial in the earth.

ciamita (Span.). Blue tourmaline.

cianita (Span.). Cyanite.

cimofano (Span. and Port.). Chrysoberyl cat's-eye.

cinnabar (sin'a-bar). A bright red to brownish red and some-times lead grey, non-gem min-eral which, however, often oc-curs as red impurities in differ-ent quartz varieties of gem-stones or in combination with such varieties. Also used in China as coloring pigment for a red lacquer. The principal ore of mercury. Hex. HgS; H. 2-2.5; S.G. 8.0-8.2. Sources widely distributed.

cinnabar matrix. A term applicable to various varieties of minerals containing numerous inclusions of **cinnabar** but especially to a Mexican variety of jasper.

cinnamite. Same as cinnamon stone.

cinnamon stone. The reddish brown variety of **hessonite.**

circle agate. Agate with circular markings.

circone (Italian). Zircon.

"Ciro pearl." An imitation pearl.

citrine (sit'-reen). The transparent yellow to red-orange to orange brown variety of **crystalline quartz,** also known as **topaz-quartz.** Together with heat-treated amethyst, it has long been sold under such false names as "topaz," "Spanish topaz" and "Saxon topaz." Most citrine of better quality is nearly flawless, but its texture and surface appearance lack the velvety quality of fine topaz. It is one of the birthstones for November. Sources: Brazil, Malagasy Republic and other localities. See **topaz-quartz.**

"City of Gems." Ratnapura, Ceylon.

clam. Word often incorrectly applied to fresh-water mussels in which pearls are found, especially those in Mississippi basin. Clam is properly a different species.

clammer. One who fishes for the fresh-water mussel for its shell or pearl or both.

clam pearl. Not **fine** pearl. Found in oysters and clams. Light drab, purplish red or blue, almost black. Sometimes incorrectly sold as **black pearl.** See **clam.**

clarified amber. More or less cloudy amber which has been clarified by heating in rapeseed oil.

clastic. Composed of fragments.

clean. A trade term usually meaning free from noticeable flaws.

clear amber. German trade term for transparent amber. See **icecolored clear amber, braunschweiger clear amber** and **common clear amber.**

cleavage. (1) The tendency of a crystalline mineral to break in certain definite directions leaving more or less smooth surface. (2) The act or process of producing such a break. See **cleaving.** (3) One of the portions of a mineral resulting from such a break, which if of comparatively large size, is known as a *cleavage mass.* (4) A term sometimes used for diamond crystals which require cleaving before being fashioned.

cleavage crack. A more or less clean and regular separation, exhibiting smooth reflective surfaces between atomic planes of a mineral, and along a **cleavage** direction.

cleavage, false. Same as **parting.**

cleaving. A process occasionally used in fashioning of diamonds and but rarely in other stones; the splitting of a stone into two or more portions to produce pieces which are of sizes or shape which will produce fashioned stones more economically or of better quality.

Cleopatra emerald mines. Emerald mines at Gebel Sikait and Gebel Zabara, in Northern Etbai, near the Red Sea. See **Egyptian emerald.**

Cleopatra Pearls. Two pearls worn as earrings by Cleopatra. One of these she was said (by Pliny) to have dissolved in vinegar (an impracticability u n l e s s first powdered). The other was said to have been bisected after her death and placed in the ears of the statue of Venus in the Pantheon at Rome.

Clerici's solution. Thallium malonate and formate in water. (Or thallium carbonate, malonic acid and formic acid in water). A **heavy liquid.** S. G. 4.15. Miscible in water to produce lower S.G.

cloud. A term used to describe a group of tiny inclusions, or of very small internal fractures, so arranged as to produce a semitransparent to semitranslucent film resembling a cloud.

cloud agate. A name applied especially to light gray transparent to semitransparent chalcedony with more or less rounded spots of darker gray which resemble dark clouds.

cloudy agate. A term loosely used for white to gray chalcedony containing any cloudy effect.

cloudy amber. A trade classification which includes translucent to opaque amber. Its comparative opacity is due to inclusions of small bubbles.

cm. Abbr. for centimeter.

Co. Abbreviation for the element cobalt.

coal jade. A descriptive term applied by Chinese to a specific color quality of jade.

coated stone. (1) A stone entirely covered by some transparent material to improve its color. (2) Same as **lacquer back.** See also **altered stone.**

cobalt. An element. Gemologically important as the coloring agent of synthetic blue spinel and of many blue glass imitations.

cobalt glass. Blue paste (glass) colored with cobalt.

cobaltite. A mineral. Usually resembles pyrite except pinkish. Cut but rarely for gem use. Iso. CoAsS; H. 5½; S.G. 6.0-6.3.

cobaltocalcite. A translucent to semitranslucent, rose-red mineral species, occasionally fashioned into attractive cabochons. Chemical composition, cobalt carbonate ($CoCO_3$); crystal system, hexagonal (crystals rare; usually spherical masses, with a concentric and radiated structure); hardness, 4; specific gravity, 4.13; refractive index, 1.60-1.85. Sources: Ligiria, Italy; Katanga district, Republic of the Congo (ex-Belgian); Jervios Range, central Australia; and Boleo, Baja California, Mexico.

coconut or cocoanut pearl. A pearl which in appearance resembles the meat of a coconut; from the giant oyster or clam of Singapore (Kunz). Another trade authority mentions it as being from a white **conch.**

cohesion. A force of attraction which holds together the atoms of a substance and which tends

44

to resist any separation of them. See **cleavage; fracture; toughness.**

collections, gem. See **museum gem collections.**

collectors (of gems). Persons who make collections of gems as a hobby or because of scientific interest.

collet. (1) Same as **culet;** (2) a flange on which a gemstone is set.

collier. A necklace consisting of one or several strings of pearls. The strings usually are of silk and have a length of between 15 and 16 inches.

collier de chein. A pearl necklace made up of several strings of small pearls in a parallel arrangement worn close to the neck. The term is French for *dog collar.*

collimator. A lens system which parallelizes incident light rays.

colloidal. Jelly-like.

Colombian emerald. Emerald from any mine in Colombia. As a trade term, any emerald of fine color quality, from any locality.

colophonite. A cloudy yellow brown common variety of andradite garnet, rarely, if ever, cut as gem. Also a nongem variety of **vesuvianite.**

color. (1) In the broadest sense, a sensation produced on the optic nerve by **light,** which varies as to (a) the wave length or combinations of wave lengths of that light, a variation described as a variation of **hue,** and as to (b) the **tone** and **intensity** of that hue. As a result of these possible variations of this sensation some authorities estimate that about 150 hues and over one million different color sensations or *colors* can be distinguished, each color being a variation in tone and intensity of one of those hues. In this broader sense white light, produced by the combination of wave lengths of all hues in the **visible spectrum,** is also considered to be a color, as well as grey, which is the lower intensity of white, black which is a total absence of color, and the purple hues, which are a blending of the red and blue or violet hues. All sensation of vision is one of light, an object being visible only because of a color variation from its surroundings. An object which reflects all wave lengths of the light which falls on it has the same color as that light e.g., blue light falling on a white object changes its apparent color to blue. Other objects absorb certain wave lengths and reflect others which produce the sensation known as the color of that object. In opaque gems this absorption occurs near the surface, in transparent gems it occurs as the rays pass through the stone. See also **absorption, primary colors.** (2) In a narrower sense, the word color is limited to hue, and the variation of such hue as to its tone and intensity, a limitation which excludes white, grey and black. Thus the term *colored birds* would exclude blackbirds. See **chromatic color, colored stone.**

Colorado aquamarine. Aquamarine from Mt. Antero, Colorado. Usually pale blue to pale blue-green, but occasionally of the most valued color, pale light blue.

Colorado jet. Jet from Colorado; of good quality.

Colorado lapis lazuli. Dark blue lapis lazuli from Sawatch Range, Colorado.

"Colorado ruby." Pyrope (garnet).

Colorado topaz. (1) Topaz from Colorado which is colorless or pale blue. (2) A misnomer for yellowish **citrine** or **topaz quartz.**

Colorado tourmaline. Pink, lilac, green and colorless tourmaline which, for a while after 1906, was found near Royal Gorge, Colorado.

Colorado turquoise. Turquoise of good color from four different localities in central Colorado. Nevada is the only state which produces more **American turquoise.**

colored pearl. A pearl which exhibits a pronounced body color, which may be red, purple, blue and gray to dead black, as distinguished from a **fancy pearl.** Usually a **fresh-water pearl.**

colored stone. A trade term in common use in North America to mean a gemstone of any species other than diamond. This usage illogically classifies all varieties of such species as colored stones, including colorless varieties, but it does not include colored diamonds. However, it has proved a practicable and satisfactory classification.

Colored-Stone Certificate. A certificate awarded to those who complete successfully the Colored-Stone and Gem-Identification Courses of the Gemological Institute of America.

color filter. Glass of a special color which, when white light passes through it, absorbs or filters out all its spectrum colors except certain ones. When emeralds, demantoid garnets and some other genuine or synthetic stones are seen through filter which absorbs all but red and green, those stones appear red. Such filters are known as beryloscopes, **emerald glasses, Chelsea filter,** etc.

color grade. The grade or classification into which a gem is placed by examination of its color in comparison to the color of other gems of the same variety.

Color Grader. An accessory designed and manufactured by the Gemological Institute of America to facilitate the color grading of diamonds under binocular magnification and to demonstrate it readily to customers.

colorless. Devoid of any color, as is pure water, a pane of ordinary window glass, or a fine diamond; therefore distinctly different from white, as is milk, or white jade. As only transparent objects can be colorless, and no opaque object can be colorless, such terms as *white sapphire* and *white topaz* are misnomers. Rock crystal is a colorless variety of quartz; milky quartz is a white variety.

color nomenclature system. A system of correlated names of colors by the use of which it is possible to more nearly describe colors than by such names as *robin's-egg blue, leaf green,* etc. In North American gemology a mathematical system has been developed and established based on 24 hues, systematically equidistant from each other, ·on the circumference of a color circle. These hues are systematically named blue, **greenish blue, blue-green, bluish green**, etc. The variations of these hues are further described as **hues** and **intensity**. To perfect this system the terms **orangy** a n d **violetish** were coined.

color play. A term usually used to mean **dispersion** and not **play of color.**

columnar. In geology, having slender prisms in close parallel grouping.

common clear amber. A German trade grade or color quality of transparent amber; light yellow. See **clear amber.**

common opal. Opal without **play of color.** Most varieties are of no gemological interest or importance, others because of their color or markings are set in jewelry. See **precious opal.**

compact. Consisting of a firm, closely united aggregate.

complex crystals. Those having many crystal forms and faces.

composite stone. An English term. Same as **assembled stone.**

comptonite. Opaque variety of thomsonite from Lake Superior region; often cut cabochon as a curio stone. Also from Italy.

concentric. Consisting of spherical layers about a common center.

conch (konk). (1) A salt-water spiral univalve or snail; a **gastropod.** The species *Strombus gigas* and the species *Cassis madagascarensis* produce conch pearl

and the former provides much of both the pink and brown shell from which cameos are carved. (2) A term sometimes used as a synonym of shell (of any mollusc).

conchoidal fracture (kon-koi'dal). *Shell-like* or *conchoidal fracture* are terms used to describe breakage which produces curved ridges like the outside markings on a shell, or the ripple marks in water.

conchologist. One who is master of or proficient in, conchology, that branch of zoology which treats of molluscs especially with reference to their shells.

conch pearl. Pearl, which may be one of several colors, from the **conch.** Only the pink, which resembles pink coral, is used in jewelry. Found principally in waters of Florida and Bahamas. Devoid of nacreous luster; not a **true pearl.**

concretions. Mechanical aggregation, or chemical union of particles of mineral forming balls or nodules in a different material.

confused. Irregular, indistinct aggregate.

conglomerate (kon-glom'er-ate). Rock composed of gravel embedded in sand, which acts as a cement.

"Congo emerald." Dioptase.

"Connemara marble." Dark green to grayish gem quality serpentine.

conical. Cone shaped. In mineralogy, usually an elongated cone as are most icicles.

conoscope. An instrument making use of convergent polarized light for gem examination; for the purpose of producing interference figures.

contact goniometer. See **goniometer.**

contact twin. See **twin.**

convex cutting. Cabochon cutting.

Coober Pedy opal. Precious white opal from Coober Pedy, South Australia. It is similar to White Cliffs opal, but with a more nearly colorless body color.

copal (koe'pal). A natural colorless, lemon yellow or yellowish brown resin from Africa, East Indies and South America. Similar in appearance to amber, soluble in alcohol, ether, turpentine or linseed oil and used principally for varnishes and lacquer, the hardest varieties being used in imitating amber (Kraus and Holden). See **kauri copal.**

copaline or **copalite.** A resinous substance, first found in blue clay at Highgate, near London, and apparently a vegetable resin, partly changed by remaining in the earth. Like resin **copal** in hardness, color, transparency and difficult solubility in alcohol. Color clear, pale yellow to dirty gray and dirty brown. Emits a resinous aromatic odor when broken

"copper emerald" Dioptase.

"copper lapis." Azurite.

"copper malachite." Chrysocolla.

coque de perle. An oval section of the rounded whorl of the shell of the Indian nautilus; because of its thinness it has to be backed with cement, and in appearance resembles blister pearl. (Smith)

corail (French). Coral.

coral. A semitranslucent to opaque material of organic origin, usually found in light to dark tones of red to orangy red, but may be more nearly orange, flesh colored or white. It is the branchlike, calcareous framework of the coral polyp and is formed by the accretion of colonies of these tiny marine invertebrates. The calcium carbonate is in the form of calcite, and this structure is radial from the center of each branch. This so-called precious coral is known technically as *Corallium Rubrum* or *Corallium Nobile.* Coral has long been popular for beads in the manufacture of necklaces, bracelets and rosaries and for carved objects, such as cameos, intaglios and figurines. Pieces of sufficient size have been carved into umbrella handles and walking sticks. Chemical composition, calcium carbonate ($CaCO_3$); crystal system (crystalline aggregate); hardness, 3 to 4; specific gravity, 2.60 to 2.70; refractive index, 1.65. Black coral from Hawaiian waters has an R.I. of about 1.37. Sources: Mediterranean Sea, Persian Gulf, Japan, Australia and Ireland.

coral agate. Any agate resembling fossilized coral. More specifically agatized or silicified coral, in which white coral skeletons appear against flesh-red background. A variety of **beekite.**

corali (Italian). Coral.

coral jade. A descriptive term applied by Chinese to a specific color quality of jade.

coralline. Aniline-dyed red chalcedony.

coraux (Fr.). Plural of coral.

cordierite. Same as **iolite.**

"Corean jade." "Korean jade."

Corean jade. See Korean jade.

corindite. Trade name for an artificial abrasive, consisting mainly of corundum.

cornelian. An alternate spelling of carnelian preferred in England.

cornalina. (Span. andPort.). Carnelian.

cornaline. French word for carnelian, sometimes used in other nations as deceptive term for analine-dyed red chalcedony.

cornerina. (Span.) Carnelian.

"Cornish diamond". Rock crystal.

corn tongs. (1) Especially in England, tweezers with somewhat blunt, rounded ends, ribbed within, with a fairly weak spring. They are particularly suitable for handling stones and pearls. (2) In the United States, a term infrequently used to describe pearl tongs.

corozo nut. The hard, close-grained, white kernel of the ivory palm (Phytelephas Macrocarpa), which bears a marked resemblance to, and is often substituted for, elephant ivory. It is one of two substances known by the general term vegetable ivory, the other being the doum-palm nut. Hardness, 2½; specific gravity, 1.40 to 1.43; refractive index, 1.583. Source: Brazil, Peru, Colombia and most of the warm, humid forests of South America.

corpse pearls. Pearls buried with Chinese dead in Sumatra, one in the mouth and one in each eye.

corrected loupe. See loupe, corrected.

Corsican green. A mineral similar to bastite; used as a substitute for it in ornamental objects.

corundolite. A name which has been suggested for (1) colorless synthetic corundum, (2) rock composed of corundum or emery.

corundum (kor-run"dum). A mineral of which ruby, sapphire and emery are varieties. Hex. Al$_2$O$_3$; S.G. 3.9-4.1; R.I. 1.76/1.77-1.77/1.78. Bi. 0.008; Disp. 0.018. Ruby from Burma, Siam, Ceylon and (rarely) N. C. Sapphire from Kashmir, Burma, Siam, Ceylon, Australia and Montana.

Coscuez (or Cosquez) emeralds. Emeralds from Coscuez mine near Muzo mine, Colombia.

cosmites. A term which has been used to designate decorative materials, ornamental stones and gems.

costume jewelry. Term used in North America to describe jewelry designed especially for use with the current mode in women's garments, and usually confined to jewelry of little intrinsic worth. Usually contains imitations of gems and metal or materials of even less value, but the term is sometimes used for jewelry containing precious stones and metals.

cowdie gum. Same as kauri copal.

Cr. Abbreviation for the element chromium.

crackled quartz. See crackled stones.

crackled stone. A gemstone in which numerous small cracks have been formed as a result of heating and sudden cooling, producing rainbow colors (as in naturally occurring **iris quartz**) by interference of light. Also, such a stone may be colored artificially, by impregnating the cracks with dye. Red- or green-stained crackled **rock crystal**, a mineral frequently used for this purpose, is sometimes called **firestone**. "Indian emerald" is a misnomer for green crackled quartz.

cradle. A trough in which placer miners wash or rock gem gravels.

craquelees (French). Rock crystal which has "crackled" producing slight iridescence. See **crackled stones**.

crazing. The tendency of opals, especially those from Nevada, to crack after being mined and exposed to the air, a condition apparently caused by a loss of moisture. The deterioration usually begins with shrinkage of the stone's surface as it loses moisture, producing a network of fine, shallow cracks on the surface. As drying continues, the cracks become deeper and the stone finally breaks. If the cracks are removed by repolishing, complete breakage may be avoided. Also known as *checking*. See **opal**.

cream fancy rosée pearl. A cream pearl with a much more pronounced rosé orient than a cream rosé pearl.

cream pearl. A pearl with a cream-colored body but without any particular hue of orient, or overtone. Light-, medium- and dark-cream pearls are distinguished.

cream rosé pearl. A pearl with a creamy body color and a pink, iridescent overtone caused by orient.

creolin. A kind of pudding stone (brecciated jasper).

creolite. A red-and-white banded jasper from Shasta and San Bernardino Counties, Calif.

crested. Consisting of groups of tabular crystals forming ridges.

crisoberilo (Span.). Chrysoberyl.

crisocola (Span.). Chrysocolla.

crisoprasa (Span.). Chrysoprase.

cristal brilliant (Span.). Rhinestone or other imitation diamond.

cristal de roca (Span.); **cristal de rocha** (Port.). Rock crystal.

Cristaria Plicata. A *fresh-water* mussel of Chinese rivers that has long been used in that country to artificially induce the production of **cultured blister pearls** and nacre-covered, knoblike pieces of bone, wood, brass and leaden images of Buddha. It is also used as one of the host molluscs for fresh-water pearl culture in Lake Biwa, Shiga Province, Honshu, Japan.

critical angle. In gemology, the angle beyond which total reflection occurs, which varies with the R.I. of the stone; the higher the R.I. the smaller the critical angle. Rays of light traveling inside the stones will be totally reflected back into the stones if they impinge upon the inside surface at an angle greater than the critical angle; but those impinging at a smaller angle will largely be refracted out of the stones.

crocidolite. A fibrous amphibole, also known mineralogically as blue asbestos. Its bluish color predominates in **sapphire quartz** and **hawk's-eye** but is altered to yellow brown or red in its **pseudo-morph, tiger-eye,** which is sometimes incorrectly called crocidolite.

crocidolite opal. A common opal containing inclusions of crocidolite. See **opal cat's-eye.**

crocidolite quartz. Tiger eye.

cross facets. Same as **break facets.** See also **girdle facets.**

cross stone. A name for (1) **chiastolite** and (2) **staurolite.**

crown. That part of any facetted stone above the girdle.

crown glass. A term which refers to a group of glasses characterized by relatively low dispersion, and used only for cheapest gem imitations except occasionally for gems of lowest dispersion. S.G. usually 2.3-2.5; R.I. usually 1.49-1.53, although extreme limits are S.G. 2.1-2.6; R.I. 1.44-1.53. See **flint glass.**

Crown of the Andes. A gold crown set with 453 emeralds, estimated to weigh 1521 carats; the principal stone weighs 45 carats. It is said to have belonged to Atahualpa (1502-1533), last of the Inca rulers. The Crown was made by the people of Popayan, Colombia, in thanksgiving for having been spared from an epidemic. After six years of labor, it was completed and placed on the statue of the Madonna at the cathedral at Popayan. Since the Crown was brought to the United States in 1936, it has been exhibited in museums, jewelry stores, gem-and-mineral shows, and by many charities for fund-raising purposes. During this time, it was owned by an American syndicate called Crown of the Andes, Inc. In 1963,

it was sold at auction to the Dutch diamond cutter and gem dealer, J. Asscher. Its present owner is Oscar Heyman & Bros., Inc., New York City manufacturing jewelers.

crucite. Same as **andalusite.**

cryptocrystalline (krip"toe-kris'tal-in). Indistinctly crystalline, in which the crystalline grains are not discernible even under magnification, although an indistinct crystalline structure can be proven by the polarizing **microscope.**

crystal. (1) A crystalline solid bounded by natural plane surfaces. (2) A trade term for diamond of a particular nuance of color.

crystal aggregate. A number of crystals grown together so that each crystal in the group is large enough to be seen by the unaided eye and each crystal is more or less perfect. In gemology it differs from a **crystalline aggregate,** as a homogenous gemstone can be cut only from an individual crystal of a crystal aggregate. Same as crystal group.

crystal faces. The flat plane surfaces on crystals.

crystal form. Form or shape in which crystals occur; the cube, the octahedron and others.

crystal form, ideal. One in which the like faces are of the same size and shape.

crystal group. Same as **crystal aggregate.**

crystal habit. See **habit.**

crystal indices. Numbers or other representations which indicate the inclination of a crystal face to the crystal axes.

crystalline (kris'tal-in). Having crystal structure. The term is often used in this book to describe a substance having crystal structure without definite geometrical external form.

crystalline aggregate. Massive crystalline material made up of many particles, each an individual crystal too small to be seen by the unaided eye. When cut as a gem, can be polished with a smooth, reflecting surface. See **crystal aggregate.**

"crystalline emerald." A deceiving name for an **emerald triplet.**

"crystalline glass". German trade term for parti-colored glass used for gem imitations.

crystalline grains. Minute crystals or crystalline particles which compose a granular crystalline aggregate. Distinguished from minute fiber-like crystals which compose fibrous crystalline aggregates.

crystalline material. Same as crystal material.

crystalline quartz. Term used to distinguish all the varieties of quartz which are not cryptocrystalline; **rock crystal; amethyst, citrine, cairngorm, rose quartz, tiger eye,** etc.

crystallite. A minute mineral form without a sufficiently definite crystal outline to indicate the species to which it belongs, but marking the first step in the crystallization process. Present in some **obsidian** and other glassy volcanic rocks.

crystallographic axes. In crystallography certain imaginary fixed lines of reference of indefinite length extending in definite directions and intersecting at the center of the crystal.

crystallographic direction (kris"tal-oe-graf'ik). Refers to directions in the various crystal systems which correspond with the growth of the mineral and often with the direction of one of the faces of the original crystal itself.

crystallographic plane. See **plane of symmetry.**

crystallography (kris"tal-og'ra-fi). The science which describes the form of crystals.

crystalloluminescence (kris'tal-oe-lue'mi-nes'ens). Light given off by certain substances in crystallizing from a solution. Arsenic oxide (As_2O_3) is an example.

crystal material. Any substance possessing crystal structure but no definite geometric form visible to the unaided eye. Also known as crystalline material.

crystal soldered emerald. Same as soldered emerald, but with rock crystal substituted for beryl.

crystal structure. An orderly arrangement of atoms; identical in all specimens of any given mineral.

crystal systems. All crystalline minerals are grouped and classified according to one of six different crystal systems, each species occurring in only one of those systems. They are: **isometric** (or **cubic), tetragonal, hexagonal, orthorhomic** (or **rhombic), monoclinic** and **triclinic.**

crystolon. Trade name for an artificially produced carbide of silicon SiC, used as an abrasive.

Cs. Abbr. for the element caesium.

ct. An abbr. for **carat.**

Cu. Abbr. for the element copper.

cube. A crystal form. Its six faces are squares and perpendicular to each other.

cubic. Having the form of a cube, as a cubic crystal; or referring to directions parallel to the faces of a cube, as cubic cleavage. See **cubic system.**

"cubic mineral or stone". Mineral or stone of the **cubic system.**

cubic system. A crystal system, same as **isometric system.**

cubo-octahedron. A crystal form which has faces of both the cube and the dodecahedron.

culasse (koo'los') (French). The base or **pavilion** of a gemstone.

culet. The small facet polished across what would otherwise be the sharp point or ridge on the **pavilion** of a faceted stone, espe cially one which is brilliant cut.

cultivated pearl. An a l t e r n a t e name for c u l t u r e d p e a r l. Thought by importers of natural pearls in U.S.A. to be misleading in its meaning.

culture pearl. A rarely used variation of the term **cultured pearl.**

cultured blister pearl. An artificially induced **blister pearl.** The Chinese forerunner of the whole c u l t u r e d pearl. Produced by placing an object, usually a hemisphere of mother-of-pearl, or a small Buddha in the shell of a fresh-water mussel which coated it with nacre. The hemispheres were cut from the shell and pegged to a hemisphere of moth-er-of-pearl, creating a round pearl doublet.

cultured pearl. A pearl produced by artificially inducing the formation of a pearl sac, usually by the introduction of a large mother-of-pearl bead and a square of mantle tissue into the body of a pearl-bearing mollusc. Over this core, layers of nacre, seldom more than $\frac{1}{2}$ millimeter in thickness, exactly like those of natural pearls, are deposited by the mollusc. Cultured pearls are produced largely in Japanese waters in the mollusc *Pinctada Martensii.* Nonnucleated fresh-water cultured pearls, in which the pearl sac is formed by a nucleus of mantle tissue, are grown in Japan's Lake Biwa; the host molluscs are *Hyriopsis Schlegeli* and *Cristaria Plicata.* Chemical composition, the outer nacreous layers are composed of calcium carbonate ($CaCO_3$); crystal structure, an aggregate composed largely of minute orthorhombic crystals of aragonite and sometimes hexagonal calcite crystals; hardness, $2\frac{1}{2}$ to 4; specific gravity, 2.72 to 2.78; refractive index, 1.53-1.69; birefringence, .156. See **cultured blister pearl, one-year pearl.**

Cultured-Pearl Association of America. The Cultured-Pearl Association of America is an organization of cultured-pearl importers and dealers who are dedicated to maintaining quality standards for the industry. It was founded in 1956. The purposes of the Association are as follows: to stimulate customer interest in the desirability of cultured-pearl jewelry through a program of national advertising and publicity; to establish ethical business standards for cultured-pearl importers and dealers, to which all members of the Association are committed to adhere; to educate the customer in the many aspects that determine the value of cultured pearls, and to direct him to the recognized professional jeweler for guidance in their purchase; to remain cognizant of both the immediate and long-range interests and requirements of the retail jeweler, and work toward stabilizing the wholesale cultured-pearl market; to spotlight unfair trade practices in the advertising and sales promotion of simulated pearl-type beads, as they relate to cultured pearls and to work to correct such practices. Headquarters: 663 Fifth Ave., New York City 10036.

cupid's darts. Fleches d'amour.
curator. One who is in charge of a department in a museum.

curio stone. Term used in this book for a stone of little intrinsic value, which, however, combines uniqueness or souvenir value with a reasonable amount of beauty or durability. Examples: **cross stone, fairy stone, Niagara spar.** In other books on gems usually classed as an **ornamental stone.**

curvette. A misspelling of cuvette, probably a result of mispronunciation. See **cuvette.**

cushion cut. Any style of cutting, either faceted or cabochon, that has a generally rectangular shape, or outline. Any such elongated stone with rounded ends and curved sides is called a **cushion-antique cut.**

cushion-shaped brilliant. The fac-

eted style from which the present circular **brilliant cut** developed. A more or less square form with rounded corners.

cut (of a gem). The style or form in which a gem has been fashioned; as brilliant cut, emerald-cut.

cut stone. A stone which has been fashioned as a gem, as distinguished from an uncut or rough stone. See **cutting, fashioning.**

cutter. A term applied to a lapidary, or any other artisan who fashions gemstones.

cutting. (1) A term in general use to mean fashioning and therefore to include the operations not only of sawing (which technically is the only cutting operation in fashioning) but of grinding, polishing and faceting.

cuvette (koo"vet'). A term sometimes applied to the **intaglio** which has a raised cameo-like figure in a concave depression.

cyclic. Circular as in certain types of **repeated twinning** that tend to produce circular forms.

cyclops agate. An eye agate with but one "eye".

cylinder (gem). Stone fashioned as a cylinder. Carved with designs, inscriptions or names, for use as seals. In the ancient business and social world drilled lengthwise for insertion of cord for carrying or wearing. Often fashioned of gem minerals.

cymophane. (sye'-moe-fane or sim'-oe-fane). (1) The variety name which includes all **chrysoberyl** with a girasol or chatoyant effect. (2) More specifically, **chrysoberyl cat's-eye** only. (3) An alternate but little used name for the entire species of **chry-**

soberyl.

cyprine. (sip'rin or sip'rene.) A light blue variety of vesuvianite.

cyst pearl. **True pearl**, which occurs in a sac or pouch within the tissues of a mollusc as distinguished from pearl, which forms outside of the tissues or mantle, such as **blister pearl**, which is not a true pearl.

D

D. Abbrevation sometimes used for density in **specific gravity**.

dactylioglyphist. An engraver of gems for rings and other ornaments.

dactyliography (dak‑til″‑e‑og′‑rah‑fe). The history and lore of engraved gems. Also (rare) the art of gem engraving.

dammar or **dammer.** A name applied to two different varieties of **resin**: (1) from the tree *Pinus dammara* of East Indian origin and marketed principally from Singapore; sometimes called cat's‑eye resin. Has resinous odor. (2) That known as **kauri copal**, which smells like turpentine. These varieties (1) and (2) are often confused. Both are used as varnish and sometimes as amber imitations, or melted with amber, and often contain real or imitation insects. Both, unlike amber, are easily softened and made sticky by ether. According to Bauer, both become sticky when rubbed briskly. See **copal**.

danburite. Dark orange‑yellow, yellowish brown, or yellowish brown to colorless, greyish, transparent to translucent, mineral, cut for collectors. Resembles topaz, more in chemical composition and physical properties than in appearance. Ortho. $CaB_2(SiO_4)_2$; H. 7‑7½; S.G. 3.0; R.I. 1.630/1.636. Phosphoresces reddish when heated. Fluoresces pale blue (Smith). First found near Danbury, Conn. Other principal localities: yellow, Burma and Madagascar; colorless, Bur‑

ma and Japan. See also "**danburyite.**"

"**danburyite or danburite.**" Has been used for light red synthetic corundum. See **danburite**.

Danish amber. Amber from coasts of Denmark. See **Baltic amber**.

daourite. Same as **rubellite**.

dark‑field illumination. A method of illuminating diamonds and other gemstones with a strong light from the side while the stone is viewed against a black background. It causes inclusions to stand out clearly and reduces confusing surface reflections. This principle, together with *light‑field illumination*, is incorporated in the *Gemolite*, or *Gemscope* (trademarks, Gemological Institute of America), the *Diamondscope* (trademark, American Gem Society), plus the *GIA Gem Detector* and the *GIA Diamond Grader*.

Darwin glass. A form of tektite rich in silica, from Tasmania. S.G. 1.8‑2.3. See **tektite**.

date stone jade. A term used by Chinese for particular color quality of jade.

datolite (dat ′oe‑lite). A transparent to translucent mineral, rarely white and opaque. Greenish, yellowish, reddish, brownish, white and mottled varieties and the white porcelain‑like variety found in Lake Superior region, which often contains copper inclusions, are sometimes cut as **a curio stone**. Mono. $HCaBSiO_5$; H. 5‑5½; S.G. 2.9‑3.0; R.I. 1.62/1.67; Bi. 0.44. From Italy,

Norway, Germany, Tasmania, Conn, N. J., and other sources.

daurite. Corrupt spelling of **daourite.**

D.C. A trade abbreviation meaning **diamond cut** or **brilliant cut.**

"dead pearl." Trade term for pearl with lusterless or dead white appearance.

decorative stone. (1) A stone used as architectural trimming in columns, mantles, and store fronts. May sometimes be set as in silver, or gold-filled jewelry, but then usually as curio stones. Examples: **malachite, marble.** (2) A term sometimes used alternately with **ornamental stone** but not in this glossary.

decrepitation. Violent breaking away of particles, with crackling sound, on sudden heating.

deer-horn pearl. Pearl from the "buck-horn clam" sometimes called the deer-horn.

deflagration (def"la-grae'shun). Sudden combustion; flashing like gunpowder.

deformed crystal. A crystal bent or twisted out of its normal shape, so that the angles between its crystal faces may differ widely from those on the regular form. See **distorted crystal.**

dehydrated stone. One from which the normal water content has been evaporated, usually by natural processes.

dekorite. Bakelite.

delatinite. Same as **delatynite.**

delatynite. A variety of amber from Delatyn in the Galician Carpathians, differing from succinite in containing rather more carbon (79.93%), less succinic

acid (0.74-1.67%), and no sulphur (English). Schlossmacher classifies among Rumanian ambers as **delatenite,** (evidently a misspelling which other authors have copied) and gives H. 2-2.5; S.G. 1.0444.

delawarite. Aventurine feldspar from Delaware County, Pa.

delphinite. Yellowish green **epidote** from France. Same as thallite or oisanite.

Deltah pearls. Trade-marked name for both solid and wax-filled imitation pearls.

demantoid. (1) A transparent green variety of **andradite** (garnet) still often bought and sold as "olivine." Rare in large sizes. Disp. .057, highest of all important gemstones. Less hard than other garnets. Iso. $Ca_3Fe_2(SiO_4)_3$; H. 6.5; S.G. 3.8 - 3.9; R.I. 1.88-1.89. From Russia only. See **andradite; olivine.** (2) *As an adjective,* diamond-like.

Demantspar. From demantspath, the German name for **adamantine spar.**

demidovite. Blue compact chrysocolla from Nizhne, Tagilsk, Russia. Has been cut as a gem.

demifin. A term meaning *half finished,* which is used principally in the wholesale costume-jewelry trade for a stone polished above the girdle; that is, a half-finished stone.

dendrite. A tree-like form as some crystal aggregates or as inclusions such as in **dendritic agate.**

dendritic. Having the form of a tree.

dendritic agate. Agate such as mocha stone and moss agate, which have inclusions of iron or manganese oxide arranged in forms resembling trees. ferns and similar vegetation.

dendritic opal. Common opal with tree-like inclusions.

density. The quantity of matter in a given space. When used in describing a property of gemstones or their substitutes, refers to their **specific gravity.**

dentelle. French word meaning lace, but in U.S.A. a misnomer for glass imitation stone.

·Derbyshire spar. Massive fluorite.

derbystone. Amethyst colored fluorite.

descriptive gemology. The classification, composition, properties, trade grades, sources, and the methods of recovery, fashioning and use of **gem minerals** and **gem materials** and their substitutes. See **gemology.**

desert glass. Obsidian or moldavite.

desert rose. A translucent to opaque, slightly pinkish, flat, flowerlike nodule of **chalcedony.** It also resembles an oyster shell in appearance. Dark-brown portions that contain minute inclusions of goethite are cut into gems called **fire agate.** Sources: Riverside Co., California, and Arizona.

determinative gemology. The science of differentiating (1) between the various gemstones (2) and between gemstones and their substitutes, and (3) between such substitutes.

detrital. Of, or pertaining to detritus.

detritus. Loose particles or fragments of rock.

devitrification. The change of a solid substance from glassy (amorphous) structure to crystalline structure, after solidification.

Devonshire Emerald. A splendidly formed crystal from' Muzo mine, Colombia, presented in 1831 to the Sixth Duke of Devonshire by Dom Pedro (once Emperor of Brazil). Now in British Museum (Natural History). Weight 1383.95 m.c.; 2" in diameter and about the same length; intense grass green.

deweylite. Eppler classifies as a reddish, greenish, light yellow, or white ornamental stone cut in U.S.A. Dana classifies as an amorphous mineral near and occurring with serpentine, in Mass., Penna., and overseas. H. 2-3.5; S.G. 2.0-2.2.

diabase. A dark igneous rock. Sometimes used as a decorative stone. Composed essentially of plagioclase and augite (a **pyroxene**).

diakon or **perspex.** A plastic used in Great Britain to imitate ivory. S.G. 1.2; R.I. 1.50

dial gauge. A measuring device with jaws, the movement of one of which is indicated on a dial. More accurately called a **dial micrometer.** See **gauge; Leveridge gauge.**

diallage. A pyroxene mineral, grayish to green or dark green, also brown, sometimes exhibiting schiller. Mono. H. 4; S.G. 3.2-3.35; R.I. 1.68; Bi .024. (Dana) Schiller varieties used rarely as ornamental stone. (Bauer) Transparent varieties sometimes cut as gems.

dial micrometer. See **micrometer.**

diamantiferous (dye"a-man-tif'er-us). Bearing or containing diamonds.

Diamond. A mineral composed essentially of carbon that crystallizes in the cubic, or isometric, crystal system. It is one of the most important gemstones and is usually transparent and nearly colorless. Tones of yellow, brown, violet, green, blue, black, and red are known. When fashioned, it is the most brilliant of gems. Diamond is the hardest of all known substances, ranking 10 on the Mohs scale. The distinguishing characteristics of diamond are the extreme hardness, specific gravity of 3.52, dispersion of 0.044, and high refractive index of 2.417. Major sources include parts of southern, western and middle Africa, north and northeast South America, and Russia.

diamond balance. A sensitive scale for weighing gemstones. It is also used for obtaining the **specific gravity** of gems by the **hydrostatic weighing method.**

Diamond Certificate. A certificate awarded to those who complete successfully the *Diamond Course* of the Gemological Institute of America, which requires passing the diamond-grading and diamond-appraising instruction and practice.

diamond cut. *In the colored stone trade* means **brilliant cut.**

Diamond Grader. An instrument designed and manufactured by the Gemological Institute of America. It consists of a binocular microscope mounted on an illuminator base and is equipped with a mechanical stoneholder, iris-diaphragm light control, light- and dark-field illumination, tiltback and a turntable. Accessories for proportion and color grading extend its use.

Diamondlux (trademark, Gemological Institute of America). A special overhead light fixture, introduced in 1959, for jewelry-store illumination. The unit consists of a combination of special fluorescent tubes, the effect of which is to produce a daylight-equivalent illumination to show objects in their true colors. A unique pattern and type of baffles produce individual light sources, yielding a degree of dispersion and scintillation in gems not seen with other present kinds of illumination. The result is the equivalent of a multitude of spots, but each corrected to true color.

diamond saw. (1) A diamond-charged blade used as a cutting edge in fashioning colored stones or in the various applications in industry. (2) A saw used for dividing, or separating, rough diamonds.

Diamondscope (trademark, American Gem Society). A binocular gemological microscope, incorporating an illuminator with an adjustable baffle that affords examination of gemstones by either dark-field or light-field illumination. It is used in both the identification of colored stones and the grading of diamonds.

diamond spar. Adamantine spar.

diaphaneity (dye"a-fa-nee'i-ti). The property of being either **transparent** or **translucent.**

diaspore (dye'a-spore). Transparent to semitranslucent colorless, grayish, yellow or violet mineral, sometimes cut for collectors. Also brown. Ortho. Al_2O_3. H_2O; H. 6.5-7; S.G. 3.3-3.5; R.I.

1.70/1.75; Bi. 0.048. From Urals, Mass., Pa. and other sources.

diaspro (Italian). Jasper.

diasteria. An asteria which exhibits a star by transmitted light only. Of little or no importance as a jewel. See **asteria.**

diasterism. Asterism seen by transmitted light. See **asterism; epiasterism.**

dichroic colors. A term loosely used to refer to either the two colors observable in a dichroic stone or the three colors in a trichroic stone. Same as **twin colors.** See **dichroscope.**

dichroic gem or **stone** (dye-kroe'-ik). One which possesses **dichroism.**

dichroism. The property of most doubly refractive colored minerals of the tetragonal and hexagonal system of transmitting two different colors in two different (right angle) directions. See **pleochroism; trichroism; dichroscope; polariscope.**

dichroite. Same as **iolite.**

dichroscope (dye'kroe-scope). An instrument designed to detect two of the different colors emerging from pleochroic (i.e., dichroic or trichroic) gems. Contains a rhomb of Iceland spar and a lens system in a short tube, and exhibits the two colors side by side.

diffraction. A modification which light undergoes, as in passing by the edges of opaque bodies or through narrow slits, or when transmitted through or reflected from a diffraction grating in which the rays of white light are broken into a series of colored spectra. The optical phenomena of diffraction also takes place

upon reflections of light from the sharp, jagged edges of broken glass and from the edges of the minute scales which make up the surface of a nacreous pearl. See also **orient.**

diffraction grating. A grating of fine parallel lines ruled on glass or metal, used to produce spectra by diffraction. See **grating.**

diffraction spectroscope. See **spectroscope.**

diffusion column. A long, narrow test tube partially filled with two heavy liquids such as methylene iodide with about five times as much benzol added. The benzol and methylene iodide gradually diffuse and a mixed liquid results whose density (S.G.) increases gradually from top to bottom. Stones of S.G.'s within the limits of the liquid settle at the levels which correspond with their particular densities. See **S.G.**

diggings. Any mineral deposit or mining camp. In U.S.A. applied to placer mining.

dike. A vertical or inclined fissure in the earth's crust which has been filled with igneous material forced upward while molten and become rock by cooling.

dimetric system. Same as **tetragonal system.**

dimorphism. See **polymorphism.**

diopside (di-op'-side). A transparent to opaque, medium-dark to very dark-green, colorless to faint green or light yellowish-green (**alalite**), pale yellow (**malacolite**), or blue to violet-blue (**violane**) mineral species. A fibrous chatoyant variety and black, four-rayed star material also occur. Chemical composition, calcium-magnesium silicate ($CaMa(SiO_3)_2$); crystal system, monoclinic (violane usually massive); hardness, 5 to 6; specific gravity, 3.27 to 3.31; refractive index, 1.678-1.701; birefringence, .024 to .028. Sources: South Africa, Italy, N.Y., Ontario, Burma, Ceylon, Malagasy Republic and other localities. See **violane, chrome diopside, mayaite, tuxtlite.**

diopside cat's-eye. Fine green chrome-diopside cat's-eye, from Burma. (Smith)

diopside-jadeite. A term sometimes used for pyroxene, intermediate between jadeite and diopside, from Mexico or Central America, as distinguished from soda-jadeite, the jadeite proper of Burma. See **mayaite.**

dioptase (dye-op'tase). A mineral often approaching emerald in color. Cut as gems for collectors but is usually imperfectly transparent and cleaves too easily for extensive commercial use. Hex. H_2CuSiO_4. H. 5; S.G. 3.3; R.I. 1.64/1.69-1.66/1.71; Bi. 0.051-0.054; Disp. 0.022. From Russia, the Congos, S. W. Africa, Arizona, and other sources. See "copper emerald."

direct weighing method. Same as **hydrostatic weighing.**

dirigem. Copyrighted trade name for green synthetic spinel.

disp. Abbreviation for **dispersion.**

dispersion. The property of a transparent gemstone or other prism to separate white or nearly white light into colored rays, white light being separated into the spectrum colors; the interval

between such colors varies in different gemstones, and is usually expressed by the measure of the difference between the refractive indices of the red ray (Fraunhofer line B) and the violet ray (Fraunhofer line G). This measure is used in this book and abbreviated **disp.** as; zircon, disp. 038. Same as **fire.**

disseminated. Scattered through a rock or other mineral aggregate in the form of grains or pebbles.

disseminated crystals. Crystals which are found not attached to the mother rock; sometimes with well-developed faces and doubly terminated.

distorted crystal. A crystal whose faces have developed unequally, some being larger than others. Some distorted crystal forms are drawn out or shortened, but the angle between the faces remains the same. See **deformed crystal.**

distrene. A polystyrene plastic. S.G. 1.05; R.I. 1.58. (Anderson) Adaptable to imitating amber.

ditroite (German). **Sodalite.**

divergent. Extending in different directions from a point; radiating.

doblete (Span.). Doublet.

doctored pearls. Pearls which have had surface cracks filled, have been artificially colored, or which have been made more spherical by removing certain portions other than an entire layer as in peeling.

dodecahedral (doe"dek-a-hee'dral). Pertaining to the rhombic dodecahedron.

dodecahedron (doe"dek-a-hee'dron). A twelve-faced geometrical crystal form of the isometric system. If the faces have four edges each of equal length, it is a *rhombic dodecahedron;* if five edges (with one longer than the others) it is a *pentagonal dodecahedron* or *pyritohedron.*

dog-tooth pearl. Tusk-like baroque pearl.

dollar value (of pearl). Same as the **once.**

domatic (doe-mat'ik). Relating to a dome; a horizontal prism.

dot agate. White chalcedony with round, colored, spots.

double cabochon. See **cabochon.**

double pearl. A pearl formed of two distinct pearls united under a nacreous coating.

double refraction. The refraction and separation of each of the single rays of light into two rays which occurs as they pass obliquely from air into minerals of any but the isometric system. The two rays then travel at different velocities and vibrate in perpendicular planes. The polariscope or dichroscope or crossed **Nicols** reveal the presence of double refraction. See **birefringence; Bi.; anomalous double refraction.**

double rose cut. Form of cutting consisting of two rose-cut forms joined along their bases. See **rose cut.**

double rosette. Same as **double rose cut.**

doublet. An **assembled** stone of two portions, bound together by a colorless cement or by fusing the parts one to the other.

doubly refractive. Possessing the property of **double refraction.**

doubly terminated crystals. See **termination.**

doum-palm nut. The hard, close-grained, white kernel of the doum-palm tree *(Hyphaene Thebaica)*, which bears a marked resemblance to, and is often substituted for, elephant ivory. It is one of two substances known by the general term **vegetable ivory,** the other being corozo cut. Hardness, 2 to $2\frac{1}{2}$; specific gravity, 1.38 to 1.40; refractive index, 1.538. Source: Upper Egypt and central Africa.

D.R. Abbreviation for **double refraction.**

Dragon Lord Ruby. See **Gnaga Boh Ruby.**

dravite. Brown tourmaline.

dreikanter. A pebble shaped by wind-driven sandblasting, having semi-planar faces bounded by three edges.

drilled pearl. Pearl through which a hole has been entirely drilled for stringing or drilled partly through for attachment on a pin or peg for use as earrings, rings, etc.

drop cut. Any form of cutting for gems suitable for use in pendants, earrings, etc., such as the **briolette** and **pendeloque.**

drop-form cut. Same as **drop cut.**

drop or **drop-pearl.** Pearl of pear or oval shape, especially suitable for pendants, earrings, etc. See **pear pearl.**

"druggists' pearls." See **Mytilus pearls.**

druse (drooze). A surface covered with small projecting crystals; a **geode.**

drusy or **drused.** Covered with minute crystals closely crowded, giving a rough surface with many reflecting faces.

dry diggings. Dry alluvial or placer mining operations.

dry ice test. A test for the detection of glass imitations. If a crystalline substance such as a gem mineral be placed in contact upon a piece of dry ice (solidified carbon dioxide, CO_2) a squeaking noise can be heard. This is not true of noncrystalline substances such as glass and plastic.

duck bone jade. Descriptive term applied by Chinese to a particular color grade of jade.

Duke of Devonshire Sapphire. A famous sapphire weighing 100 m.c. last reported in possession of the Duke.

dull. Lacking in brightness or intensity; almost devoid of luster.

dumortierite (du-mor'-te-er-ite). A transpararent to translucent, intense-blue to greenish-blue to violet-blue mineral species, infrequently used as a gem material. It is the coloring agent in **dumortierite quartz.** Chemical composition, an aluminum borosilicate; crystal system, orthorhombic (usually fibrous or columnar aggregates); hardness, 7; specific gravity, 3.20 to 3.40; refractive index, a single vague reading at about 1.68. Sources: Nev., Ariz., France, Norway, Brazil, Malagasy Republic and elsewhere.

dumortierite quartz. A massive, opaque, intense blue to greenish-blue to violet-blue variety of crystalline quartz, colored by inter-grown crystals of dumortierite. It is also known by the misleading name of "California lapis."

dupa xaga. Term used by Pomo Indians of California for harder obsidian than **bati xaga.** The term means obsidian, which cuts. The variety was used for razors.

Duplex Refractometer. A refractometer made by the Gemological Institute of America that employs a large, high-index hemicylinder, slotted to reduce parallax. Using an auxiliary eyepiece for flat-surface readings, it is the first refractometer designed for both spot and facet readings. A new model eliminates the movable mirror necessary in the first model. See **refractometer.**

durchscheinend (German). Translucent.

durchsichtig (German). Transparent.

dust pearls. Small seed pearls weighing less than 1/25 of a grain.

Dutch East Indies pearls. Similar to, and often classed in trade, as **Australian pearls.**

dyed pearl. Pearl which has been dyed any one of various colors, the usual process being to force dye into the pearl by way of the drill hole.

dyed stones. Minerals which are artificially dyed to improve their color or to imitate a more valuable stone. Usually fade or discolor.

dyke. Same as **dike.**

dysluite. Zinc-manganese-iron, brownish **gahnite** from Mass. and N. J.

E

Eacret Benitoite. A 7.6-c. flawless benitoite. Found by discoverer of mine and purchased by Godfrey Eacret of San Francisco, it is the largest gem quality benitoite known. Now in Roebling Collection, U. S. National Mus., Washington, D. C.

eaglestone or **aetites.** A concretionary nodule of ironstone of the size of a walnut or larger. The ancients believed that the eagle transported these stones to her nest to facilitate the laying of her eggs (Webster). Evidently a **quartz** pebble

ear-shell. The popular name for *Haliotis.* See **abalone.**

earth amber. A term rarely used to distinguish mined amber from sea amber. Also to describe amber, the outer portion of which has deteriorated in luster, transparency, and color.

earth stone. A term sometimes applied to mined **amber** to distinguish it from sea amber.

earthy. Consisting of minute particles loosely aggregated; claylike, dull.

East African pearl. See **African pearl.**

ebonite. A name for vulcanized rubber used sometimes in mourning jewelry.

ecaille. French word meaning shell and used by the trade in France and some other nations to describe tortoise shell. Often applied by unscrupulous dealers to imitation of tortoise shell.

eclat. The splendor or flash of a gem.

Edelstein. German word for precious stone. Literally "noble stone." See **Schmuckstein.**

Edelsteinkenner or **Edelsteinkundiger** (German). Gemologist.

Edelsteinkunde (ae'del-shtine-koonda) (German). The science of precious stones, gemology.

Edith Haggin de Long Ruby. A star ruby, measuring 1½ inches (4 cm.) and 1 inch (2.5 cm.) across and weighing 100 metric carats. From Burma. In Am. Mus. of Nat. Hist., N. Y.

edible oyster. See **Ostrea edulus.**

edinite. Prase.

edisonite. A name proposed for a mottled blue turquoise.

Edwardes Ruby. A fine ruby crystal presented to British Museum in 1887.

effervescence. Evolution of gas in bubbles from a liquid.

egeran. A variety of vesuvianite. Found near Eger in Western Bohemia, in region annexed by Germany from Czechoslovakia in 1939.

egg jade. A descriptive term applied by the Chinese to a particular color grade of jade.

egg pearl. Pearl shaped like an egg.

egg-shell turquoise. Turquoise with crackled appearance due to fine, irregular arrangement of matrix which appears like cracks in an egg shell.

Egyptian alabaster. Banded calcite found near Thebes, Egypt. Same material as **onyx marble.**

Egyptian emerald. Emerald from the ancient Egyptian mines of

Gebel Sikait, Gebel Zarbara in northern Etbai, near the Red Sea, which were rediscovered in 1818, but principally produce cloudy stones of light color.

Egyptian jasper. (1) Banded yellow, red, brown or black jasper from Egypt. (2) Misnomer for an orbicular jasper from beaches in the state of Washington.

Egyptian pearls. Pearls from Egyptian shore of Red Sea. Cream to yellowish body color. See **Red Sea Pearl.**

Egyptian pebble. (1) Jasper pebbles usually from deserts of Egypt. (2) Same as **Egyptian jasper.**

Egyptian peridot. Term properly applied only to peridot from St. John's Island in the Red Sea.

Egyptian turquoise. Term properly applied to turquoise found on the Sinai Peninsula, Egypt, from which turquoise has come since Biblical times; usually greenish blue, sometimes fine blue and unusually translucent.

eight cut or **eight side cut.** Same as **single cut.**

Eisenberg. A trade name for gowns and dress accessories, including jewelry called Eisenberg Ice. This contains some genuine, but principally imitation, gems, which because sold as "genuine Eisenberg" is sometimes thought to be some unusual genuine gemstone.

Eisenhower Sapphire. A bust of Dwight D. Eisenhower carved from a 2097-carat black star sapphire found at Anakie, Queensland, Australia. The finished carving weighs 1444 carats and measures $2\frac{1}{2}$ inches high, $2\frac{1}{16}$ inches wide, and $2\frac{1}{4}$ inches deep. A star is visible at the base of the neck. The sculpter was Harry B. Derian and the technical advisor, Lincoln Borglum. This carving, together with those of Presidents Lincoln, Washington and Jefferson and the *Black Star of Queensland,* were presented as a gift to the American people by the Kazanjian Foundation of Pasadena, California, a charitable, nonprofit organization founded by Kazanjian Bros., Los Angeles gem dealers. The *Eisenhower Sapphire* is presently on display at the Smithsonian Institution, Washington, D.C.

Eisenkies (German). Pyrite (Dana).

ekanite. A semitransparent, light greenish-brown to dark yellowish-green metamict calcium-thorium silicate, first discovered in Ceylon in 1953 by F. D. L. Ekanayake, gem dealer of Colombo, Ceylon. This rare mineral is highly radioactive. Some specimens exhibit a 4-rayed star. Hardness, 6 to $6\frac{1}{2}$; specific gravity, 3.28; refractive index, 1.597.

elaeolite. A mineral sometimes cut as an ornamental stone. Translucent specimens sometimes exhibit a chatoyant effect. Reddish, brownish, greenish, or grayish. See **nephelite.**

El Aguila Azteca Opal ("the Aztec eagle"). Fine 32 c. fire opal carved with head of Mexican sun god. In Field Mus. of Nat. History. Once in **Hope collection**

elastic. The property of springing back to its original form when bent, as in thin sheets of mica.

El Doradoite. A locally coined trade name for a blue quartz, sometimes cut as a gemstone. From El Dorado Co., Calif.

electric calamine. Same as **hemimorphite.**

"electric emerald." A glass imitation of emerald.

electromagnetic spectrum. The entire range of electrical energy, extending from the extremely long rays of radio and electricity at one end to the extremely short X rays at the other. The visible spectrum (visible light) is included.

electrons. The particles or electric charges which make up the greater portion of the atom and which revolve about the nucleus of the atom. See **protons.**

electrum. (1) An obsolete name for amber. (2) The alloy of gold and silver.

elektron. Ancient Greek word for amber.

element. A form of matter which cannot be decomposed by any chemical means; for example, carbon, oxygen, silicon, etc.

element stone. Opal.

elephant jasper. Dark to light-brown jasper with scattered small, black dendritic inclusions.

elephant-tooth ivory. An unusual kind of ivory from the molar teeth of the elephant, having a mottled or banded appearance in tints of cream and brown. It is sometimes used for knife handles and small carved objects.

"Elie ruby." Red pyrope (garnet) from Elie, Scotland.

elixerite (e-lix′-er-ite). A local fanciful name for a kind of **wonderstone** (banded rhyolite) found near Truth or Consequences, Sierra

Co., New Mexico. It is harder, more compact, and takes a much better polish than ordinary wonderstone, and is attractively banded in purplish brown, brown, yellow-brown, yellow and orange-yellow.

Elster pearl. Pearl from a mussel native to the Elster River, Saxony, a part of Germany.

"Ely ruby." Same as **"Elie ruby."**

emaldine. Same as **emildine.**

ematite (Italian). Hematite.

emerada. Trade-marked name for a yellowish-green synthetic spinel.

emerald. (1) The medium-light to medium-dark tones of slightly bluish-green or slightly yellowish-green **beryl.** There is no standard dividing line between emerald and either **aquamarine** or the lighter green variety known as **green beryl.** Colored by chromium, a fine emerald is one of the three most valuable gems; its color is possessed by no other gemstone except top-quality jadeite. The finest emeralds come from Colombia, good ones from Russia, and a few others from Brazil, India and Africa. It is the birthstone for May. See **synthetic emerald, synthetic stone.** (2) A color designation meaning the color of an emerald, as in **emerald jade, emerald glass,** etc., although the meaning is often extended incorrectly for any color approaching the green of emerald.

emerald cut. A form of step cutting. Favored for diamonds and emeralds and many other colored stones when the principal purpose is to enhance the color in contrast to the brilliancy or to emphasize the absence of color in diamonds. Rectangular or square with rows (steps) of elongated rectangular facets on the crown and pavilion, parallel to the girdle; usually with corner facets. Corresponding facets are generally placed on the girdle. The number of rows or steps may vary. See **square emerald cut; sharp-cornered emerald cut.**

emerald filter. Same as **emerald glass.**

emerald glass. (1) The usual trade name for a color filter through which genuine emeralds and some other genuine stones appear reddish to violetish while glass imitations and some genuine stones appear green. Same as **beryloscope.** See also **Walton filter; Detectoscope.** Also (2) any green glass such as used in manufacture of imitation stone. (3) A glass of emerald color made by fusing beryl. S.G. 2.5; R.I. 1.52. (Anderson)

emeraldine. A coined name for green dyed chalcedony.

"emeraldite." An incorrect and misleading spelling of **emeralite.**

emerald jade. Semitransparent to translucent jadeite of emerald color; most desired color in North America. Also called **imperial jade.** See also **Fei Ts'ui.**

"emerald malachite." Same as **dioptase.**

emerald matrix. Any rock embedded with emerald, especially one composed of feldspar and quartz

en cabochon. See **cabochon.**

endomorph. A crystal of one species inclosed within one of another, as one of rutile in quartz

(Webster). Here rutile is an endomorph and quartz is a **perimorph,** and rutile is said to be endomorphic and to be **endomorphous** in quartz.

endomorphous. Of, or pertaining to, **endomorph.**

endoscope. In gemology, an instrument which affords a magnified image of the drill hole of a pearl. Used to distinguish between genuine and cultured pearl. A modification of it directs onto the walls of the drill hole a tiny beam of light, the subsequent path of which through the pearl reveals whether the structure of its core is concentric (real pearl) or parallel (cultured pearl). See also pearl-testing **microscope.**

endoscopic stage. A special microscope stage used for distinguishing between drilled genuine and cultured pearls. Incorporates the principle of the **endoscope.**

"endura emerald." A coined name used for glass imitation sold by a particular distributor and still sometimes used for any glass imitation of emerald.

engelardito (Span.). Zircon.

English amber. See **British amber.**

English brilliant cut. A cushion-shaped brilliant with eight star facets, eight upper break facets, eight lower break facets, four pavilion facets, a table and a culet. See **star cut.**

"English crystal." A term used for fine tableware, including "cut glass." See also **imitations; glass.**

engraving. That branch of the lapidary art confined to comparatively small gems on which are incised various kinds of figures or designs and that are generally mounted and used as articles of personal adornment (cameos, intaglios, etc.).

enhydros. (Greek, "holding water"). Term used in describing nodules of chalcedony containing water. Such chalcedony is found in Uruguay, Australia and India, and is a **curio stone** of no gem value.

enstatite (en′stah-tite). A transparent to translucent, light- to dark-green, brownish-green, yellowish-green, yellowish-brown, brownish-yellow or gray-green magnesium-rich member of the **pyroxene** group of minerals, closely related to **hypersthene.** Some material, particularly the dark-green variety, exhibits chatoyancy. **Bronzite** is a massive, nearly opaque brownish variety that contains a multitude of fibrous inclusions, giving it a bronzelike appearance; it occasionally is cut in the cabochon form, when it may exhibit 6-rayed asterism. Chemical composition, magnesium silicate ($Mg_2Si_2O_6$); crystal system, orthorhombic; hardness, $5\frac{1}{2}$; specific gravity, 3.25; refractive index, 1.658-1.668; birefringence, .010. Sources: South Africa, Burma, India, Ceylon, Calif. and elsewhere. See **bronzite.**

"emerald triplet." An **assembled stone,** two parts of which are quartz, pale beryl or synthetic spinel and the third part a layer of green cement, serving both as colorant and adhesive.

emeralite. Light green tourmaline from Mesa Grande, Calif.

"emeraudine." Misnomer for dioptase.

emeraud soudé (French). **Soldered emerald.** Same as **soudé emerald.**

Emerita. An obsolete trade name for *synthetic* emerald-coated prefaceted natural **beryl.**

emery. An impure variety of **corundum,** often used as an abrasive.

emildine. A variety of **spessartite;** from South Africa.

emilite. Same as **emildine.**

emission spectrum. The spectrum of the radiation produced by a given source. For example, if a diamond is heated to a white heat, an emission spectrum will be produced that is characteristic of carbon and the impurities within the stone. A second kind of emission spectrum results from fluorescence; i.e., a secondary radiation caused by exitation by X-rays, ultraviolet rays, cathode rays or visible radiation. Emission spectra may be continuous or seen as a series of bright lines in the spectroscope.

enamel. A vitreous glaze. In jewelry, it is usually fused to a base by heat. The base used in jewelry is always of metal, but it may also have a glass or pottery foundation. It is applied to the metal in the form of powdered glass, often preserved in distilled water. It is dried, placed in a furnace and heated to a pale-orange heat. The particles of glass melt and run together into a smooth coating. This process is repeated until the desired thickness is obtained. The enamel is then stoned down flush with the metal walls and polished with abrasives. The principal kinds of jewelry enamels are cloisonné, plique à jour, champlevé, basse taille, niello, painted enamels and lacquer.

"enstatite cat's-eye." Enstatite which, when cabochon cut, has a **chatoyant effect.**

eosite. A trade name for a rose-colored **Tibet stone.**

epaulet (cut). A five-sided modern cut of the step cut which resembles an epaulet in outline.

epiasteria. An asteria which, cut cabochon and in the correct crystallographic direction and observed by **reflected light,** exhibits the optical phenomenon of a star. See **asteria, diasteria.**

epiasterism. Asterism seen by reflected light, as in star ruby or sapphire which is cut cabochon to reveal the asteria.

epidosite. A mixture of epidote and quartz sometimes cut cabochon as a curio stone.

epidote (ep'i-dote). A mineral of which the more transparent, pistachio-green variety has sometimes been cut as a gem for collectors. Epidote is also yellow, red, brown, black, gray or colorless. Mono. $HCa_2(Al,Fe)_3$ Si_3O_{13}. H. 6-7; S.G. 3.2-3.5; R.I. 1.73/1.77. Bi. 0.039; Disp. 0.030. From Italy, Norway, France and other sources.

epithelial sac (ep"i-the'li-al). A sac composed of **epithelium,** as is the **pearl sac.**

epithelium (ep-ih-thee'-le-um). Cells in the outer body wall, or **mantle,** of a mollusc that secrete its shell-building material.

Erb & Gray refractometer. A gemological refractometer made in two models, one (1) with a fixed hemisphere of glass and (2) with a rotating hemisphere similar to the **Tully refractometer.** See also **Rayner refractometer, Smith refractometer.**

erinide. Trade-mark name for a yellowish green synthetic spinel.

erinoid. A **casein** plastic used for moulding many common objects and sometimes for inferior gem imitations. S.G. about 1.33; R.I. about 1.53-1.54.

escarboucle (Fr.). Carbuncle (garnet).

esmeralda (Span. and Port.) Emerald.

espectroscope (Span.). Spectroscope

espinela (Span, and Port.). Spinel.

essence d'orient (e "sans'doe" rian). A substance used as coating for **imitation pearls** which resembles luster and orient of natural pearl; made from scales of various fish such as the bleak, herring, etc. Used in manufacture of most **imitation pearls.**

essonite. Same as **hessonite.**

estealita (Span.) Soapstone.

etched. Having the surface roughened by solution or corrosion.

ethical gemology. The study of the correct and incorrect nomenclature of gems, with emphasis on names and terms which may mislead or deceive purchasers.

euclase (ue'klase). A very rare gem, the light blue variety being held in great esteem by collectors, but lacking in toughness usually desirable in gemstones. Transparent, pale blue, pale bluish-green and colorless. Mono. $Be(Al, OH)SiO_4$. H. 7.5; S.G. 3.0-3.1; R.I. 1.65/1.67. Bi. 0.019; Disp. 0.016. From Russia, Brazil and other sources.

euxenite. A mineral species belonging to the group of minerals often called rare earths. Has, in rare instances, been fashioned as a gem. Brownish black. H. 6½ ; S.G. 4.7-5.0.

even fracture. When the surfaces of the fracture are smooth and even.

"evening emerald." Peridot, which loses some of its yellow tint by artificial light, appearing more greenish.

exfoliation. Splitting apart and expansion of flakes or scales on being heated.

extinction; extinction position. When employing a polarizing microscope, or polariscope for the examination of gemstones in parallel polarized light, upon rotation, the field changes from light to dark every 90 degrees, provided the stone is doubly refractive and sufficiently transparent. The change to dark is known as extinction. Singly refractive stones either exhibit no change, or if they possess anomalous double refraction, the change almost always occurs at irregular intervals.

extraordinary ray. In a uniaxial mineral, the ray which, depending upon its direction through the crystal, varies in refractive index. See **ordinary ray.**

eye agate. Agate with concentric bands which may be of various alternating colors, about a dark center.

eye glass. Any glass worn over the eye to aid vision. The term is also often used by jewelers to mean an eye loupe.

eye loupe. Any loupe so constructed that it can be held in the eye socket; used in watch making, gem grading and setting, engraving, etc. See **loupe.**

eyestone. Thomsonite.

F

F. Abbr. for the element fluorine.

"Fabulite." A trademarked name for **strontium titanite.**

face. In crystallography, one of the plane surfaces which form the sides, and often theoretically at least, the ends or **termination,** of a **crystal.**

facet. One of the small, plane, or approximately plane, polished surfaces which are placed upon gemstones fashioned as **brilliant cut, step cut** or any other **faceted cut.**

faceta (Spanish). Facet.

facet cut or **faceted cut.** A type of cut gem bounded by plane faces as distinguished from **cabochon** cut or other unfaceted cut. See **facet; cutting.**

faceting machines. Mechanical devices for holding stones during grinding or polishing facets upon them. By their use facets can be placed at the exact angles which theoretically result in producing the most brilliant stone. Rarely used in fashioning diamonds or the more valuable colored stones where recovery of a greater amount of weight is more important than maximum brilliancy. See **grinding; polishing.**

faceting tool. See **faceting machine.**

facsimile. An exact copy or reproduction. See **imitations; synthetic stones.**

fading. A term loosely used to refer to loss of color, or to any undesirable change of color in a gemstone.

Fahrenheit. Pertaining to the scale used by Fahrenheit in the graduation of his thermometer; as, 40° Fahrenheit (or 40° F).

faience. A term now applied to all kinds of glazed pottery, including the type which was used in the ancient world to imitate opaque stones such as lapis lazuli and turquoise. See **ceramic.**

fairy stone. A name for (1) **staurolite,** or (2) the variety of staurolite which occurs in the form of a **twinned crystal.**

falcon's-eye. German name (Falkenauge) for hawk's-eye.

fales. Stones with two, or more, differently colored layers.

"false amethyst." Purple **fluorite.**

"false chrysolite." Same as **moldavite.**

false cleavage. Same as **parting.**

false doublet. See **doublet.**

"false emerald." Green **fluorite.**

"false hyacinth." Same as **hessonite.**

false lapis. (1) **Lazulite.** (2) Blue-dyed agate or jasper. See **"Swiss lapis."**

false nephrite. A misnomer for serpentine, "Transvaal jade" or other green mineral similar in appearance to **nephrite.**

"false ruby." Red **fluorite.**

"false sapphire." Blue **fluorite.**

"false topaz." Same as (1) **topaz quartz;** (2) yellow **fluorite.**

falun brilliants. Name for theatre jewelry made of a lead-tin alloy.

fancy agates. Agates showing delicate markings and intricate patterns.

fancy cut. A term used for styles of cutting which are little used, or are new at the moment. Includes those defined in this book as **modern cut.**

fancy pearl. A pearl with a body color of white or cream and a **rosé orient** superimposed on an **overtone** of some hue such as blue-green, violet, purple, blue or green. (*Gems & Gemology*). See **colored pearl.**

fancy sapphire. (1) A sapphire of any hue other than blue or colorless, although colorless is included by some. See page 258.

fancy stone. (1) A variety of a gemstone which is less often encountered commercially, such as a **fancy sapphire,** or (2) an unusually fine gemstone, particularly a diamond of unusually fine **color grade.**

Fasergips (German). Fibrous gypsum, i.e., **satin spar.**

fashioned gemstone. One which has been cut and polished. See **fashioning.**

fashioning (of gems). Includes slitting, cleaving, cutting, polishing, and other operations employed in preparing rough gem material for use in jewelry; also the determination of the proportions.

Fashoda garnet. Dark red to brownish-red pyrope garnet from Tanganyika.

"Fashoda ruby." (1) Iron-rich pyrope garnet from Tanganyika (Smith). Same as **Fashoda garnet.** (2) In the trade refers usually to any red garnet.

fat amber. Opaque yellowish amber.

fat stone. A name for **nephelite.**

Its fractured s u r f a c e s have greasy luster.

fatty amber. Same as **flohmig amber.**

fault. Anything within, or on the surface of a stone which decreases its beauty or value.

faulty structure (of stones). Irregularities of crystallization; also subsequent breakage or separation between the atomic planes, such as a **cleavage crack, cloud,** or **feather.**

Fe. Abbr. for the element iron.

feather. (1) A trade term (a) commonly applied to almost any flaw inside a stone, and (b) more specifically, to a jagged irregularly shaped fracture which is white in appearance. (2) In **determinative gemology,** a series of liquid inclusions which under the microscope are elongated and irregular in shape, and grouped together in orderly proximity to each other in a manner which makes them resemble the over-all pattern of the feathers on a bird's wing.

feather gypsum. Same as **satin spar.**

Federal Trade Commission. A United States government body that oversees interstate commerce and cooperates with representatives of various industries, including the gemstone and jewelry trades, to establish trade-practice rules that govern the representation to the public of the products of those industries.

Federgips (German). Same as **Fasergips.**

Fei Ts'ui. Chinese name once applied only to kingfisher jade, and more recently to bright green or bluish greens. Like quality names of diamonds in U.S.A., the term has become meaningless and sometimes is applied to all qualities with the possible exception of dark opaque jadeite. See **kingfisher jade; Pi Yü; Pai Yü.**

feldspar. A group of closely related mineral species, the only gemologically important of which are **albite, labradorite, microcline, oligoclase** and **orthoclase,** which yield several gem varieties. See also **plagioclase.**

feldspar-apyre (French). Andalusite.

felspar. A British spelling of feldspar.

felted structure. See **matted.**

fereto (Span.). Hematite.

ferozah or **firozah (firuza).** Persian word for turquoise; means "victorious", and is derived from the word *feroz* or *firoz*, "victory, victorious, successful."

ferriferous. Containing iron.

ferri-turquoise. A variety of crystallized turquoise containing 5% Fe_2O_3. From Lynchberg, Va.

ferrolite. A name for a black iron slag, said to be satisfactory for fashioning into gemstones.

ferrous mineral. Any mineral having a considerable portion of iron in its composition.

ferruginous. Stained by or containing iron.

fiber. In crystallography a hair-like or thread-like crystal. See **fibrous.**

fibrolite or **sillimanite.** A transparent to translucent gem mineral. Often a fibrous aggregate, greenish or brownish varieties, used as an inferior substitute for jade. Pale sapphire or violetish blue variety sometimes distinguished as fibrolite; fibrous varities as sillimanite. Ortho. Al_2SiO_5.H.6-7 or 7.5 for crystals (Smith). S.G. 3.2; R.I. 1.66/1.68. Bi. 0.019; Disp. 0.015. See "fibrolite cat's-eye."

'fibrolite cat's-eye." Pale greenish fibrolite with fibrous inclusions which, when cut, produces a chatoyant effect but not a well defined cat's-eye.

fibrolithoid. A substitute for celluloid.

fibrous. Having a hair-like, thread-like, or fiber-like form as a fibrous crystal, or in a mineral, a structure composed of such crystals.

fibrous aggregate. A crystalline aggregate composed of closely packed **fibers.** Takes a good polish.

fibrous calcite. Translucent calcite composed of fibrous crystals, which like fibrous gypsum, with which it is often confused, causes a silky sheen. When cut cabochon produces a girasol or chatoyant effect, but not a true cat's-eye. Also like fibrous gypsum, it is called **satin spar** but less correctly.

fibrous gypsum. Satin spar. See **fibrous calcite.**

"fictile ivory." An imitation of an artistic ivory object. It is made by casting the article in plaster-of-Paris, tinting it with yellow ochre, and treating the surface with a mixture of waxes.

"figure stone." Agalmatolite.

Fijian soapstone. A soapstone from Fiji Islands.

Fiji Islands pearl. A good quality

fine pearl from Fiji Islands, So. Pacific.

filter. Colored glass used in determinative gemology to filter out certain colors of the spectrum. See **color filter.**

filtered light. A term commonly used to refer to light which has passed through a colored glass (a filter) which absorbs the rays of some hues, allowing those of other hues to pass through.

fine-grained or **fine-granular mineral.** Consisting of small **crystalline grains.**

fine pearl. (1) A **true pearl** which possesses all the qualifications of a gemstone, such as oriental pearl. (2) A translation of **perle fine,** the French trade term for a natural pearl as distinguished from a cultured pearl.

fingerprint inclusions. Clouds of hollow inclusions filled with liquid and gas that form patterns that resemble fingerprints. They are common in ruby and sapphire.

finish. Term referring to certain details of fashioning, such as the placing and polishing of the girdle, culet, and facets. See **make.**

Finnish amber. Amber from the shores of Finland. See **Baltic amber.**

fiorite. A common opal occurring near hot springs. If with pearly luster is called pearl sinter. A **curio stone** only.

fire. (1) Flashes of the different spectrum colors seen in gemstones as the result of dispersion; the presence or the vividness of which depend upon **refractive index, fashioning, transparency** and color. (2) A term used by practical jewelers in U.S.A. for **play of color,** a gemologically incorrect usage.

fire agate. **Chalcedony** containing layers of minute inclusions of goethite or limonite, producing an iridescent, firelike appearance when a cabochon is ground so that only a very thin layer of chalcedony covers the inclusions. Sources: Riverside Co., California, and Arizona.

fired stones. Same as **heated stones.**

fired zircon. (1) Any zircon, the original natural color of which has been changed or entirely eliminated by heating. The induced colors often fade.

Fire Eye. A trademarked name for a chaytoyant **glass** imitation that contains tubes oriented in a parallel fashion, so that a very sharp band of light ("eye") is produced on the apex of a cabochon-cut stone.

fire marble. A variety of marble emitting fire-like chatoyancy, which resembles opal matrix. See **lumachelle** or **lumachella.**

fire opal. Transparent to translucent orangy-yellow to red, sometimes brownish-orange or brownish-red opal, generally classed as precious, whether or not it displays a **play of color.** R.I. about 1.45. Principally from Mexico.

"fire opal glass." Translucent glass imitating fire opal. Usually S.G. 2.4 or more.

fire stone. Flint (quartz).

firmament stone. Precious opal.

fish belly jade. A descriptive term applied by the Chinese to a particular color grade of jade.

fish eye. (1) A little-used name for moonstone, also for opal with a girasol effect. (2) A popular trade term for any transparent faceted stone so cut that its center is lacking in brilliancy.

fish eye stone. Apophyllite, which is not a gem or ornamental stone.

fish pearl. Term rarely used to describe the common imitation pearl made wholly or partly from fish scales.

fish silver. Same as **fish pearl.**

fissure. (1) Separation along cleavage plane which slightly penetrates the surface of a stone. (2) Geologically, a narrow opening formed by a parting of the earth's crust.

Five Great Gems. Called the *Maharatnani* by the Hindus, these consist of diamond, emerald, pearl, ruby and sapphire.

flag. In determinative gemology, same as **feather.**

flame opal. Opal in which red play of color occurs in sweeping bands or more or less irregular streaks, much like wind-blown flames.

flame-polished synthetic corundum. A method of polishing synthetic corundum rods and balls by rotating them in an oxygen-gas flame, which melts the surface slightly and obliterates scratches.

Flame Queen Opal. A 253-carat black opal, found in the Lightning Ridge district, New South Wales, Australia, in 1918. Measuring 2¾ x 2½ x ½ inches, it has a high-domed, bronze-red center and a green border. In order to preserve this unusual pattern, frequently referred to as resembling a poached egg, it has only been partly cut. The *Flame Queen* was once owned by Kazanjian Bros., Los Angeles gem dealers; it is now owned by a Milwaukee chemist.

flame spinel. Intensely bright orange-red **rubicelle.**

flash fire opal. Same as **flash opal.**

flash opal. Opal in which the play of color is pronounced only in one direction.

flat. A term which used in connection with the price of pearls or other gemstones means price per grain or carat regardless of size.

flat double cabochon. Same as **lentil.**

flaw (in a gemstone). Inclusion of another substance, internal cleavage, or fracture or visible imperfect crystallization.

fleches d'amour. (Fr., arrows of love). (1) A name formerly used in Russia for amethyst containing brown needles of **goethite;** from Russia and North America (Bauer; also Schlossmacher). (2) The acicular crystals contained in any variety of **sagenitic quartz.** (3) A term used loosely and questionably as a synonym of **sagenitic quartz.** Same as cupid's darts.

flint. A translucent to opaque, compact, fine-grained variety of **cryptocrystalline quartz,** usually occurring in gray, brown or black. Long the favorite material of primitive peoples for making arrowheads, spearheads, knives and other useful objects, flint is occasionally cut and polished by amateurs. Source: widespread.

flint glass. A name used for any one of a group of glasses characterized by relatively high **dispersion**, usually the result of lead in the composition. May be light flint, medium flint, heavy silicate flint, extra-heavy silicate flint or other classifications. The last three classes mentioned, and others, are also called **lead glass.** H. 5; S.G. (usually) 3.1-4.2; R.I. (usually) 1.57-1.68, although either property may be higher or lower (Shipley). H.5; S.G. 2.9-5.0; R.I. 1.54-1.78 (Anderson). H. about 5; S.G. 3.15-4.15; R.I. 1.58-1.68 (Smith). See also **beryl glass; crown glass; borosilicate glass; strass; thallium glass.**

floaters. Pieces of fair-quality weathered opal, also called **color floaters,** found lying loose on the ground in the Australian opal-mining fields. Floaters are often used to indicate the presence of an opal-bearing seam nearby.

floating opal. Small pieces of gem opal, placed in glycerine in transparent drop-shaped or spherical glass container, for use principally as a drop on a neck ornament.

float stone. A variety of opal that will float on water.

flohmig amber. Fatty amber, resembling goose fat; full of tiny bubbles, but not as opaque as **cloudy amber.**

flower agate. (1) Any moss agate. (2) Translucent chalcedony from Oregon. Contains inclusions of minerals, sometimes red, brown, or yellow and green, arranged in flower-like forms, often of both red and green colors. (3) Term is often applied to any

moss agate or mocha stone with flower-like markings.

flower stone. (1) Flower agate. (2) Incorrect term for beach pebbles of chalcedony.

flow lines. Curved lines within a *glass imitation* gem, resembling the appearance of a viscous, flowing liquid. This effect may be caused by an improper mixture that comprised the glass melt, or by the disturbance of the melt as it cooled. Also called **swirl marks** or **swirl lines.**

fluor. Same as **fluorite.**

fluorescence. A variety of **luminescence.** The phenomenal property of changing the short invisible wave lengths into longer visible ones, and reflecting them as visible colors when exposed to the influence of X rays, cathode rays, ultra-violet rays, including those in sunlight, etc., possessed by ruby, kunzite, yellow-green synthetic spinel, some diamonds and opals, and many other substances. Colorless fluorite fluoresces violet; diamond various colors. See **phosporescence.**

fluorite. A transparent-to-translucent green, blue, violet, yellow, orange, red, brown or colorless ornamental mineral, occurring principally in pale to light tones. The compact, massive variety is especially adaptable for carving as figurines, lamp bases, snuff bottles, boxes, etc., and is rarely cut as gems. Iso. CaF_2; H. 4; S.G. 3.2; R.I. 1.43. From England, Arizona, and other sources.

fluoroscope. (1) In general a screen coated with fluorescent material to make possible the direct observation of the effect of X-rays, cathode rays, etc. (Shipley, Jr.)

(2) In popular usage, the term is sometimes applied to a closed chamber in which specimens, such as pearls, may be exposed to X-rays, cathode rays or ultra-violet light, and observed for the presence of **flourescence**. See **pearl fluoroscope.**

fluorspar. Same as **fluorite.**

flux. To melt; to fuse. As a noun, a fluid or substance which may be used to fuse some other material, as in making glass imitations.

flux-fusion method. A technique used to manufacture certain synthetic gem materials (e.g., emerald and ruby) and other materials, in which crystal growth occurs in a high-melting flux, such as lead oxide, cryolite or lithium molybdate. Materials with the composition of the desired synthetic are mixed with the flux and heated to a temperature above that at which the ingredients of the synthetic dissolve. The temperature of the melt is then slowly lowered to a temperature below that at which the synthetic begins to crystallize and above the melting point of the flux. The synthetic then crystallizes in the flux. Used to make synthetic emerald and ruby.

flux-melt method. Same as **flux-fusion method.**

foamy amber. Frothy amber. Almost opaque chalky white amber. Will not take a polish.

foil back. Trade name for an **assembled stone.** (1) *Genuine foil back:* a genuine gemstone backed with colored or silver foil to improve its color or brilliancy or both. (2) *False foil back:* one in which a stone of a different species is backed with a color to imitate a more desirable one. (3) *Imitation foil back:* one in which glass is substituted for a stone. See also **lacquer back.**

foiling. A thin leaf of metal silvered and burnished and afterwards coated with transparent colors; employed to give color or brilliancy to pastes and inferior stones. See **foil back.**

folia. Thin flakes or leaves; lamellae.

foliated. Composed of, or easily splitting into, thin plates or flakes.

"fool's gold." A popular name for **pyrite.**

formation striae or **formation striations.** Color bands in synthetic corundum or spinel, which, since they are distinctive and almost always curved, differ from the straight color zones in genuine.

fortification agate. Agate with parallel zigzag lines which are heavier than in **topographic agate.**

fossil. Originally, any rock, mineral or other objects dug out of the earth. Now, any remains, impression, or trace, of an animal or plant of past geological ages, which has been preserved in a stratified deposit or a cave. The term frequently further restricted to remains of a stony nature, as those which have undergone more or less petrifaction. See also **petrifaction.**

fossil coral. Same as **beekite.**

fossiliferous. Containing fossils, remains of plants or animals.

fossil ivory. Ivory obtained from the tusks of the wooly mammoth *(Elephas Primigenius)*, the remains of which are found buried in the frozen ground, primarily in Siberia. It is not a true fossil, however, since it has not been altered by mineralization. An insignificant quantity comes from the mastodon, an earlier animal found in the Yukon River region of Alaska and elsewhere. Only about 15% of the material found is suitable for use and of fairly good quality. Its properties are essentially the same as those of recent ivory.

fossilized. Preserved by burial in rock or earthy deposits.

fossilized wood. Same as **petrified wood.**

fossil resin. Geologically preserved resin or gum of long-buried plant life. All of the harder, tougher varieties have been questionably called amber, including **ajkaite, beckerite, chemawinite, delatynite, glessite, krantzite, retinite, and stantienite.** See **true amber, dammar.**

fossil turquoise. Same as **odontolite.**

foundation stones. The wall of the New Jerusalem rested on twelve foundation stones as described in Apocalypse (Revelation XXI). There is a close connection between these and the stones of the High Priest's breastplate. See **birthstones.**

fowlerite. Variety of rhodonite from Sussex Co., New Jersey; cut and polished locally as a gemstone.

Fr. Abbr. used in this book for French.

fracture. Term used to describe the chipping or breaking of a stone in a direction other than that of cleavage plane or across cleavage planes. In mineralogy, fracture is classified as **conchoidal fracture, splintery fracture,** etc. See also **cleavage.**

frangible. Capable of being broken; breakable; brittle; fragile.

Fraunhofer lines. A group of dark lines (absorption bands) in the solar spectrum. The position of certain Fraunhofer lines, denoted by letters, is useful in **spectroscopy.** See **absorption.**

Frederician cut. A style of cabochon cut with one or two rows of facets around the girdle, frequently applied to chrysoprase.

"Frémy rubies." Synthetic rubies once made by the French chemist, Frémy.

"French color" rubies. Rubies of light color. See also **Ceylon ruby.**

French cut. A variety of mixed cut. Square in shape with a square table placed at a 45° angle to the edges of the stone. Also on the crown 24 smaller facets are usually placed, consisting of 8 star facets, 4 bezel facets and 12 girdle facets. The pavilion is either a step cut or a variation of the brilliant cut.

French stones. A deceptive term for glass imitation stones.

fresh-water pearl. A concretion with orient and pearly luster, found in a fresh-water mollusc. The *Unio Margaritifera* genus is the principal host in North American and European waters. Such pearls usually have strong colors and luster and are often baroque in shape.

fresh-water pearls. Pearls from the Unio.

friable. Readily broken into grains; crumbling easily.

"friable amber." Gedanite.

frictional electricity. Electricity developed by rubbing (with a cloth) amber, tourmaline, topaz, diamond, and some plastic imitations.

front (of a gemstone). The crown.

frost agate. Grey chalcedony with white markings which resemble frost or snow. See **frost stone.**

frothy amber. Same as **foamy amber.**

fruit flesh jade. A descriptive term applied by the Chinese to a particular color grade of jade.

FTC. Abbr. for **Federal Trade Commission.**

fuchsite. A green mica (chrome mica) which, as inclusions, colors verdite and aventurine quartz. See **muscovite.**

"full crystal." See **"English crystal."**

full cut brilliant. The term correctly used for a brilliant cut diamond or colored stone with the usual total of 58 facets, which total consists of 32 facets and a **table** above the **girdle** and 24 facets and a **culet** below. On colored stones the **girdle** is usually polished, but not on diamonds. See also **standard brilliant.**

furrowed. Having deep grooves or striations.

fused beryl. Same as **beryl glass.**

fused quartz. See **quartz glass.**

fused stone. (1) Any gem substitute produced by means of fusion; especially synthetic stone or glass. (2) An assembled stone such as **soldered emerald.**

fusible. Capable of being fused or melted by the blowpipe.

futuran. Trade-marked name for a phenol aldehyde plastic; used as imitation amber.

G

G. Abbr. sometimes used for **specific gravity**.

Gablonz jewelry. Glass imitation jewelry made in Gablonz, Czechoslovakia.

Gachala emerald. Emerald from the Gachala Mine, Department of Cundinamarca, Colombia. They are nearly the equal of the Muzo product and of better color than the usual Chivor production. See **emerald**.

Gagat (German). Jet.

gahnite. Semitransparent-to-opaque, yellowish, greenish to black **spinel** in which zinc has replaced magnesium. Rarely, if ever, cut as gem. S.G. and R.I. higher than **gahnospinel**.

gahnospinel. Zinc-rich, blue-green, gray-green or light violet spinel with greater S.G. (as high as 3.98) and higher R.I. (as high as 1.748) than other (magnesium) spinel fashioned as gems.

gair. Burmese term for large opaque rubies.

galalith. A **casein** plastic of various colors, used in imitations of amber, coral, jet, ivory, and tortoise shell.

Gambier pearl. Pearl from Gambier in Tuamotu Archipelago, South Pacific. Of unusual and almost chalky whiteness.

gamma zircon. That type of zircon which possesses lower properties than the **alpha** and **beta zircon**. Amorphous or nearly so, due to deteriorated crystal structure. S.G. 4.0; R.I. (single) 1.79-1.84. Bi. approximately zero. Rarely fashioned as a gem. See **zircon**.

gangue (gang or ganj.) The minerals associated with metallic ores in a deposit. Usually worthless although some minerals such as apatite occur. See **veinstone**.

garden (in emerald). See **jardin**.

Gargun (German). Same as **jargoon**.

garnet. (1) A name that encompasses a number of closely related mineral species. Several chemically similar elements replace one another freely in the garnet group; as a result, the properties and appearance of the different members differ appreciably. The garnet group is comprised of the following species and varieties: **pyrope, almandite, rhodolite, andradite** (variety demantoid), **grossularite** (variety hessonite), **spessartite** and **uvarovite**. Garnet is the birthstone for January, and it is correct to use any member of this group for this purpose. See **demantoid, andradite, grossularite, hessonite, rhodolite, spessartite, topazolite, uvarovite, isomorphous replacement**. (2) As an adjective, a color designation meaning *dark red*, as in the term **garnet glass**.

garnet blende. Same as **sphalerite**.

garnet doublet. The most common doublet: that with a very thin top of red garnet and a glass base. It is made in every color in which glass is made.

"garnet jade." A name applied to the several varieties of so called **Transvaal jade**, and also to the translucent to semitranslucent light green **grossularite** garnet, sometimes almost emerald green

80

in hue and closely approaching fine jadeite in appearance, a small deposit of which was found in Oregon about 1930.

garnetoid. A substance (silicate, phosphate, etc.) which has a structure similar to garnet, including hydrogarnet, grossularoid, and others (Spencer).

garnet shell. See **shell** (cut).

garnierite (gar'nee-er-ite). A mineral resembling **steatite** (Eppler) or **serpentine** (Dana). Pale apple to emerald green, apparently amorphous. H. 2-3; S.G. 2.3-2.8; R.I. 1.59 (Kraus and Hunt).

gas bubbles. Bubbles seen as inclusions in glass, synthetic corundum and synthetic spinel, which reveal their difference from genuine corundum, spinel and most other genuine gems, in which inclusions are more angular.

gas inclosure. A gas **inclusion** in a stone, such as can be found in all **synthetic corundum.**

gastropod. A division of **univalve** molluscs which includes land and sea snails, the **abalone,** etc.

gauge. *In general,* a measure of dimensions, distance or capacity or a device for measuring, registering or marking. *In the gem trade,* the word usually refers to a device for measuring diameter, thickness, height and other dimensions of a gemstone and is then more accurately called a **micrometer.** See also **Leveridge, Moe gauge; caliper.**

gaungsa. Burmese term applied to pale, inferior rubies of mixed sizes up to six carats.

gawdone. Burmese term for star sapphire.

gedanite (jed'a-nite). A brittle fossil resin sometimes classed as amber, but not by those who specify the presence of succinic acid as a requirement, although Schlossmacher mentions a trace of it in gedanite. Lacks toughness and ability to take as high polish as succinite. Rarely used as gem except for beads. H. 1.5-2; S.G. 1.06-1.07. See **fossil resin; Baltic amber.**

gem. (1) A cut and polished stone which possesses the durability and beauty necessary for use in jewelry; or a **fine pearl.** (2) A term often applied to an especially fine specimen, as a *gem emerald.* (3) As an adjective, a prefix, as in **gem crystal, gem quality, gem material,** etc. (4) As a verb, to decorate with gems (Standard).

gem collections. See **museum gem collections.**

gem collector. See **collectors.**

gem color. The most desirable color for a stone of its particular variety. Perfection color.

gem crystal. A crystal from which a gem can be cut.

Gem Detector. An inexpensive binocular microscope mounted on a dark-field illuminator base and equipped with a mechanical stoneholder.

gem gravels. Gem-bearing gravels of present or former river or lake beds.

gem jade. Same as **jewel jade, emerald jade.**

gemmary. (1) (Rare) The science of gems (Standard). (2) A house or receptacle for gems or jewels; also gems collectively. (3) An engraver of gems

Gemma Star. A trademarked name for synthetic star corundum made in West Germany.

gem material. A term used particularly by Kraus and Slawson to mean (a) any synthetic or other important substitute for a **gemstone,** or (b) any rough mineral from which a gemstone can be fashioned, such as a piece of uncut jade.

gem mineral. Any mineral species which yields either a **gem variety** or individual specimens which meet the qualifications of a **gem.**

Gemmological Association of Australia. An organization for the furtherance of gemology in Australia. It is affiliated with the Gemmological Association of Great Britain. Headquarters: Box 1532, GPO, Sydney, New South Wales, Australia 2060.

Gemmological Association of Great Britain. Established in 1933 as the educational branch of the National Association of Goldsmiths. Actually, the second body to be established for the furtherance of the study of gems. Since its inception, the Association has conducted the gemological courses previously offered through the National Association of Goldsmiths. Headquarters: Saint Dunstan's House, Carey Lane, London, E.C.2, England.

gemmologist. (The English spelling ing of **gemologist**). One who has mastered **gemmology.**

gemmology (jem-ol'oe-ji). The spelling of **gemology** as used in Great Britain where it was formed from the Latin *gemma* (a gem), and the suffix *-ology* de-

rived from the Greek meaning a science. Introduced previous to the time of the establishment of the gemological courses in England in 1910, probably about 1900. See **gemology; gemmary.**

Gem of the Jungle Sapphire. Unusually large blue sapphire found just below the grass, in Burma, in 1929. Weighed 958 carats. Cut into nine gems.

Gemolite (trademark, Gemological Institute of America). An illuminator-magnifier combination for diamonds and other gems. It utilizes wide-field binocular magnification with the StereoZoom method of magnification change and a base designed for the magnification of gems by either darkfield or light-field illumination. The base contains a diffuser; an adjustable baffle; a diaphragm, to adjust to various lighting needs; and a turntable, to permit the instrument to be turned around to the customer. Accessories enable demonstration of proportions and color to be made to customers.

Gemological Institute of America. A nonprofit, endowed, educational institution controlled by a board of trustees and maintained for the benefit of the industry and the public. In addition to home-study courses or resident classes in diamonds, colored stones, pearls, jewelry designing, diamond setting, jewelry retailing and jewelry display, the Institute publishes books, pamphlets and periodicals, manufactures diamond-grading, gem-testing and other instruments, identifies gemstones and grades diamonds for the industry and the public. Classwork is offered in

Los Angeles, New York City and cities throughout this country and elsewhere. Headquarters: 11940 San Vicente Blvd., Los Angeles, California 90049. Eastern Division: 580 Fifth Ave., New York City 10036.

gemological laboratory. Laboratory equipped with instruments which are especially designed for testing fashioned stones, and especially **mounted stones.**

gemological microscope. See **microscope.**

gemological polariscope. See **polariscope; Shipley polariscope.**

gemologist. One who has successfully completed recognized courses of study in gem identification, grading and pricing, as well as diamond grading and appraising; e.g., a *Gemologist* or *Graduate Gemologist* of the Gemological Institute of America or a *Certified Gemologist* of the American Gem Society.

Gemologist Diploma. A diploma awarded to those who complete successfully the correspondence courses in gemology that are prepared and conducted by the Gemological Institute of America.

gemology. The study of gemstones; their identification, grading and appraising.

gem pearl. (1) A term often used for those better quality pearls that possess a rosé or other particularly desirable orient. Does not include **white pearl.** (2) A term more specifically used to mean an iridescent pearl, really spherical, of maximum luster of even intensity, free from all visible blemishes, and of a decided and desirable orient, such

as pink rosé.

gem-peg. A rest for the gemstick, in gem cutting (Standard).

gem quality. Possessing the qualifications of a gem.

Gems & Gemology. A scientific periodical published four times each year by **Gemological Institute of America.** Established 1933.

gem species. A gem-bearing mineral **species.**

gem-stick. A stick on which a gem is cemented while being cut (Standard).

gemstone. Any mineral or other natural material that has the necessary beauty and durability for use as personal adornment.

gem-testing laboratory. See **gemological laboratory.**

Gem Trade Laboratories, Gemological Institute of America. The two research and testing laboratories maintained and operated by GIA to provide diamond, gemstone and pearl identification and grading for the jewelry industry, Better Business Bureaus, jewelers' organizations, insurance companies and the public. They are located at 580 Fifth Ave., New York City 10036, and 11940 San Vicente Blvd., Los Angeles, California 90049.

gem variety. That variety of a mineral species which yields gemstones.

genera. Plural of **genus.**

genesis (gemological). Origin or formation of a natural gem mineral.

"Geneva ruby." (1) An obsolete trade name given to the earliest reconstructed ruby, probably first made in 1882 in a small Swiss town near Geneva. (2) The name deceivingly applied to the first rubies made synthetically in 1891.

genuine doublet. See doublet.

genuine pearl. A natural pearl in contrast to a cultured pearl.

genuine triplet. See triplet.

genus (jee'nus or jen'us). A group of two or more species of animals or plants. Plural *genera* or, rarely, *genuses*.

geo-chemistry. The science of the chemistry which treats of the materials of the earth.

geode. Cavities in clay or other formations which have been incrusted with a wall of quartz or other mineral and which (later) separate as a hollow mass, the interior walls of which are usually studded with crystals. See amygdule.

geology. The science which treats of the history of the earth.

"German gold." Amber (S. H. Ball).

German jet. Jet from Swabian Aips and Saxony; of inferior quality.

"German lapis." Incorrect term; same as "Swiss lapis." Originally jasper from Nunkirchen, Germany, dyed blue.

German silver or nickel silver. An alloy of copper, nickel, zinc, and sometimes other metals, but no silver, in which gemstones are but rarely set.

geyserite or siliceous sinter. A porous variety of common opal deposited by geysers.

ghost crystal. Same as phantoms.

G.I.A. Gemological Institute of America.

Gibraltar stone. A light colored onyx marble found at Gibraltar and elsewhere. See "Mexican onyx."

gibsonite. Fibrous pink thomsonite (English), from Renfrewshire and Dumbartonshire, Scotland.

gigaku. Japanese name for jade or for precious stones in general.

Gilson-Created Emerald. A trademarked name for a flux-fusion synthetic emerald manufactured in France by Pierre Gilson. See synthetic emerald.

gilsonite. Same as uintahite.

giogetto. Italian name for black coral.

girasol (jir'a-sol). (1) A name which has been applied to (a) moonstone, (b) fire opal, (c) an almost transparent opal with a bluish floating light; see girasol opal; and (d) to many other stones (Bauer-Spencer). (2) In North American gemology and in this glossary an adjective, used as in girasol sapphire, to describe any gem variety which exhibits a billowy, gleaming, round, or elongated area of light which floats (i.e. moves about as the stone is turned or as the light source is moved). When the elongated light forms an uneven or indistinct band the stone is said to have a chatoyant effect. Only when the band is sharp and distinct is it a cat's-eye. (3) A trade name for glass spheres used in manufacture of imitation pearls.

girasol chrysoberyl. Cymophane with girasol effect but lacking true chatoyancy.

girasol opal. A term which has been been used for (1) an opal with blue to white body color and a red play of color as well; (2) the varieties of opal described under **girasol.**

"girasol pearl." An imitation pearl with a glass base. See **girasol** (3).

girasol sapphire. Sapphire with a floating cloud of light or with a wide indistinct light band. Often incorrectly called sapphire **cat's-eye.**

girdle. The outer edge or periphery of a fashioned stone; that portion which is usually grasped by the setting or mounting; the dividing line between the crown and pavilion. In most diamonds it is left unpolished. On emerald cut diamonds, on almost all **colored stones** and on some brilliant cut diamonds, **polished girdles** are placed. On the latter these often consist of a series of more or less flat polished surfaces which are more or less accurately termed **girdle facets.**

girdle facets. (1) In a brilliant-cut stone, (a) in traditional trade usage, the same as **break facets,** or (b) a term more or less correctly applied to the polished or partly polished flat surfaces which often are placed on a polished **girdle.** (2) In other styles of cutting, especially emerald cut, the girdle is usually polished, producing well-defined rectangles or other parallelograms in contrast to the outline of those on brilliants, which are usually uneven and unsymmetrical in comparison.

glass. An amorphous substance, ordinarily consisting of a mixture of silicates. Glass is usually manufactured by fusing silica, an alkali, and lead oxide or another metallic oxide. The better glass imitation stones contain a large proportion of lead and may contain oxides of rarer elements, such as thallium. Some glass imitations are made according to very complex formulas. The properties of glass used in **imitations** vary widely. H. 5-6½ ; S.G. 2.0-5.0; R.I. 1.44-1.69 (rarely 1.77). Usually contains air bubbles and often **whorls.** See also **beryl glass; borosilicate glass; flint glass; paste; strass; thallium glass.**

glass agate. A name applied to transparent to semitransparent, slightly gray chalcedony; also, even less correctly to obsidian.

glass lava. An undesirable name for obsidian.

glass meteorite. An undesirable name for moldavite.

glass opal. Hyalite.

glass quartz. A little-used name for rock crystal.

glass schorl. Axinite.

glass stone. A glass imitation stone. Also a term applied to axinite.

glassy lustre. Vitreous lustre. See **vitreous.**

glessite. A fossil resin.

globular. Having spherical or rounded form.

glow stone. Chalcedony.

glyptography. The art or process of engraving gems; also, the description or study of engraved gems.

Gnaga Boh Ruby (Dragon Lord Ruby). A fine Burmese ruby which weighed 44 carats, rough, and when fashioned, 20 carats.

gnat stone. Dendritic quartz (moss agate or mocha stone) with small black inclusions.

gneiss (nice). A crystalline rock of metamorphic origin with its mineral content bedded so that the rock appears in crude, irregular layers or laminae; similar to granite in composition.

goethite or **göthite.** A yellowish, reddish or brownish mineral (often blood red by transmitted light), thin needles of which sometimes occur as prominent inclusions in sagenitic quartz; also, according to G. F. H. Smith, as inclusions in sunstone. FeO(OH); Ortho. H. 5-5.5; S.G. 4.3; R.I. 2.26/2.40. Named for the poet Goethe, and similarly pronounced.

gold. A metallic element and precious metal. See **gold jewelry.**

golden beryl. Yellow to greenish beryl. See **heliodor.**

golden sapphire. Yellow to greenish yellow sapphire.

golden stone. Greenish-yellow peridot.

Golden Willows Sapphire. A 322-carat golden-yellow sapphire found in the Willows field, Anakie district, Queensland, Australia, in 1952. The largest stone cut from the rough, called the *Golden Queen*, weighed 91.35 carats, but its present whereabouts is unknown.

gold glass. Term sometimes applied to "goldstone."

gold jewelry. Term used in U.S.A. for jewelry made wholly or principally of **solid gold**; also designates gold-filled or gold-plated jewelry.

gold matrix. Gold in a matrix of

milky quartz. Same as **gold quartz.**

gold opal. Opal which exhibits only an over-all color of golden yellow.

gold quartz. Milky quartz containing inclusions of gold. Same as **gold matrix.**

"gold sapphire." Lapis lazuli containing flecks of pyrite. See also **golden sapphire.**

goldstone. A translucent, reddish-brown, soda-lime glass containing a multitude of tiny metallic-copper tetrahedra or hexagonal platelets that exhibit bright reflections, producing a poor but popular imitation of **sunstone** (quartz or feldspar). Despite the copper content, the specific gravity is only between 2.50 and 2.80, and the refractive index is 1.53. It is also produced in a blue color.

"gold topaz." (1) Heat treated topaz-quartz. (2) Naturally colored citrine.

goniometer. An instrument used to measure angles between facets of a gem or faces of a crystal. The *contact goniometer* is a physical instrument incorporating a protractor; the *reflection* or *reflecting goniometer* uses light reflected in a fixed system, the specimen being turned on a calibrated table. Probably the most valuable to the gemologist is the *horizontal single-circle goniometer* which is used to measure the index of refraction by the method of **minimum deviation.**

goodletite. A name for Burmese marble forming matrix of rubies.

gooseberry stone. A name for **grossularite,** and more specifically for its yellow-green to yellowish green varieties.

goshenite (goe'shen-ite). Colorless beryl.

gota de aceite (Spanish). The best quality of emerald.

göthite. Same as **goethite.**

goutte de eau. Colorless topaz.

goutte de sang. Blood-red spinel.

goutte de suif. Same as **tallow top.**

gr. Abbr. for **grain** (weight).

graduated cut. Step cut.

graduated necklace. A necklace on which beads of gradually increasing size are strung, with the smaller ones near the clasp and the largest at the center. Normally, there is a several-millimeter differential between center and end beads.

Graduate Gemologist. One who holds the *Graduate in Gemology Diploma*, awarded by the Gemological Institute of America, after successful completion of both its correspondence and residence courses in gemology.

Graduate Gemologist in Residence. One who holds the *Graduate Gemologist in Residence Diploma*, awarded by the Gemological Institute of America, after successful completion of its entire gemology curriculum in residence.

grain. (1) A unit of weight; one-quarter of a metric carat, or 0.0500 metric gram; commonly used for pearls, sometimes for diamonds; rarely for other gemstones. (2) A popular trade term for cleavage direction in a gem mineral or gemstone. (3) In mineralogy, a minute crystalline particle. See **crystalline grains.**

gram. A unit of weight in the metric system, commonly used for many kinds of rough gem materials. One gram equals the weight of a cubic centimeter of water at 4° C., .03527 ounce avoirdupois, 15.4324 grains, 5 carats or 1000 milligrams.

granada (Port.). Garnet.

Granat (German). Garnet.

grandite. A name suggested for garnets, the chemical composition of which is between grossularite and andradite.

granite. A granular igneous rock containing principally quartz and feldspar.

granitic. Granite-like, or composed in part of granite.

granular. Composed of or resembling **crystalline grains.**

graphic granite. A variety of granite containing quartz crystals arranged so that their cross sections resemble cuneiform and Hebrew writings.

grave jade. Same as **tomb jade.**

gray-blue, gray-green, gray-purple, gray-violet. In color nomenclature **system** of North American gemology, colors which, respectively, are midway between **neutral gray** and blue, green, violet, purple.

grayish blue, grayish green, grayish purple, grayish violet. In North American gemology, colors which are, respectively, more grayish than vivid blue, green, purple or violet, but not as grayish as **gray-blue, gray-green, gray purple, gray-violet.**

gray sapphire. The gray variety of sapphire popular as a gem only if asteriated.

grease stone. A name for **steatite.**

greasy luster. Luster resembling that of oily glass. Produced by reflection from a non-plane surface. Seen on polished jade.

Great Mogul. Title of the native sovereigns (1526-1857) of the empire founded in India by the Mongols in the 16th Century. Their chief seat was at Delhi. The Moguls had vast stores of gems, especially diamonds.

Great Southern Cross. Group of nine Australian pearls forming a cross and said to have been found naturally in this exact form, but claim later discredited. Said once to have sold for $135,000, and to have been in possession of the Vatican. Same as **Southern Cross Pearl.**

green beryl. A term applied to the lighter green varieties of beryl as distinguished from the full green **emerald** and the light blue-green **aquamarine.**

green-blue. In **color nomenclature system** of North American gemology, the **hue** midway between green and blue. Same as **blue-green.**

green chalcedony. Usually some cryptocrystalline variety of quartz stained green. Also may be chalcedony of natural green color.

"green-ear." A name which has been applied to **fresh-water pearl.**

green garnet. The demantoid variety of andradite garnet. The green grossularite garnet is usually known as gooseberry garnet. Also a misnomer for **enstatite.**

greenish blue. In North American gemology, the hue midway between blue and **green-blue.**

greenish gray. In North American gemology, a color midway between green-gray and **neutral gray.**

greenish yellow. In North American gemology, the hue midway between yellow and **green-yellow,** therefore more yellow than green.

green-gray. In color nomenclature system of North American gemology, a color midway between vivid green and **neutral gray.**

green jasper. The color of this jasper is usually caused by inclusions of iron silicate, chlorate or chromium salts. It is popular as an ornamental stone. The chief source is the Ural Mountains of Siberia. See **jasper.**

green-john. Green fluorite.

"green onyx." In U. S. A. jewelry trade, a widely accepted, but otherwise incorrect term for artificially colored green **chalcedony.** Not as light green as **chrysoprase.** See **onyx.**

greenovite. A reddish or pinkish variety of sphene.

green quartz. (1) Transparent greenish quartz. (2) Sometimes incorrectly used for green **fluorite.**

green starstone. Chlorastrolite.

greenstone. (1) Correct name for **nephrite.** (2) A little used misnomer for **chiastolite** or for **fuchsite.**

Green Vault. The Grüne Gewölbe in Dresden, Germany, where are exhibited the gem collections of Augustus II, a former Elector of Saxony and King of Poland.

green-yellow. In **color nomenclature system** of North American gemology, the hue midway between green and yellow. Same as **yellow-green.**

grenat (Fr.). Garnet.

grenat noble (Fr.). Almandine.

grenat Siriam (French, meaning *Siriam garnet*). According to Kunz, a trade name for any red garnet

DICTIONARY OF GEMS AND GEMOLOGY

with tinge of violet.

grey, greyish. Alternate spelling of gray, grayish.

grinding. The preliminary shaping of a rough **colored stone;** followed by polishing. Grinding is done on carborundum wheels or on metal laps, and diamond powder or carborundum is usually used, depending on hardness of stone.

griqualandite. Mineralogical name for the yellow silicified crocidolite which appears in parallel layers in tiger eye.

grossular. A British term for grossularite garnet.

grossularite (gross'-u-lar-ite). A species of the **garnet** group, of which the transparent yellow-brown to orangy-brown **hessonite** is the principal variety. It is also found in a transparent green color. Massive, translucent to semitranslucent green, white, yellow and pink varieties are sometimes sold incorrectly as "jade," "African jade" or "Transvaal jade," because of its principal occurrence near Pretoria, Transvaal, South Africa. Chemical composition, calcium-aluminum silicate $(Ca_3Al_2(SiO_4)_3)$; crystal system, isometric; hardness 7 to $7\frac{1}{2}$; specific gravity, 3.57 to 3.73 (hessonite), 3.45 to 3.50 (massive); refractive index, 1.74 to 1.75 (hessonite), 1.70 to 1.73 (massive); birefringence, none; dispersion, .028. Garnet is the birthstone for January, and it is correct to use grossularite or any other member of the garnet group for this purpose.

grothite. Sphene.

Grubstake Opal. A fine example of **precious opal** pseudomorphous after wood. A $4\frac{1}{2}$ x$\frac{3}{4}$-in. polished slab. From Virgin Valley, Nevada. Pawned by prospector who failed to reclaim it. Now in Amer. Mus. of Nat. History, N. Y. (Whitlock)

Grünes Gewölbes. Same as **Green Vault**.

"Guadalcanal cat's-eye." Same as "shell cat's-eye."

guanin. Guanine or guango. Constituent of **essence d'orient** which causes its iridescence.

guarnaccine garnet. A trade term for yellowish red garnet. Same as **vermeille garnet** (Kunz).

Guilds. The periodical of the **American Gem Society.**

gum anime. A recent fossil resin, often containing insects; sometimes mistaken for amber.

gun-metal pearl. (1) The variety of so-called **black pearl;** the color and luster of which resembles polished gun metal. (2) A gun-metal imitation of such a **pearl.** A misnomer.

gypsite. Same as gypsum.

gypsum (jip'sum). An ornamental, decorative and curio mineral, the light colored varieties of which are easily dyed. A white opaque variety is **alabaster;** the fibrous white variety is **satin spar.** Mono. $CaSO_4 2H_2O$; S.G. 2.2-2.4; R.I. 1.52/1.53. Bi. 0.010. Sources widely distributed.

gyu. Tibetan name for **turquoise.**

H

H. (1) Abbreviation for the degree of hardness of a substance. (2) The symbol, in a chemical formula, for the element hydrogen.

Habachtal emerald. Emerald from the Habachtal Valley in the Austrian Alps, a commercially unimportant source but one of the famous emerald localities. See **emerald.**

habit. Crystal form or forms in which a mineral usually is found.

hackle back pearl. A fresh-water pearl of the Mississippi Valley, found, rarely, in the mussel *Symphynota complanata*, popularly known as the hackle back, hatchet back, or heel splitter.

hackly fracture. Breaking with a rough surface having many sharp points, like most metals.

haematite. Same as **hematite.**

hair (rare). Trade term for hairlike fractures or needlelike inclusions in gemstones.

hair amethyst. Sagenitic amethyst. See **amethyst, sagenitic quartz.**

hair crystal. Same as **hair stone.**

hair stone. Any variety of crystalline quartz containing fibrous or thread like inclusions of other minerals. See **Thetis hair stone; Venus hair stone.**

Haiti pearl. Pearl mentioned by Cattelle in 1906 as being from south and west coasts of Haiti, and of good quality.

hakik. General name for agate in India.

half-bored pearls. A pearl drilled partly through for use in earrings, scarf pins, etc.

"half carnelian." Yellow carnelian.

half facets. Same as **break facets,**

cross facets. See **girdle facets.**

half moon. A style of cutting which produces a stone shaped as a half circle.

half opal. Semiopal.

half pearl. (1) Half of a round pearl; (2) rarely used to mean a cultured blister pearl.

half tin. A term meaning that only one-half of an imitation stone, the crown, has been polished on a tin lap.

Haliotidae. A family of gastropods, with deep oval shell with a row of perforations and a flat lip; ormers or ear-shells.

Haliotis. A genus typical of haliotidae; an ear shell.

halo. See **pleochroic halo.**

halves facet. Same as **half facet.**

hamaage. A Japanese word that refers to the crop of cultured pearls before any form of processing.

hambergite. Grayish white or colorless mineral. Colorless variety from Madagascar, cut as gems for collectors only. Looks like rock crystal. Ortho. $Be_2(OH) BO_3$; H. 7.5; S.G. 2.35; R.I. 1.55/ 1.62; Bi. .072.

hammered pearl. Pearl with tiny indentations in its surface, which resemble the hammer marks on hammered silver. See also **hammer pearl.**

hammer pearl. Pearl shaped like head of a hammer. See also **hammered pearl.**

Han or **Han jade.** Same as **Han Yü.**

hand loupe. See **loupe.**

Han Yü. Chinese name for (1) jade of the time of the Han dynasty. (2) In trade, **tomb jade** or any jade which resembles it in color and texture even though it be artificially treated to accomplish that resemblance.

hard clam pearls. From hard clam or quahog *(Venus mercenaria)*, from Atlantic Coast. U.S.A.

hard mass (or masse). A trade term used originally for a special glass of an unusual hardness of 6 or more. Now misused to mean any glass, especially green glass artificially flawed to imitate emerald; and sometimes to mean synthetic sapphire or spinel.

hardness. The resistance a substance offers to being **scratched,** a property that is sometimes useful in the identification of gemstones and their substitutes. See **Mohs' scale.**

hardness gauge. Same as **hardness points.**

hardness pencils. Same as **hardness points.**

hardness plates. A series of small pieces of minerals of differing hardness, polished flat, and set side by side in cement, for testing hardness of another mineral which is drawn across one after another piece, beginning with the hardest, until it scratches one.

hardness points. Small pieces of minerals of differing hardness, with one end pointed and affixed to small handles of wood, metal or plastic, to be held in hand and used for testing hardness of another mineral, by ascertaining which points will scratch it. Minerals of hardness 10 to 6 are usually used as points for testing gemstones.

hardness scale. Same as **hardness table.** See **Mohs scale.**

hardness table. Any listing of substances as to their comparative **hardness.**

hardness wheel. A hand instrument in which **hardness points** are set as equidistant spokes of a rimless wheel, permitting more rapid selection of points in testing hardness.

harlequin opal. Usually white opal with close-set, angular (mosaiclike) patches of color, of similar size. See **cat's-eye opal; pin fire opal.**

Harlequin Prince Opal. A fine-quality, 215.85-carat, harlequin-type black opal owned and displayed by the American Museum of Natural History, New York City. The predominate play of color consists of red, yellow and orange, as well as the more common green, blue and violet. It is considered the most important opal in the Museum's collection.

Harz cat's-eye. Name sometimes used to mean any quartz cat's-eye, but more especially a variety from Harz Mountains (Germany). Is usually inferior to the better qualities of Bavarian and Ceylonese quartz cat's-eye.

hatchet back pearl. Same as **hackle back pearl.**

hatchet stone. Nephrite.

haüyne or **haüynite** (ha′win or ha′-win-ite). A constituent of lapis lazuli. Hardness 6; translucent to opaque; bright blue to green-blue. See **lapis lazuli.**

"Hawaiian golden yellow topaz." Clear plagioclase feldspar.

Hawaiian peridot. Peridot from near Hilo, Hawaii, in cut stones, sizes averaging about one-half carat. Same as hawaiite.

hawaiite. *Gemological:* A name given to a pale green variety of **peridot** from Hawaiian Island lavas (English). *Geological:* A variety of basalt.

hawksbill. The marine turtle *(Chelone Imbricata)* that provides the **tortoise shell** of commerce.

hawk's-eye. Also spelled *hawk-eye.* Transparent colorless quartz containing closely packed, parallel fibres of **crocidolite** which impart to it a blue color. In form and sheen it resembles **tiger-eye** to which it alters geologically. Differs from **sapphire quartz,** in which fibres are not parallel.

haystack or **haystack pearl.** Term applied by American river fishermen to high-domed button pearls.

He. Abbr. for the element helium.

healed pearls. Those in which surface or subsurface cracks have been repaired by experts.

heart-shaped brilliant. A heart-shaped variation of the **pendeloque;** usually with a large table and a shallow crown.

heated stone. A stone that has been artificially heated to the proper temperature with the intention of improving or completely altering its color. The induced color is permanent in varieties such as **hyacinth, burnt amethyst,** etc.; less permanent in **blue zircon.** See also **stained stone.**

heat treated stone. Same as **heated stone.**

heaven stone. Benitoite.

heavy liquid. Liquid having high S.G., such as methylene iodide, in which different species either float if their S.G. is lower than that of the liquid, or sink if higher. See **diffusion column.**

Hebrew stone. Graphic granite. An intergrowth of crystals of feldspar and quartz in which the arrangement of the latter suggests letters of Hebrew alphabet.

hedgehog stone. Transparent quartz containing larger needles of göethite or some other hydrous iron oxide than those in **sagenitic quartz.**

heel splitter pearl. Same as **hackle back pearl.**

hei-tiki. A carved image for the neck; jade amulet, often buried with Maoris of New Zealand. (Kunz)

heliodor (he'-le-oh-dor). Another name for brownish-yellow **beryl.**

heliodore. An alternate spelling of **heliodor.**

heliolita (Span.). Aventurine feldspar.

heliolite. Sunstone.

heliotrope (hee'li-oe-trope). Dark green chalcedony containing spots or patches of red jasper (Kraus). Sometimes fades to grayish green and spots are earthy hematite (Schlossmacher) From India and other sources. Less desirable yellow spots also occur. Same as **bloodstone.**

hemachate or **haemachate.** A light-colored **agate** spotted with red jasper.

hematinon or **haematinon.** A dark red glass, known to the ancients, to which metal filings are added to produce **aventurine glass.** Same as purpurin.

hematite. An opaque mineral; yielding pigments when red and earthy; fashioned as intaglios and other carved gems when dark gray to black with metallic luster. The latter variety is translucent and red in very thin sections. Leaves red **streak** which identifies from most imitations. The principal ore of iron. Hex. Fe_2O_3; H. 5½-6½; S.G. 4.9-5.3; R.I. 2.94-3.22; from England, Scandinavia, U.S.A. (Lake Superior region). Incorrectly called "bloodstone," (its ancient name), also "black diamond." Sometimes used to imitate black pearls. See **bloodstone, specular hematite.**

Hemetine. A trademarked name for a sintered imitation of **hematite.** The raw material used to manufacture early material was galena (lead sulphide), resulting in a black streak and a heavy specific gravity (7.00). More recent material contains mainly iron and titanium oxides, resulting in a redbrown streak and nearly the same specific gravity (about 5.20) and hardness (5½ to 6½) as hematite. It is used mostly as intaglios of Greek or Roman warrior's heads. The name Hemetine was enjoined by the Federal Trade Commission many years ago, but comparable imitations have continued to be made under various names.

hemihedral. Having a lower grade of symmetry than, and only half as many faces as, the corresponding form of full, or normal, symmetry for that system.

hemimorphic. Having no transverse plane of symmetry and no center of symmetry, and composed of forms belonging only to one end of the axis of symmetry.

hemimorphite. Translucent to opaque yellow to blue-green specimens have been cabochoncut for gem collectors. When pure or mixed with smithsonite, from which it differs but slightly, it sometimes appears in the trade as **smithsonite.** Ortho. $H_2Zn_2SiO_5$; H. 4.5-5; S.G. 3.3-3.6; R.I. 1.614-1.636; Bi. 0.022. Also called calamine. From Montana, Utah, Nev., Ariz., and other states and countries.

hemiopal. Same as **semiopal.**

Herbert Smith Refractometer. Same as **Smith Refractometer.**

Hercules stone. A name for **lodestone.**

herrerite. Copper-stained blue and green smithsonite from Albarradon, Mexico. (Schlossmacher)

hessonite (hess'on-ite). A transparent to translucent variety of **grossularite.** Yellow to red-orange varieties known as **hyacinth garnet;** yellow-brown to reddish brown as **cinnamon stone.** Usually has a loupe-visible granular structure unlike true **hyacinth** (zircon).

hessonite glass. An orange-colored glass, used for imitations.

Hex. Abbreviation used in this book for hexagonal crystal system.

hexagon cut. Any style of cut the outline of the girdle of which is six sided, i.e., hexagonal. Called *square hexagon* if all sides are of equal length; *pointed hexagon* if two parallel and equal-length sides are much longer than others; called *oblong hexagon* if those sides are but slightly longer.

hexagonal mineral or **stone.** A mineral or stone of the **hexagonal system.**

hexagonal system. A system in crystallography, a division of which is known as the rhombohedral system; has four axes, three in one plane intersecting each other at 60°, the fourth perpendicular to this plane. Corundum, beryl, tourmaline, and quartz are important gems in this system. See also **crystal systems.**

hexahedron. A solid bounded by six plane faces. The regular hexahedron is the cube, a common crystal form.

Hf. Abbr. for the element hafnium.

Hg. Abbr. for the element mercury.

hiddenite (hid'n-ite). Green spodumene found only in small crystals in North Carolina. Intense but pale yellowish-green to yellow-green. See **spodumene.**

High Priest's Breastplate. See **Breastplate of High Priest.**

Hindoo or **Hindu cut.** Schlossmacher describes this as a style of unsymmetrical over-all faceting of stones to preserve maximum weight and size of the rough.

hinge pearls. (1) Pearls of elongated shapes from the hinge of the fresh water mussel. (2) A trade term for pearl shapes cut from the hinge.

"Hinjosa topaz." Brownish red citrine from Hinjosa del Duero, District of Cordova, Spain. Heat treated to fiery red-orange color as distinguished from the Madeira wine color of so-called **"Madeira topaz."** See also **"Spanish topaz."**

hippopotamus ivory. Ivory from the tusks of the hippopotamus *(Hippopotamus Amphibus)*. It is denser, has a finer grain, and is a purer white and is less likely to split than elephant ivory. Since the tusks are hollow, little solid material is available; consequently, it is used only for small objects. The texture is often described as between ivory and pearl shell.

Hardness, $2\frac{1}{2}$ to $2\frac{3}{4}$; specific gravity, 1.80 to 1.95; refractive index, 1.545. Source: the rivers of central Africa.

historical gemology. History of the discovery and production of gemstones and their substitutes and of their use as personal, and other ornament.

hmyaws or **hmyaudins.** Mining term used in Burma for a deep open mine in a gently sloping hillside or between hills, situated in a sloping valley.

hollow doublet. A doublet which contains a colored liquid in a concave depression hollowed out of the lower surface of its top section or the upper surface of its bottom section, or both.

hollowed cabochon. Cabochon-cut stone with a concave depression in its under surface, to lighten its color.

hollow pearl. Same as **wax-filled pearl.**

holohedral forms. Those which are holohedrons.

holohedron. A form having the full number of symmetrically arranged faces possible in its crystal system.

hololith ring (hoe'loe"lith). An entire finger ring made from a single piece of gem material.

holomorphic. Uniformly or completely symmetrical.

Holzstein. The German name for **petrified wood.**

"Honan jade." Same as **"Soochow jade."**

Hope Cat's-eye. A large, nearly hemispherical stone, about $1\frac{1}{2}$ inches in diameter, once in the **Hope collection.** A chrysoberyl cat's-eye.

Hope Chrysoberyl. A 45-ct., flawless, yellowish-green, oval, brilliant-cut chrysoberyl, now in the British Museum (Natural History), called by it a matchless specimen. Once in **Hope collection.**

Hope collection. A collection of gems made by Thos. P. Hope, a wealthy British banker of the early 19th Century.

Hope Opal. See **El Aguila ·Azteca Opal.**

Hope Pearl. An 1800-grain pearl somewhat cylindrical, but swelling at one end, white, but brown tinted at one end. Once in Hope collection, and now in British Museum (Natural History). It is thought to be the largest known precious pearl; length 2½ inches, circumference, 3½ to 4½ inches. See also **Pearl of Asia.**

"Hope sapphire." Term originally applied to blue synthetic spinel, and later used extensively for synthetic blue sapphire.

Hope stone. A trade name applied by an American importer to any synthetic corundum or spinel. See **"Hope sapphire."**

hornbill ivory. So-called ivory from the helmeted hornbill *(Rhinoplax Vigil)*, one of about 45 species of this large, old-world, enormous-billed bird from Indonesia. The bill is predominantly yellow, and the helmet, or casque, surmounting the head is brownish red. The material is sometimes used for snuff bottles and other small objects.

hornblende. (1) A dark green brown non-gem **amphibole;** (2) A term used by most German mineralogists to refer to the entire amphibole group. See **nephrite.**

hornblende jade. A term sometimes used overseas for **smaragdite.**

horn coral. See **black coral.**

hornstone. An impure, flintlike, non-gem cryptocrystalline **quartz.**

hot-point test. When a red-hot metal point is applied to an unknown material, the nature of the vapors given off may be analyzed for color and odor, and the nature of the spot left may also be characteristic.

hot-point tester. An instrument that provides an electrically heated metal point to detect oiling, paraffin treatment, plastic imitations, etc.

howdenite. Chiastolite with fern-like markings, from South Australia. (Merrill)

howlite. An opaque white mineral species, usually with brown or dark veins and dendritic markings, occurring in compact, nodular masses resembling unglazed porcelain; sometimes chalky and earthy. Chemical composition, silico-borate of calcium ($H_5Ca_2SiB_2O_{14}$); crystal system, monoclinic (crystals very rare; commonly massive); hardness, 3½; specific gravity, 2.53 to 2.59; refractive index, 1.586-1.605 (a single vague reading at 1.59). It is in demand for making bookends, spheres, ash trays and similar ornamental and utilitarian articles. Material stained blue is often used as a substitute for turquoise. Outstanding localities are Nova Scotia and Tick Canyon, near Saugus, Los Angeles Co., California.

Hsi jade (Hsi Yü). A Chinese name for either clear water or clear black jade.

Hsieh jade. Hsieh Yü, a Chinese name for ink black jade.

Hsiu Yen. A Chinese name for green and white jasper. Often sold to tourists as jade.

hue. The principal attribute by which a color is distinguished from black, white or neutral gray. The attribute by which colors, when they are arranged in their orderly spectrum sequence, are perceived as differing from one another. Thus, technically, each wave length in the **visible spectrum** propagates a different hue. Thus, red, yellow and green, as well as greenish yellow, green yellow, and yellowish green, are different hues, while pink (light red), maroon (dark red), and brownish red, are colors which have the same hue but which differ in other attributes. See **tone, intensity.**

huinzo. Peruvian Indian name for lapis lazuli. (Ball)

hulls. The very thin outer coatings or nacreous layers of pearl.

"Hungarian cat's-eye." An inferior yellowish green variety of **quartz cat's-eye,** from Bavaria, not Hungary.

Hungarian opal. (1) A white opal with fine play of color. From Czerwennitza, near Presov, Czechoslovakia (formerly Hungary). (2) A widely used trade name for any white opal, regardless of source.

"hyacinth." Incorrect when applied to hessonite, unless full name *hyacinth garnet* is used. See **hyacinth.**

hyacinth (hye'a-sinth). A variety of zircon. The term is by some authorities applied only to the red and orange variety, many of which have been heat treated.

Others use it interchangeably with jacinth to mean yelloworange or red or brown zircon. It is sometimes loosely used to mean any zircon. The word is also used as a color designation meaning orange-red to orange, as in hyacinth garnet, hyacinth sapphire. See **"hyacinth."**

hyacinth garnet. Hessonite. See **hyacinth,** and **"hyacinth."**

hyacinth of Compostella. Reddishbrown **citrine** from the gypsum beds near Santiago de Compostella, northern Spain.

"hyacinth of Vesuvius." Brown or honey-yellow **vesuvianite** from Mt. Vesuvius.

hyacinthozones (hye'a-sinth"oezone-is). Sapphire-blue beryl.

hyacinth quartz. Red to reddish brown citrine.

hyacinth sapphire. Reddish orange to red-orange sapphire.

"hyacinth topaz." An incorrect name for hyacinth (a zircon).

hyaline. Opalescent milk quartz (Eppler).

hyalite. Colorless common opal; not gem quality.

hyalithe. An opaque variety of glass, frequently black, green, brown, red, etc. Resembles porcelain. (Standard).

hyalosiderite. Rich olive-green olivine, containing much iron (Merrill).

hydrolite. Same as **enhydros.**

hydrophane. A dehydrated, yellowish, brownish or greenish variety of common opal which when immersed in water, becomes more translucent or transparent. Sometimes may exhibit **play of color.** Similar and more permanent results are sometimes obtained by immersing or boiling in oil. See **oculis mundi; pyrophane.**

hydrostatic weighing. Weighing of a substance first in air, then in water. The S.G. is then obtained by dividing the weight in air by the difference between the weights.

hydrothermal method. A technique for synthesizing materials, in which compounds of the chemical composition of the desired material are dissolved in water at high temperature and pressure. As the temperature and/or pressure is lowered, crystals of the desired type form. This technique is used to synthesize some emeralds and rubies.

hydrous (hye'drus). Containing hydrogen or water, and therefore, yielding water on heating.

hypersthene (hi' - per - stheen). A translucent to opaque, dark-green, brown or black iron-rich member of the **pyroxene** family of minerals, closely related to **enstatite.** It exhibits a metallic, iridescent effect caused by minute inclusions of what may be brookite, goethite or hematite, producing interesting cabochon material. Chemical composition, magnesium-iron silicate $(FeMg)SiO_3$; crystal system, orthorhombic; hardness, 5 to $5\frac{1}{2}$; specific gravity, 3.40 to 3.50; refractive index, 1.715-1.731; birefringence, .016. Sources: Bavaria, Norway, Greenland, Labrador, Quebec, Colo. and other localities.

Hyriopsis Schlegeli. A large fresh-water mussel used in Lake Biwa, Shiga Province, Honshu, Japan, for producing both nonnucleated and conventionally nucleated **cultured fresh-water pearls.**

I

I. Abbr. for the element iodine.

ice-colored clear amber. (German trade grade). Best color quality of transparent amber. Colorless or very pale. See **clear amber.**

"Iceland agate." (1) Obsidian from Iceland. (2) A brownish or grayish variety of obsidian. (3) An alternate name for obsidian.

Iceland crystal. Same as **Iceland spar.**

Iceland spar. Transparent calcite. Because of its strong double refraction its more flawless qualities are used in optical instruments and research and known as **optical calcite.**

ice spar. Term has been incorrectly applied to adularia (moonstone) but is an alternate name for colorless sanidine, a different variety of orthoclase.

ice stone. Name used by Ojibways (American Indians) for white flint. Name doubtless applied to rock crystal. (Ball).

icy flakes. A seldom used trade name for small cracks along cleavage planes sometimes caused by overheating stones during polishing.

Idar agate. Name for any of the small agates the discovery of which resulted in the establishment of the gem cutting industry at **Idar-Oberstein.**

Idar-Oberstein. Twin towns in southwestern Germany. One of the world's largest cutting centers of less valuable colored stones. See **Idar agate.**

ideal crystal form. See **crystal form, ideal.**

identification (of a gemstone). The testing of the physical properties of a stone to determine whether genuine or not and, if genuine, its species; as distinguished from the former method of rendering of opinions based on the appearance of the stone to the eye. See **determinative gemology; gemological laboratories.**

idiochromatic stone (id'i-oe-kr e-mat'ik). Stone in which the substance producing the color is an inherent constituent of the mineral. Limited to such stones as **chrysocolla, malachite, diopside, azurite, turquoise** and **peridot.**

idiophanous. Exhibiting interference figures without the aid of the polariscope.

idocrase (i'doe-krase). Also known as **vesuvianite,** the varieties of this mineral species are **californite** (massive, translucent to opaque, yellowish-green to dark green, mottled with white or gray), **ciprine** (transparent to translucent, light blue to greenish blue), and **zanthite** (transparent yellow to yellowish brown). Californite is often used as a substitute for jade. Transparent greenish-brown, yellowish-brown or green single-crystal material also occurs and is sometimes cut for collectors. Chemical composition, a complex calcium-aluminum silicate $(Ca_6Al-(AlOH)(SiO_4)_5)$; crystal system, tetragonal; hardness, $6\frac{1}{2}$; specific gravity, 3.30 to 3.50; refractive index, 1.713-1.718; birefringence, .005; dispersion, .019. Sources: Siberia,

Calif., Italy, Canada, Switzerland and Norway.

igmerald. Coined name of the I.G. Farbenindustrie of Germany for the variety of synthetic emerald made by it.

igneous rock (ig'nee-us). A rock formed by the solidification of a molten magma, either at the surface, as volcanic lava or within the earth as plutonic rock or intrusive igneous rock.

illam. Singhalese name for the local sedimentary gem gravels.

illusion cut. This is a novelty form of cutting and engraving. It is made by cutting a transparent material (usually rock crystal) into the shape of a triangular block and placing grooves of varying widths and inclinations on one edge of the block. When the grooves are viewed through the opposite flat surface, a three-dimensional effect is observed, due to reflection of the grooves from the other two surfaces, which are inclined toward the engraved edge.

ilmenite. An opaque black mineral rarely cut for collectors or substituted for hematite. (Its streak is brown, hematite's is red). Hex. $FeTiO_3$. H. 5-6; S.G. 4.5-5.

image stone. Agalmatolite.

imitation cameo. See **cameo.**

imitation doublet. See **doublet.**

imitation foil back. See **foil back.**

imitation lacquer back. See **lacquer back.**

imitation opal. A poor-quality assembled imitation of opal, made with a cabochon of rock crystal or glass and backed with mother-of-pearl or abalone shell. A glass sandwich with a metallic film on one surface is also made for this purpose.

imitation pearls. Beads made of glass, wax or other substances coated or lined with **essence d' orient,** as distinguished from natural and cultured pearls. See **Roman pearls;** "indestructible pearl."

imitation star sapphire. See **star doublet.**

imitation triplet. See **triplet.**

imitations or **imitation stones.** (1) In the broadest sense, any material other than genuine gem material. A genuine stone that imitates a more desirable one is sometimes called its imitation; preferably its substitute. (2) More specifically, **glass, plastic,** or other amorphous substitutes or reproductions as distinguished from synthetic and reconstructed stones (which are crystalline) and from genuine **assembled stones** (portions of which are crystalline). See also **reproduction; simulated stone.**

immersion cell. Any cell used to immerse a gemstone in a liquid as a means of overcoming reflection and refraction from its surface, thus providing more efficient observation of its interior. Immersion cells usually have glass bottoms, to facilitate their use with microscopes, polariscopes, etc.

imperfection. A trade term used to refer to an inclusion or faulty structure of any kind which is visible to the eye whether observed with or without the aid of a magnifier.

Imperial Chinese jade. Same as **emerald jade.**

imperial jade. (1) In China, a term properly applied to the finest emerald green color of jadeite.

The term has been adopted in the American trade. See **emerald jade**. (2) In other countries, a term which also has been used for a substitute, green aventurine quartz.

"Imperial Mexican Jade." Green-dyed calcite.

Imperial Yü-Stone. Green aventurine quartz. See **Yü**.

inanga (Maori). A highly prized grey variety of New Zealand nephrite.

Inca rose. Rhodochrosite.

Inca stone. Pyrite.

incident light or ray. That which strikes the surface or enters a stone, as distinguished from the light which has subsequently entered the stone and, in most cases, been refracted or reflected.

inclusion. Any foreign body, whatever its origin, enclosed in a substance, such as liquids or small crystals of one mineral in another, or air or gas bubbles in glass or synthetic stone, visible to the unaided eye or with a magnifier only. See **determinative inclusion**.

incrustation. A crust or coating.

"indestructible pearl." An imitation pearl consisting of a solid opalescent glass bead covered with layers of pearl essence, the quality of the imitation depending upon the number of coats, the quality of **essence d'orient**, etc. Fairly durable, but not indestructible.

index of refraction. A numeral which expresses the ratio of the speed of light in air to its velocity in a substance, and also, the ratio of the sine of the angle of incidence to the sine of the angle of refraction. In mineralogy this index is indicated by the symbol n; in gemology, by the abbreviation R.I. Thus the index of amber is expressed as either n 1.54, or R.I. 1.54. Same as **refractive index**.

Indian agate. A name for **mocha stone** or **moss agate**. Same as **dendritic agate**.

Indian cat's-eye. Cymophane. Same as **chrysoberyl cat's-eye, Ceylon cat's-eye.**

Indian cut. A clumsy form of the **single cut**, adopted by East Indian cutters for the purpose of retaining maximum weight in the cut stone.

"Indian emerald." Crackled quartz.

Indian garnet. Almandite.

"Indian jade." Aventurine quartz.

Indian pearl. (1) Pearl from East Indian waters, including Ceylon. (2) Any **Bombay pearl** or **Madras pearl**. (3) Rarely used to mean any **oriental pearl**.

Indian rule. Same as **Tavernier rule**.

"Indian topaz." A misnomer for **citrine** or yellow **sapphire**.

indicators. Term used in determinative gemology for minerals or other substances of known S. G., pieces of which are used to indicate or calibrate the approximate S. G. of heavy liquids. See also **diffusion column**.

indicolite (in-dik'oe-lite). Blue tourmaline. Very light to dark violet-blue to blue. Frequently almost black, sometimes greenish-blue.

indigolite. Same as **indicolite**.

indigo sapphire. Very dark blue sapphire.

indra. A casein resin (plastic).

infrared. That part of the electromagnetic spectrum beyond the red end of the visible spectrum, containing the so-called heat rays, which produce **luminescence** in some gems and other substances. Infrared extends from wavelengths of about .7 to 100+ micron.

inherent vice. If an insured gemstone is said to have suffered damage, the insurance adjustor must determine whether damage has occurred and, if so, whether it is attributable to some prëexisting weakness in the stone (e.g., an earlier cleavage); such weakness is called *inherent vice.* If damage has occurred, it is fully recoverable from the insurance company only if inherent vice is not involved.

inky sapphire. Very dark blue sapphire.

ins or **in-byes.** Excavations in the Burma ruby mines, larger than **kobins.**

in situ (in sigh'tue). A term used to describe the location of minerals when found in the place where they were originally formed.

intaglio (in-tal'yoe or en-tal-yoe). A carved gem which may be used as a seal, in which the design has been engraved into the stone. Intaglios differ from cameos, in that the edges of cameos are lower than the figures.

intensity (of a color). The comparative brightness (vividness) or dullness or brownishness of a color; its comparative possession or lack of brilliance; therefore, the variation of a hue on a vivid-to-dull scale. See **hue, tone.**

interfacial angle. In crystallography the internal angle between any two faces of a crystal form.

interference (of light). Explained by the undulatory theory as the reinforcement or the partial or complete destruction of certain of the rays of the spectrum when the undulation of the light rays traveling in the same direction coincide (and reinforce one another) or interfere (and tend to destroy each other). This complete or partial destruction or reinforcement of certain of component (colored) rays of white light causes **iridescence, labradorescence, orient,** and **play of color.**

interference colors. Colors made visible by the reinforcement of some wavelengths of white light and the cancellation of others by the effects of light interference. See **iridescence, labradorescence.**

interference figures. Figures caused by the interference of light, which can be seen in most doubly refractive minerals when examined along an optic axis. The resulting appearances differ markedly between uniaxial and biaxial gemstones.

intergrowth. A mutual interlocking of crystals, during their crystallization. The crystals may be of same or different minerals and in more or less close contact. See **crystal aggregate, crystalline aggregate.**

interlaced or **interwoven.** Confusedly interwined, as are fibres or slender crystals in some minerals.

interpenetration twins. Two or more crystals in twinned positions which penetrate each other. Same as **penetration twin.** See **twin.**

intumescence (in"tue-mes'ens). The property of bubbling and swelling upon fusing.

invelite. A plastic similar to bakelite.

Inverell sapphire. Blue sapphire from New South Wales, marketed through Inverell. Lighter blue than typical **Anakie sapphire.**

"invisible light." A term used to refer to certain radiations of light traveling in wave lengths too short or too long to be distinguished by the human eye such as **ultra-violet, infra-red.** See also **visible light.**

iolanthite. Local trade name for a banded reddish jasper-like mineral from Crooked River, Ore.

iolite (i"-oh-lite). A transparent to translucent, light- to dark-blue to violet-blue mineral species also called **dichroite** or **cordierite** and, incorrectly, "water sapphire." It may also be colorless, yellowish white, green or brown. The mineral is noted for its very strong **trichroism.** A weak cat's-eye or star effect is sometimes present, and inclusions of hematite sometimes cause reddish **aventurescence.** Chemical composition, a hydrous silicate of aluminum and magnesium ($Mg_2Al_4Si_5O_{18}$); crystal system, orthorhombic; hardness, 7 to $7\frac{1}{2}$; specific gravity, 2.57 to 2.66; refractive index, 1.542-1.551; birefringence, .008; dispersion, .012. Sources: Ceylon, Burma, Brazil, India, Norway and Calif.

ion. An electrically charged atom or atomic group.

Iran or **Iranian lapis.** Same as **Persian lapis.**

Iran or **Iranian turquoise.** Same as **Persian turquoise.**

iridescence. The exhibition of prismatic colors in the interior or upon the surface of a mineral caused by interference of light from thin films or layers of differing refractive index.

"iridescent cat's-eye." Unsatisfactory term sometimes used for **chrysoberyl cat's-eye** to distinguish it from quartz cat's-eye.

iridio-platinum. An alloy usually containing 90% or more of platinum. The remaining percentage is of iridium which is necessary to produce an alloy sufficiently stiff for use in gem **mountings.**

iris agate. Banded agate which in thinly fashioned sections displays iridescence. Of almost no gem importance.

iris quartz. Rock crystal containing thin air-filled cracks which produce iridescence. Same as **rainbow quartz.**

"Irish diamond." Rock crystal from Ireland.

iron-aluminum garnet. Same as **almandine.**

iron opal. Same as **jasper opal.**

"iron pyrites." Popular name for pyrite.

ironstone. Any hard earthy ore of iron, such as **hematite.**

irregular inclusion. See **inclusion, irregular.**

iserine (i"-zer-in). A blackish ferruginous mineral (probably **rutile**), with a brownish-black streak and a higher metallic luster than **hematite,** for which it has been substituted. Hardness, $5\frac{1}{2}$ to 6; specific gravity, 4.50 to 5.20. Source: Czechoslovakia.

Isle Royal greenstone. Chlorastrolite.

Iso. Abbr. used in this book for

isometric system.

isochromatic (eye"soe-kroe-mat'-ik). Possessing the same color.

isometric (eye"soe-met'rik). Equal in measure, as the **isometric system.**

isometric mineral or **stone.** Mineral or stone of the **isometric system.**

isometric system. The cubic system of crystallization. Substances of this system are all isotropic and their axes are of equal length. An **ideal crystal form** of this system is therefore a cube or a variation of it such as an octahedron. Diamond, spinel and the garnets are the most important gem minerals of this system. Same as cubic system. See **crystal system.**

isomorphism (eye"soe-mor'fiz m). The property of crystallizing together in variable chemical proportions possessed by some minerals (and other substances) of like **atomic structure.** See **isomorphic replacement.**

isomorphous. Exhibiting isomorphism.

isomorphous replacement. Replacement of one element by another of the same **valency** in the chemical composition of a mineral, as in tourmaline, where iron, lithium and magnesium, etc., replace each other with resulting wide ranges of colors but little variation in other properties, iron producing no gem qualities. In other cases of isomorphic replacements wide variations in physical properties result. See **garnet.**

isotropic (eye"soe-trop'ik). Singly refractive. Affecting light similarly in all directions as it passes through the mineral. See also **anisotropic.**

"Italian chrysolite." Vesuvianite.

Italian coral. Coral from sea waters of Italian mainland and neighboring islands, as distinguished from **Algerian coral, Tunisian coral.**

"Italian lapis." Same as **"Swiss lapis."**

itatli. An Aztec name for obsidian.

ivory. The translucent to opaque, fine-grained, creamy-white substance that comprises the tusks of the African elephant *(Elephas Africanus)*, the Asian elephant *(Elephas Maximus)* and certain other mammals; viz, hippopotamus, walrus, sperm wale, narwhal, wart hog, mammoth and mastadon. It has long been a favorite material for carving, and is esteemed for a wide variety of ornamental and utilitarian articles. Properties of elephant ivory: hardness, $2\frac{1}{2}$ to $2\frac{3}{4}$; specific gravity, 1.70 to 1.85; refractive index, 1.535.

ivory, artificial. Any substitute for ivory, such as bakelite, cederon, celluloid, fibroc, invelite, micarta, redmanol, and others.

ivory jade. A descriptive term of the Chinese for jade of a particular color and texture.

"ivory turquoise." Odontolite.

ivory, vegetable . The hard white kernel of the nut of certain palm trees (R. Webster).

iztac chalchihuitl. White or green Mexican onyx (Merrill). See **chalchihuitl, "Mexican onyx."**

iztli. Aztec name for obsidian which because of its many uses, was surnamed *teotetl* (divine stone).

J

jacinth (jae'sinth or jas'inth). A name which was originally an alternate spelling of **hyacinth,** but which has been used for (1) yellow or brown **zircon,** (2) red or orange **zircon,** (3) any **zircon,** or (4) **hyacinth garnet.** Having become meaningless, the name is now obsolete in the American trade.

jacinto (Spanish). Hyacinth.

Jacumba hessonite. Hessonite from near Jacumba Hot Springs, San Diego Co., Calif.

jade. A gemological group of two minerals, jadeite and nephrite, of differing chemical composition but rather closely related in appearance, in physical properties, especially their unusual toughness, and in uses which include jewelry, carved objects, and various ornamental objects. Occurs in large compact masses, and its color is often unevenly distributed. See **jadeite; nephrite.**

jade fisher. Chinese name for an alluvial jade miner.

jade glass. A green translucent to opaque glass, usually a lead ("flint") glass; S.G. about 3.73. (Anderson)

jadeite. A semitransparent to opaque mineral species that furnishes the most valuable and desirable **jade.** It occurs in a wide variety of colors, including green of high intensity (so-called **Imperial jade),** white, mottled green and white, violet, brown, orangy red, yellow and gray-green. The black to dark-green variety is known as **chloromelanite.** Chemical composition, silicate of sodium and aluminum $(NaAl(SiO_3)_2)$; crystal system, monoclinic (but always a massive, granular to fibrous crystalline aggregate); hardness, $6\frac{1}{2}$ to 7; specific gravity, 3.30 to 3.38; refractive index, 1.66-1.68 (a single, hazy reading near 1.66 is most common). Principal world source: region of Mogaung, Upper Burma. Minor sources include Gautemala, California, Mexico and Japan. See **jade, nephrite.**

jadeite triplet. A hollow cabochon of translucent white jadeite into which is cemented an accurately fitted piece of the same material with an organic green cement that simulates the color of fine-quality jade. The base is completed with a third piece of jadeite.

jadeolite. A deep-green chromiferous **syenite** cut as a gemstone and resembling jade in appearance, from the jadeite mine at Bhamo, Burma. Possibly the same as **pseudojadeite.**

"jade tenace." Saussurite.

jais, jai, jayet (French). **Jet.**

jamb peg. An upright post, positioned at the side of a polishing lap, used to facet colored stones, and containing a number of suitably placed holes into which is placed the end of the gem holder, thus regulating the angle and inclination of the facet being cut.

Japan (or Japanese) **pearl.** (1) A term originally used for **cultured blister pearl** but later used for whole **cultured pearl.** (2) A correct name for any pearl from Japanese waters whether cultured or genuine. The latter occasionally is marketed with the former, and not distinguished

104

from it.

Japanese coral. Coral from Japanese waters. Usually pink in color with white centers. Beads and cut specimens pink, often flecked with white.

jardin. (French, garden). Term applied to a group of mossy inclusions typical of fine **Colombian emerald.**

jargoon or **jargon.** A name used (1) infrequently for any variety of **zircon,** (2) more generally for colorless to grayish yellow or pale yellow **zircon,** (3) most specifically and correctly for colorless **zircon** only.

jaspagate. A banded jasper that is less translucent than agate.

jaspe (Fr. and also Span.). Jasper.

jaspe fleuri (obsolete). Vari-colored jasper agate.

jasper. A semitranslucent to opaque, red, yellow, brown, green, grayish-blue or lavender (or any combination thereof), fine-grained impure **chalcedony** (cryptocrystalline quartz). Widely distributed. It often is dyed blue and sold incorrectly as "Swiss lapis" and "German lapis."

jasperated agate. Jasper mixed with agate.

"jasper fleuri." Jaspe fleuri.

jasperine. Bandéd jasper of varying colors.

jasperite. Same as **jasper.**

"jasper jade." Term used by Chinese dealers for jade substitutes, including serpentine, quartz or combinations of quartz and jade. See **"Soochow jade."**

jasper opal. An almost opaque common opal, most commonly yellow-brown; almost reddish brown to red, due to iron oxides.

Resembles jasper in appearance.

jasper ware. A semiporcelain employing a granulated dip invented by Josiah Wedgwood, adaptable to various types of ceramic ware, but especially to the moulding of cameos, the most popular of which in jewelry, are of white figures on a blue ground.

jaspe sanquin (French). Black jasper.

jaspidean. Consisting of or containing jasper; like jasper.

jaspilite. A term used in Lake Superior region for bright red jasper alternating with bands of black, commonly, specular hematite.

Jaspis (German). Jasper.

jasponyx. An opaque onyx, part or all of whose layers consist of jasper, or near jasper like chalcedony.

jaspopal. Same as **jasper opal.**

Jefferson Sapphire. A bust of Thomas Jefferson carved from a blue, 1743-carat sapphire found at Anakie, Queensland, Australia. The finished carving weighs 1381 carats and measures 2½ inches high, 2¼ inches wide, and two inches deep. The sculptor was Harry B. Derian and the technical advisor, Lincoln Borglum. This carving, together with Presidents Lincoln, Washington and Eisenhower and the *Black Star of Queensland*, were presented as a gift to the American people by the Kazanjian Foundation of Pasadena, California, a charitable, non-profit organization founded by Kazanjian Bros., Los Angeles gem dealers. The *Jefferson Sapphire* is presently on display at the Smithsonian Institution, Washington, D.C.

jet. A black variety of lignite (brown coal); a fossilized coniferous wood. Inflammable. H. 3-4; S.G. 1.10-1.40; R.I. 1.64-1.68. From England and Spain.

jet glass. Black, opaque glass. H. about 5.

jet stone. Black tourmaline. (Power).

jewel. (1) A fashioned gemstone or a pearl. (2) Any ornament made of the platinum metals or gold of more than 10 karat fineness whether or not set with a genuine or synthetic gemstone, or with a genuine or cultured pearl. (3) A badge or ceremonial ornament containing genuine or artificial gems, enamel or the like. See **jewelry, solid gold.**

jeweler (British, jeweller). Term applied in U.S.A. to any merchant selling genuine or imitation jewelry or to any maker or repairer of jewelry. See **Registered Jeweler, A.G.S.**

Jewelers' Security Alliance of the United States. The Jewelers' Security Alliance, which was organized in 1883, is a mutual, nonprofit, voluntary association of jewelers. It coöperates with all law-enforcement agencies; prevents the commission of crimes, by advocating burglar alarms and protective devices; supplies guards to traveling salesmen when suspicious circumstances arise; issues an encyclopedia to each member, explaining how to prevent the various kinds of crimes committed by jewelry thieves. Headquarters: 535 Fifth Ave., New York City 10017.

"jeweler's topaz." Citrine or **topaz quartz.**

Jewelers' Vigilance Committee. Or-ganized in 1913, the Jewelers' Vigilance Committee is composed of representatives of every branch of the jewelry industry. The principal objectives of the Commission are as follows: to be prepared to meet promptly any situation that imperils any broad interest of the trade; to protect the trade's prestige and endeavor to maintain public confidence in the jewelry industry, particularly the retailers; to fight any discrimination against the trade through government action; to help maintain fair competition within the industry; to develop and help maintain trade standards on the highest possible level; to assist in the prosecution of violators of the various laws, rulings and regulations pertaining to advertising, correct nomenclature and quality markings; to assist the government to combat smuggling and protect the industry from it; and to keep the trade informed of laws and regulations affecting its business. Headquarters: 156 E. 52nd St., New York City 10022.

jewel jade. Same as **emerald jade.**

jewel land. See **Mogok Stone Tract.**

jewelry (British, jewellery). In North America, any personal adornment wrought from precious metals, or any ornament which can be worn as a substitute for it, such as shell jewelry, plastic jewelry, etc. See **costume jewelry.** In trade usage, the term jewelry includes (1) any article worn or carried wholly for personal adornment, or (2) any article worn or carried for utilitarian needs which is (a) made of precious metals, (b) set with precious gems or (c) made in imitation of any utilitarian article made of precious metals and set with gems. Differs in meaning from **jewel.**

Jewelry Industry Council. This is the nationwide publicity and promotional organization of the entire industry, with a membership consisting of jewelry retailers and suppliers. Its basic objective is to keep retail jewelry sales at the highest possible level. This is accomplished by the following activities: it prepares and releases for newspapers, magazines, radio and television and other communications media a steady stream of publicity stories about the desirability of jewelry-store merchandise. It creates and furnishes sales-promotional material for retailers, including booklets for public distribution, advertising and display ideas for newspapers, direct-mail service, radio commercials, window displays, Christmas portfolios, display cards for gift occasions, speech manuscripts and fashion reports. Headquarters: 608 Fifth Ave., New York City 10020.

jig. A sieve shaken vertically in water to separate gem gravel from worthless material. Also, a pulsator.

joaillerie. The French term for jewels, separate and distinct from the term *bijouterie*, which refers to jewelry, containing, no gems. See also **bijouterie.**

jobber. A wholesaler as distinguished from an importer or manufacturer, either of whom may sell to jobbers or retailers or both.

jobbing stones. A jeweler's assortment of unmounted stones, kept for use in repair, remodeling or rehabilitating jewels.

Job's tears. Local name for peridot from Arizona and New Mexico.

johnite. A variety of vitreous or scaly turquoise.

jolite. Iolite.

Jolly balance (jol'i; prop., yole'e). A spiral spring balance especially adaptable to rapid determination of specific gravity of medium to very large-sized specimens of cut and rough gems.

Juan jade. A mixture of fine white and red jade.

junk box. Term used by jewelers for a collection of damaged or temporarily useless gem materials, for the most part salvaged from worn-out or out-moded jewelry.

K

K. Abbreviation for (1) the element potassium; (2) Karat; see **carat.**

kahurangi. A pale-green translucent variety of New Zealand nephrite jade; rare. (Smith)

Kaiyéral. Ceylonese trade name for a dark-colored treble pearl, not quite round. (Kunz)

kalanchu. (1) A Ceylonese measure of weight used in pearl trade; the equivalent of 67 grains troy. (2) A term applied to the four inferior classes of **true pearl** from Ceylon, i.e., kalippu, pisal, kural, and tul. See **chevvu; vadivu.**

Kalette (German). Culet.

kallainite. Same as **callainite.**

kallait. Same as **callait.**

kallipo or **kalippu.** Ceylonese trade grade of pearls; includes lens shaped or elongated pearls usually flattened, (Kunz) and with external blemishes (Boutan). Similar to **masanku,** but of poorer quality (Cattelle).

kalmuck opal or **agate.** Same as **cacholong.**

Kan C'hing jade. A Chinese name for pale bluish jade.

kand or **kann.** Same as **cand.**

"Kandy spinel." Almandite from Ceylon.

Kaneelstein (German). Hessonite.

Kan Huang jade. A Chinese name for light yellowish jade.

Kan jade. Kan Yü, a Chinese name for jade which is the color of boiled chestnuts.

kann. See **kand.**

Karfunkel (German). Carbuncle.

Karlsbad Spring stone. A banded red, white and brown gypsum used in small carved objects and cheap jewelry. (Pough)

Karneol (German). **Carnelian.**

Kashgar jade. Nephrite of inferior qualities from the jade market and cutting center of Kashgar, Chinese Turkestan. Best qualities from this area are usually sold to cutters in Peiping, Shanghai or Canton.

Kashmere or **Kashmir sapphire.** Same as **Cashmere sapphire.**

kauri copal, kauri gum or **kauri resin** (cow'ree). Resin from the Kauri pine *(Dammara australis)* from Australia, New Zealand, and other sources. Occurs in whitish yellow masses. Used in some inferior imitations of amber. According to Bauer has dirty appearance compared with amber. Smells like turpentine. See also **copal; dammar.**

kawakawa. Maori name for ordinary green variety of **nephrite.** (Smith)

kawk. Cornish name for fluorite.

kelve. Cornish name for fluorspar.

keystoneite. Blue chrysocolla or chalcedony colored by copper silicate.

khesbet. Egyptian word for lapis lazuli but probably of Babylonian origin. (S. Ball)

Khiraj-i-Alam Ruby. See **Timur "Ruby."**

Khorog lapis. Lapis lazuli from near Khorog, Russian Badakshan, and usually sold as **Badakshan lapis.**

Khotan jade. Nephrite of inferior

qualities from jade market and cutting center of Khotan (Sinkiang), Chinese Turkestan. The best qualities mined in the neighborhood are usually sold to cutters in China.

"kidney stone." Nephrite.

kikukwaseki (Japanese). A radial aggregate of xenotime and zircon. Also called chrysanthemum stone. From Ishikawa, Iwaki province, Japan (English).

"Killiecrankie diamond." Colorless topaz from Tasmania.

kimpi (East Indian). A red or brownish variety of jadeite.

kindradite. Mis-spelling for a spherulitic jasper-like quartz from California. See **kinradite.**

King Croesus stone. Same as **simav opal.**

kingfisher jade. Jade resembling the color of the brilliant blue-green back of the kingfisher. See **Fei-Ts'ui.**

king's coral. Black coral formerly abundant in Persian Gulf and on Great Barrier Reef of Australia. Not used in Occident. See **black coral.**

king stone. Same as **"king topaz."**

"king topaz." Term used in Ceylon for deep yellow sapphire, but elsewhere in Orient for orange or even brownish sapphire, and for pale yellow citrine.

kinradite. A local trade name for jasper containing spherulites of colorless or nearly colorless quartz. Much of it is the same as orbicular jasper. From California and Oregon.

klaprothine. Same as **lazulite.**

Klein's solution. Boro-tungstate of cadmium; melts to an aqueous solution of S.G. 3.55 which is lowered by dilution with water. R. Webster places S.G. of Klein's solution at 3.28.

kobins. Reinforced pits from four to five feet in diameter in Burma ruby mines.

kochenite. A fossil resin, like amber. Kochenthal, Tyrol. (English)

kodai pearl. Ceylonese trade grade for a pearl with no nacreous luster; formed of prismatic shell. It may be large, is usually spherical, and includes pearls' of various colors. The name is also used for white pearls with black or brown marks. *Van kodai:* a kodai pearl with one side nacreous. *Karunk kodai:* a black or blue-black slag-like pearl. (Kunz) In this definition prismatic shell probably has same meaning as **prismatic layers.**

Koenigskrone mine. An old mine in Saxony which was the source of the topazes in the crown jewels of the King of Saxony. See **Green Vaults.**

Kollin garnet. Almandite from Kollin (Bohemia). See **Bohemian garnet.**

Kongo emerald. Same as Congo emerald.

"Korean or Korea Jade." Term used for (1) various impure jades; (2) bowenite (Smith); (3) artificially colored soapstone or other minerals; (4) glass imitations of jade.

kornerupine (kor"-neh-roo'-pin). A transparent brown, green, yellow or colorless mineral species, seldom cut except as a curiosity for collectors. It is characterized by strong pleochroism. A star effect is sometimes encountered. Chemical composition, magnesium-aluminum silicate ($MgAl_2SiO_6$); crystal system, orthorhombic; hardness, $6\frac{1}{2}$; specific gravity, 3.27 to 3.44; refractive index, 1.667-1.680; birefringence, .013; dispersion, .019. Sources: Ceylon, Malagasy Republic, Burma and elsewhere.

korowell. A Ceylonese trade grade of pearls; includes double pearls (Boutan). Apparently same as **kuruval.**

krantzite. A fossil resin.

Künstlicher Edelstein (German). Artificial stone.

kunzite (koonz'ite). Transparent pink to lilac-colored **spodumene** named for **Kunz.** A comparatively new gemstone, discovered in 1902 or earlier in Southern California; later found in Madagascar.

kural. A Ceylonese pearl trade grade said to include (1) very small and misshapen pearls (Boutan; Kunz), or (2) deformed or double pearls (Cattelle who probably confused with **kuruval**).

kuruval. Ceylonese trade grade consisting of deformed or double pearls (Kunz). See **vadivu.**

kyanite (ki'-ah-nite). A transparent to opaque, light- to dark-blue (its most common hue), yellow, gray, green, brown or colorless mineral species, occasionally cut as a gemstone. It is characterized by its extreme variability of hardness: 4 to 5 in one direction and 6 to 7 at right angles. Chemical composition, aluminum silicate (Al_2SiO_5) — trimorphous (same chemical composition) with andalusite and sillimanite); crystal system, triclinic; specific gravity, 3.56 to 3.57; refractive index, 1.716-1.731; birefringence, .016; dispersion, .011. Sources: India, Ceylon, Burma, Brazil, Tanzania and other localities.

kyauk-ame (East Indian). Black variety of jadeite.

kyauk-atha (East Indian). White translucent jadeite.

kyauk-me (East Indian). Term applied to dark stones at the Burma ruby mines.

Kyushu. The southernmost island of Japan, which is becoming increasingly important in pearl cultivation because its warmer waters afford excellent pearl-culturing conditions. It is to this area that Ago Bay rafts are removed for the winter months, because the water temperature is higher. Presently, over one-fourth of the cultured-pearl production comes from Kyushu waters, and, in all probability, a greater percentage will be grown there in the future.

L

labradorescence (lab"-rah-door-ess'-ence). The phenomenon possessed by **labradorite** that displays flashes of a laminated iridescence of a single bright hue that changes gradually as the stone is moved about in reflected light. The effect is created by light interference set up in thin plates of feldspar that result from repeated twinning. See **labradorite.**

Labrador feldspar. Labradorite.

Labrador hornblende. Same as **hypersthene.**

labradorite (lab'-rah-door-ite). An opaque, massive, gray **plagioclase feldspar** that displays the phenomenon of **labradorescence** (flashes of a laminated iridescence of a single bright hue that changes gradually as the stone is moved about in reflected light). The colors produced are usually brilliant blue or green, although yellow, red, orange and bronze occur less frequently. Labradorite is also found in a transparent yellow form that does not display labadorescence; it has little gemological interest or value. Crystal system, triclinic; hardness, 6; specific gravity, 2.65; refractive index, 1.559-1.568, birefringence, .011. Sources: Labrador, Finland, Malagasy Republic, N.Y., Russia and Colorado. Pale-yellow material occurs in Utah, Calif., Oregon and Texas. See **feldspar.**

Labrador moonstone. A variety of labradorite. Specimens from Madagascar are translucent, yellow-brown with fine bluish **adularescence.** (Schlossmacher).

Labrador rock. Labradorite.

Labrador spar. Labradorite.

Labrador stone. Labradorite.

lacquerback. A transparent or translucent stone, the pavilion of which has been covered with colored lacquer, cement or similar material to change or improve its color. A glass imitation so treated is an **imitation lacquerback.**

ladjward-jui (Afghan for *Lapis Lazuli Brook*). The name of the stream near Faisabad near which **Badakshan lapis** is found.

Lake Biwa. A large reservoir in Shiga Province, Honshu, Japan, that is the site of the cultured fresh-water pearl-farming industry in that country.

Lake Superior agate. (1) Any agate from Lake Superior region. (2) Incorrect name for **thomsonite** from same region which is marked or banded as is agate.

"Lake Superior fire agate." A glass imitation of opal.(Kraus and Slawson)

Lake Superior greenstone. Chlorastrolite.

lamellae (la-mel'ee). Thin plates or layers; **laminae.**

lamellar (la-mel'ar or lam'e-lar). Consisting of laminae; tabular.

laminae (lam'i-nee). Thin plates or layers, usually, but not always, of repeated or polysynthetic **twinning.**

laminated (lam'i-nate"ed). Consisting of, or arranged in, plates or layers.

landerite. Pink grossularite from Xalostoc, Morelos, Mexico. Same as rosolite and xalosticite.

landscape agate. White or gray chalcedony with inclusions of irregular arrangements of manganese oxide which bear fanciful resemblance to a landscape.

Lao Kan C'hing jade. A Chinese name for bluish jade. See **Kan C'hing jade.**

Lao Kan Huang jade. A Chinese name for deep yellowish jade.

lap. Horizontally revolving metal circular disc, usually 12″ to 18″ in diameter, against which gems are held to be ground or polished or faceted. Soft iron for diamonds. Copper, gun metal, lead, pewter, wood, cloth-covered, leather-covered, etc., for colored stones.

La Paz pearl. A trade term for pearl fished in the Gulf of California and Pacific coastal waters of Mexico and Central America. Usually **black pearl** of grayish or bronzy varieties but sometimes **white pearl** of fine quality. Formerly marketed through La Paz, Mexico, but most of the molluscs have disappeared. They were variously reported to be found in the species *Margaritifera m. mazatlanica* (Kunz), or the species *Meleagrina californica* (Boutan). Schlossmacher mentions the mussel *Malleus* as producing the bronze pearl. Same as Panama pearl. See also **Venezuela pearl.**

La Pellegrina Pearl. A 111½-grain, perfectly round, unpierced pearl of a silvery transparent sheen brought from India to Russia in the 18th century. A book of 48 pages devoted to it alone was published in 1818 by a German in praise of it. Whenever *La Pellegrina* was displayed it was said to be so stunning that it met with as-

tonished silence. Considered one of the loveliest pearls in the world, it was last known in Russia in 1827.

La Peregina Pearl. A pear-shaped pearl of 203.84 grains, found in the Gulf of Panama in 1560 and presented to Philip II of Spain, who gave it to his wife, Mary Tudor. After her death, the great pearl, often called *The Incomparable*, was owned by such personalities as Margarita of Spain, Joseph Bonaparte, Louis Napoleon and the Marquis of Abercorn. In 1969, it was purchased by actor Richard Burton as a gift for his wife, actress Elizabeth Taylor. It is also called the *Philip II Pearl*.

lapis (lape′is). Latin, a stone. Often used in the trade as an abbreviation for lapis lazuli.

lapis ardens. A Latin name for **amber.**

lapis crucifer. A name for the variety of **staurolite** that occurs in the form of an interpenetrating twin crystal. Used as a curio stone, without fashioning, for amulets, charms, rosaries, etc. See **staurolite.**

lapis-lazuli (lap′-iss laz′-u-li). A semitranslucent to opaque **rock,** composed principally of **luzurite** and **hauynite,** plus variable amounts of pyrite and calcite and lesser quantities of diopside and other minerals. The finest color is an intense, slightly dark blue to violetish blue. Less valuable qualities are various tones and intensities of blue with or without pyrite inclusions, and light blue to greenish blue with white calcite inclusions. "Swiss lapis" and "German lapis" are misleading terms for blue-dyed jasper or chalcedony. Chemical composition of lazurite, Na_4Si_2-$Al_3Si_3O_{12}$; crystal system, isometric (gem material, a granular crystalline aggregate); hardness, 5 to 6; specific gravity, 2.50 to 3.00; refractive index, 1.50. Sources: Afghanistan, Chile and Russia. See lazurite.

lapis lazuli ware. A variety of Wedgwood, colored and marked to resemble lapis lazuli.

lapis lazzale (Italian). Lapis lazuli.

lapis matrix. Lapis lazuli containing prominent patches of calcite. See Chilean lapis.

lapis mutabilis (L.) Hydrophane opal.

lapper. A person who operates a lap.

lapping. The grinding or polishing of colored stones on a lap, by the use of water and (1) diamond dust rolled or hammered into a soft metal lap, or (2) a mixture of abrasive grit, usually silicon carbide.

lardite. Agalmatolite.

lard stone. Agalmatolite.

La Régente Pearl. Egg-shaped pearl of 337 grains, once a French court jewel. Sold in May, 1887.

La Reine des Perles (The Queen of Pearls). A fine, round oriental pearl weighing 27.5 c. stolen with other French crown jewels in 1792. Thought by some to have been purchased and renamed La Pellegrina Pearl.

La Tausca pearls. Trade-marked name for both solid and wax-filled imitation pearls.

lathi (Burmese). Term applied to 1 ¾ -carat gemstones.

lattice. The pattern in which atoms or molecules are arranged in crystal structure.

lat yay (East Indian). Clouded jadeite. Used for making buttons, hat pins, etc.

Lauégrams. A name for Laué photographs or diagrams. The X-ray photographs used in identifying gemstones and pearls. Named for the noted physicist Max von Laué who discovered them.

lava. Molten rock, as that which flows from volcanos; also the same rock after solidification.

lazulite. A transparent-to-opaque mineral, light to a dark sky-blue, which somewhat resembles lazurite in color. Rarely cut except for collectors. Mono. $(Fe,Mg)Al_2$ $(OH)_2 (PO_4)_2$; H. 5-6; S.G. 3.1; R.I. 1.61/164; Bi. 0.031. From Brazil, Germany, Calif., N. C., and Ga.

lazurfeldspar. A blue variety of orthoclase, found in Siberia.

lazurite (laz'-u-rite). A semitranslucent to opaque, intense, blue to violetish-blue mineral; the principal constituent of lapis-lazuli. Chemical composition, $Na_4S_2Al_3$-Si_3O_{12}; crystal system, isometric (commonly compact, massive); hardness, 5 to 5½; specific gravity, 2.38 to 2.45; refractive index, 1.50. Lazurite often contains, by isomorphous replacement, molecules of the closely related minerals hauynite and sodalite and occasionally noselite. See lapis-lazuli.

lazurquartz. Blue quartz. See sapphire quartz.

lazurspar. Lapis lazuli.

lazurstone. Lapis lazuli.

lead glass. Any glass which contains a large proportion of lead oxide; the inclusion of this oxide raises the refractive index and dispersive power over that of ordinary glass. The lead glass most often used for gem imitation is flint glass (or strass). See **flint glass.**

lechosos opal (lay'-cho-sos). Milky opal showing green play of color only, characteristic of the Mexican deposits.

lemanita (Span.). Jade.

lenbouk. Burmese term for a first water ruby exceeding four carats.

lens system. Same as **optical system.**

lente acromatic (Span.). Achromatic lens.

lente aplanática (Span.). Aplanatic lens.

lenticular. Lens-shaped; of tabular form, thick at the middle, and thinning toward the edges.

lentil. A form of cabochon cutting approximately symmetrical about the girdle plane, with comparatively thin convex top and base. This style is used especially for fashioning opal.

leonite. A trade name for a yellowish **Tibet stone.** Also a mineralogical name for a mineral of no gemological interest.

leopard jade. A descriptive term applied to spotted jade resembling the colors and marking of a leopard.

lepidolite (lep'i-doe-lite). L i g h t reddish violet lithia mica; a matrix of tourmaline.

Leshem. Seventh stone in the breastplate of the high priest. Translated as *ligurius*; probably amber, but other authorities

give jacinth, others a brown agate. Engraved with the name Joseph.

leuco-sapphire (lue'ko). Colorless sapphire.

leukorite. Bakelite (Eppler).

Leveridge gauge. A millimeter dial micrometer, designed by A. D. Leveridge, for measuring various shapes of mounted and unmounted diamonds and colored stones, as well as spherical pearls. An accompanying set of tables is used for translating measurements into weights. It is the most accurate of the gauges designed specifically for weight estimations.

levin opal. A variety of opal characterized by long, thin, lightninglike flashes of play of color. See **opal.**

Li. Abbreviation for the element lithium.

Lichtbrechung (German). Refraction (of light).

ligament pearl. Elongated misshapen pearl formed near hinge of a mussel.

light. A form of radiant energy that, like X-ray, radio and other similar radiations, travels through space. Visible light has a wavelength range of about 4000 A.U. to 7000 A.U.

Light of the World Opal. A black opal from the Lightning Ridge district, New South Wales, Australia. Found in 1928, it weighed 16 ounces and measured 6 x 3 x 1 inches in the rough. After fashioning into a convex-topped stone, it weighed 252 carats and measured about 2½ x 1½ x ⅞ inches. The play of color is predominantly red, with a lesser amount of gold and

114

green. Today, it is reported to be owned privately in the United States.

light-field illumination. A kind of illumination in which the light source is directly behind the gemstone being observed. This principle, together with *dark-field illumination*, is incorporated in the *Gemolite*, or *Gemscope* (trademarks, Gemological Institute of America), the *Diamondscope* (trademark, American Gem Society), plus the *GIA Gem Detector* and the *GIA Diamond Grader.*

light opal. Term which has been used to distinguish White Cliffs opal and other Australian white opal from **black opal.** See **white opal.**

ligurite. An apple green **sphene.** (Dana)

Ligurius. See **Leshem.**

lime jade. A descriptive term applied by Chinese to a lime-green color of jade.

limestone. A sedimentary rock composed chiefly of calcium carbonate (calcite). See also **marble.**

limonite. A brown iron oxide sometimes coating gem minerals, and usually an associated mineral with turquoise, in which it is often seen as brownish inclusions. With large pieces of turquoise it is fashioned as turquoise matrix. S.G. 3.8.

limpidity. Water-like transparency.

Lincoln Sapphire. A bust of Abraham Lincoln carved from a dark-blue, 2302-carat sapphire found at Anakie, Queensland, Australia. The finished carving weighs 1318 carats and measures 2$\frac{1}{16}$ inches high, 1$\frac{3}{4}$ inches wide and two inches deep. The sculptor was Norman Maness and the technical advisor, Dr. Merrill Gage. This carving, together with those of Presidents Washington, Eisenhower and Jefferson and the *Black Star of Queensland*, were presented as a gift to the American people by the Kazanjian Foundation of Pasadena, California, a charitable, nonprofit organization founded by Kazanjian Bros., Los Angeles gem dealers. The *Lincoln Sapphire* is presently on display at the Smithsonian Institution, Washington, D.C.

Linde Star. A trademarked name for synthetic star ruby and synthetic star sapphires of various colors, made in the United States by the Linde Co.

Linde Synthetic Emerald. A trademarked name for a hydrothermal synthetic emerald manufactured in the United States by the Linde Co.

Lingah pearl. Same as **Persian Gulf pearl.** See also **zinni pearl.**

Linschoten. Famous 16th Century Dutch traveler in Orient who formulated a rule for the valuation of gems. (S. H. Ball).

lintonite. An agate-like variety of **thomsonite** greenish or with alternating bands of pink and green. From Lake Superior region where it is cut and sold as a gemstone.

lion's-eye. A name used in some nations for cat's-eye.

liquid inclusion. A space in a gemstone filled or partially filled with a liquid.

liroconite (lye-rok'oe-nite). A translucent to opaque blue to greenish-yellow mineral occasionally used as an ornamental stone, and more rarely as substitute for turquoise. A hydrous arsenate of aluminum and copper. H. 2-2½; S.G. 2.9; R.I. 1.61/1.67; Mono. From Arizona and other sources.

"Lithia amethyst" (lith'i-a), Kunzite.

"Lithia emerald." Hiddenite.

lithia lazuli. Same as **lithoxyle.**

lithion beryl. Beryl containing lithium but no caesium, purely a chemical distinction.

lithomancy. Divination by minerals or gems.

lithoxyle, lithoxyl, or **lithoxylite.** Opalized wood in which original woody structure is observable.

liver opal. Same as **menilite.**

llusvisnados (u-vees-nah'-doz). A Mexican term that refers to a highly transparent opal with a very light-yellowish or light-bluish body color showing thin, lightninglike or sheetlike shafts or flashes of intense play of color within the stone. The flashes may be comparatively small or fairly coarse and bold. This colorful effect is sometimes likened to myriads of individual, minute rainbows produced by a shower of raindrops through the rays of the setting sun. It is the most highly prized type of Mexican opal. See **opal.**

loadstone. Same as **lodestone.**

lodestone. The highly magnetic variety of the iron-oxide mineral **magnetite.** Small specimens have long been sold as good-luck charms.

loodwins (Burmese). Mine workings in caves or fissures. (V. Ball).

loop. See **loupe.**

loose diamond, pearl, or **other gem.** A gem not set in a jewel.

Los Cerrillos turquoise. From Los Cerrillos mines (near Mt. Chalcichnite), close to Santa Fe, N. M., possibly worked by Indians for centuries but now almost inactive; produced fine q u a l i t y **American turquoise.**

loss of color. Becoming lighter, or darker in tone, as when blue becomes darker when observed under artificial light or becomes lighter when exposed to sunlight. Any loss in intensity of color or change to a less desirable hue.

lot pearls. Small pearls, under 1 carat each.

loup. See **loupe.**

loupe (French), **lupe** (German), **loup,** or **loop.** The French word is accepted as correct spelling in English - speaking nations. Any small magnifying glass mounted for use in the hand as a **hand loupe,** or so that it can be held in the eye socket or attached to spectacles as an **eye loupe.** Loupes may contain a single lens or a system of lenses, and in commercial usage range in magnifying power from 2 to 20, the usual jeweler's or watchmaker's loupe being from 2 to 3 power, and aplanatic loupes from 6 to 20 power. See **loupe, corrected.**

loupe, corrected. A loupe in which the lens system has been corrected for either spherical or chromatic aberration, or both. See **aberration, aplanatic loupe, apochromatic lens, G.I.A. Registered Loupe.**

loupe-visible. Visible with aid of a **loupe.**

love's arrows. Same as **fleches d'amour.**

love stone. Aventurine quartz.

low relief. When inclusions in a transparent mineral have a refractivity near or the same as the host, they are said to have low relief. Also caller **bas-relief.** Example: corundum crystals or grains enclosed in corundum.

lozenge cut. A modern style of gem cutting; shaped like a playing card diamond.

lucinite. Variscite from near Lucin, Utah.

lucite. DuPont's trade name for a transparent methyl-methacrylate plastic. S.G. 1.19; R.I. 1.49. See **plexiglass.**

lucky stone. Same as staurolite.

Lu jade. Lu Yü, a Chinese name for bluish green jade.

luli. Local name for imitation pearl made in Egypt in the Roman era, by silvering a glass bead and then flashing over it another coat of glass.

lumachella. See **fire marble.**

lumachelle. Same as lumachella.

luminescence. A general term used to describe the emission of light by a substance when excited by rays (particularly ultra-violet or X rays), electrical discharge, heat, friction, or similar agency.

lumpy girdle. A too-thick girdle.

lumpy stone. Refers to one cut with too great depth in proportion to its width.

lunaris (lue-na'res) Latin, meaning moonstone.

lunar stone. A phosphorescent variety of barite.

lus. Mining term used in Burma ruby mines for deep underground excavations or shafts into the hillsides, sometimes several hundred feet in depth.

luster. The appearance of a surface in reflected light. It depends principally upon the relative smoothness (texture) of the surface and upon the refractive index, which governs the amount of light reflected. Schiller, play of color, orient and other such optical phenomena are distinct from luster, but luster is related to **sheen.** See **adamantine luster; metallic luster; pearly luster; resinous; silky; vitreous; waxy.**

"luthos lazuli". Violet fluorite.

Lydian stone. Same as **basanite.**

lynx eye. Green **labradorite.**

lynx eye labradorite. Labradorite with a green schiller.

"lynx sapphire." Dark blue iolite (Schlossmacher). See **lynx sapphire.**

lynx sapphire. (1) Term applied to dark blue sapphires in Ceylon (Smith). (2) Very pale blue sapphire with a girasol effect (Schlossmacher). See **"lynx sapphire".**

lynx stone. Iolite.

M

mabe. An artificially induced blister **pearl,** made by inserting a hemisphere of mother-of-pearl against the shell of a fresh-water mussel. After a few years the resultant formation is cut from the shell, the half-bead removed, and the nacre-covered half-dome is cemented over a mother-of-pearl bead of appropriate size and shape. The result is called a **mabe** or **mabe pearl.**

machastone. Same as **mocha stone.**

machchakai. See **vadivu.**

macle (mak'l). Same as maacle. (1) A seldom-used name for chiastolite. (2) A twin crystal.

macroscopic (mak"roe-skop'ik). Large enough to be observed without the microscope.

Madagascar aquamarine. As a trade grade, any aquamarine that is darker and more violetish blue than the usual light greenish-blue variety.

Madagascar morganite. Morganite of fine color and large size, from Madagascar.

Madagascar pearl. Fine pearl from Island of Madagascar, sold through Indian pearl markets as Indian pearl. (Boutan)

madanku. A Ceylonese trade grade for pearls. Literally, folded or bent. Pearls of small or **vadivu** class, but imperfect in form and color (Kunz). See **mondogoe.**

Madeira stone. Same as "Madeira topaz."

"Madeira topaz." Originally, citrine of fiery Madeira wine color, from Salamanca. Since 1900, similar colored stones have been produced by heating amethysts (Schlossmacher). See **burnt amethyst.**

Madonna of the Star. A 545-carat gem creation of the Madonna and Child carved from a black star sapphire. The rough stone, found at Anakie, Queensland, Australia, weighed 1100 carats and measured 1¼ inches high, 1¾ inches wide and 1½ inches deep. The polished back exhibits a strong star and a second, smaller, star has been polished on the upper right of the front of the piece. The artist was Harry B. Derian. The *Madonna of the Star* was presented to the American people as a gift by the Kazanjian Foundation of Pasadena, California, a charitable, nonprofit organization founded by Kazanjian Bros., Los Angeles gem dealers. The piece is occasionally on exhibit at art museums and elsewhere in the United States.

Madras pearl. (1) Any **oriental pearl** marketed through Madras, India. (2) Any oriental pearl found in the Madras area. (3) As an *American trade grade*, a white pearl with faint bluish **overtone** and a **rosé orient,** a combination which produces a lavender tint. See also **Madras white pearl.**

Madras white pearl. Trade term for slightly rosé pearl with whiter body color than **Bombay pearl** (Kunz). Other authorities describe as slightly more metallic. Came principally from the now-dormant Ceylon fisheries. See **Ceylon pearl.**

magic stone. A white, opaque variety of hydrophane, in rounded lumps, with a chalky or glazed coating; from Colorado.

magma (mag'ma). Molten (liquid) rock material within the earth; the molten mass from which any igneous rock or lava is formed.

magnesium-aluminum garnet. Same as **pyrope.**

magnetic. Capable of either attracting a magnetic needle or of being attracted by a magnet.

magnetic twin. Same as **polysynthetic twin.**

magnetite. Opaque iron-black mineral of no gemological importance. See **lodestone.**

Mahabharata (ma-ha-ba'ra-ta). A Hindu epic containing early information regarding India.

Mahar. See **Lingah pearl.**

Maharani Cat's-eye. A 58-carat, green chrysoberyl cat's-eye on display at the Smithsonian Institution, Washington, D.C. It is said to be one of the finest in existence. From Ceylon.

Maharatnani. The five great gems of the Hindus, which for centuries have been the diamond, pearl, ruby, emerald and sapphire. (S. H. Ball)

maiden pearl. Pearl newly fished and not yet worn.

main facets. The **crown** and **pavilion** facets of a brilliant-cut gemstone that extend from table to girdle or girdle to culet. On step-cut stones, the **center** row of facets on the pavilion.

make. Trade term referring to proportions, symmetry, and polish; as a *well-made stone,* a *lumpy stone,* a *swindled stone,* etc.

malachite (mal'-ah-kite). A semi-translucent to opaque, intense, light to dark, slightly bluish-green to yellowish-green decorative and ornamental mineral species, often banded in two tones of these colors. It is often intimately associated with **azurite,** when it is called **azurmalachite.** A radial fibrous structure with a high luster on the individual needlelike crystals produces an attractive sheen on some specimens. Malachite is an important ore of copper. Chemical composition, copper carbonate $(Cu_2(OH)_2CO_3)$; crystal system, monoclinic (microscopic crystals only; usually, massive and fibrous); hardness, $3\frac{1}{2}$ to 4; specific gravity, 3.30 to 4.10; refractive index, 1.66-1.91 (massive material yields an indistinct reading at about 1.66); birefringence, .026. Sources: Russia, France, Rhodesia, the Congo, Arizona, New Mexico and other localities.

malaquita (Span.). Malachite.

"malchit-jade." Same as **chrysodor.**

male ruby, sapphire, etc. Any dark-colored ruby, sapphire, etc. See **female ruby, sapphire, etc.**

malleable. Capable of being shaped by hammering or rolling.

Malleidae. The family of salt-water **bivalves** which include both the hammer shells and the so-called pearl oysters. Same as Aviculidae or Pteriidae. See also **Malleus; Meleagrina pearl.**

Malleus. The genus of **Malleidae** containing the hammer shells. See also **LaPaz pearl.**

maltesite (mol-teze'ite). A variety of andalusite resembling chiastolite in its markings; from Finland.

mammillary (mam'i-lae-ri). Having a smooth, hummocky surface, with curved protuberances larger than botryoidal. See **botryoidal; reniform.**

manchadi. A Ceylonese weight, the equivalent of 3.55 grains troy.

Manchurian jade. Soapstone.

manganese-aluminum garnet. Same as **spessartite.**

manganese garnet. Spessartite.

manganese spar. (1) Rhodonite. (2) Rhodochrosite.

manganoandalusite. Same as **viridine.**

mangelin (man'g'lin). Hindu weight equal to 1⅜ carats.

Manila gum. Fossil resin from the Philippines.

Manila pearl. Pearl marketed through Manila. Principally of same quality as **Philippine pearl.**

Man jade. Man Yü, a Chinese name for jade of blood red hue.

mantle. External body wall or skin of a mollusc; that portion of the body which secretes the shell-building material.

manufactured stone. In gemology, any man-made substitute for a genuine gemstone. It may be an **imitation,** a **synthetic stone** or any other man-made reproduction.

manul (Ceylonese). Loose or soft sand sea-bottom.

Maori stone (ma'oe-ri), colloq. mou'ri). Name given nephrite of New Zealand from its use by the Maori natives.

marble. Crystalline limestone, a massive form of **calcite.** A building and **decorative stone.** Many varieties are ornamental stones, as Parian marble and Carrara marble used in sculptured figures and figurines, lamp bases,

etc. Some varieties are used in costume jewelry, as the onyx marble called "Mexican onyx" or "Mexican jade." Never a gem stone.

marcasite (mar'-kah-site). An opaque, metallic, very light brownish-yellow or grayish mineral. The name is often applied incorrectly to **pyrite,** which is used extensively in "marcasite" jewelry. Hematite is used less often for the same purpose. On exposure, the surface color of marcasite darkens and becomes unattractive. Chemical composition, iron sulphide (FeS_2); crystal system, orthorhombic; hardness, 6 to 6½; specific gravity, 4.85.

margarita (Latin). Pearl.

margaritaceous. Pertaining to or resembling pearl.

Margaritifera (Mar"-gah-rih-tif'-erah). Another, but older name for *Pinctada,* the most important genus of salt-water pearl-bearing molluscs. The name is from the Greek word **margarites** (pearl).

margaritiferous. Pearl-bearing.

margaritomancy. Divination by use of pearls.

marialite. A variety of **scapolite.**

marmol (Span.). Marble.

Marmor (German). Marble.

marquise. A term loosely used in the trade to mean either a **marquise cut** or a **marquise ring.**

marquise (mar-keez'). A style of cutting gemstones in which the girdle outline is boat shaped. The shape and placement of the facets is of the **brilliant** style. The word marquise is preferred in the diamond trade; **navette** and **boat shaped** in the colored-stone trade.

masaku or **masanku.** Ceylon trade grade which includes (1) pearls somewhat irregular in shape and slightly faulty in shape or color (Cattelle). (2) Badly colored pearls, usually symmetrical, grey and with luster (Kunz).

"mascot emerald." Trade name for genuine beryl triplet. See also **"emerald triplet."**

masculine. Term applied to stones of a deep and rich color.

masitúl, (meaning "ink-dust," or "chalk powder"). Generally used for medicinal purposes, or burnt and eaten with areca-nut and betel by the natives. A Ceylonese trade grade of pearls (Kunz).

mass aqua. Trade term for borosilicate crown glass imitation of aquamarine. H. 6; S.G. 2.35-2.37; R.I. 1.50-1.51.

massive. Not occurring in crystal forms, but not necessarily noncrystalline. In mineralogy, a compact crystal aggregate showing no exterior crystal form is said to be massive.

massive amber. A compact, almost colorless to dark orange-yellow variety of **Baltic amber.**

mass opal. Opal matrix.

matched pearls. A term often interpreted to mean pearls exactly duplicated in color as to all of the color attributes—**hue,** tone and intensity—which is practically an impossibility with the number of pearls necessary in a necklace. Pearls may, however, be matched as to body color and predominant color of orient. Thus a necklace may consist entirely of light cream rosé pearls, but those pearls vary slightly in one or more color attributes, usually tone and intensity. See **blended pearls.**

matinee length. A pearl necklace 20 to 24 inches in length.

matrice. Same as **matrix.**

matrix (mae'triks). The rock in which a mineral is contained, portions of it containing pieces of the mineral being known as **turquoise matrix, opal matrix,** etc.

matriz. (Span.). **Matrix.**

matted. Tangled closely together. Said of **crystalline aggregates** in which the crystals are closely packed together, as in nephrite. Same as felted structure.

Matto Grosso (mat'oo grose'oo). A gem-bearing state or territory of Brazil.

mawing. The process of grinding and polishing strategically placed cuts, about one inch wide and three-fourths of an inch deep, on a jadeite boulder at the Burma mines. The purpose is to expose the interior for better, although still speculative, examination for the benefit of the buyer.

maw-sit-sit. An opaque, fine-grained **albite feldspar.** It is a vivid, medium tone of slightly yellowish green, with veins and patches of dark green to black. The miners' name for lighter tones of maw-sit-sit is *kyet tayoe.* The source of its green color is chromium-rich jadeite inclusions. Source: Upper Burma.

Maxixe aquamarine or **beryl.** A name which has been applied to a deep blue, boron-bearing beryl from the Maxixe Mine, Minas Geraes, Brazil.

Maxwell Stuart Topaz. A colorless topaz from Ceylon which, when brilliant cut about 1897, weighed 369 m.c. and created much comment (Kunz). Since then many larger colorless, yellow and blue topazes have been cut.

mayaite (ma'ya-ite or my'a-ite). Diopside jadeite from Central America such as found in ancient tombs of the Maya nation. Grades from tuxtlite to nearly albite. White to gray green or yellow-green. See **diopside-jadeite.**

m. c. Abbreviation for **metric carat.**

mean birefringence. The numeral which represents the average between the greatest strength of **double refraction** and the least strength of double refraction possessed by a species or variety. R.I. of sphene is 1.885/1.990-1.915/2.050; hence the **birefringence** varies from 0.105 to 0.135. The average, or mean, is 0.120. See also **refractive index.**

mean refractive index. The R. I. which is equidistant from the least R. I. and the greatest R. I. which is possessed by any substance. The mean R. I. of singly refractive gem **species** is expressed by one figure as 1.50; or doubly refractive substances by two R.I.'s as 1.50/1.55. (Anderson defines mean R.I. of a singly refractive gem as its most usual R.I.) See **refractive index.**

medfordite. A local Oregon name for massive white quartz with streaks and patches of green and brown moss.

"medina emerald." Green glass.

medwins. Open cuttings in East Indian alluvial hill deposits over which water is led.

meerschaum (meer'-shum). A white, light-gray or light-yellow, opaque, compact, massive, claylike, partly amorphous hydrated silicate of magnesium. The material is noted for its lightness and porosity. It is an ornamental mineral, used for pipes, cigar and cigarette holders and carvings. The mineralogical name, **sepiolite,** comes from the Greek word meaning **cuttlefish,** because the bones of this fish are equally light and porous. Hardness, 2 to 2½; specific gravity, 2.00; refractive index, 1.52 to 1.53. Sources: Eski Shehr in Asia Minor, Moravia, Greece and Spain.

megascopic (meg"a-skop'ik). Visible to the unaided eye in contrast with miscroscopic. Same as **macroscopic.**

Mei-kuo Lu jade. Same as **American green jade.**

meionite. A variety of **scapolite.**

melanite. Black andradite garnet. Has been used in mourning jewelry.

Meleagrina (Mel"-e-ah-gre'-nah). An alternate but little-used term that is synonymous with *Pinctada* or *Margaritifera,* the most important genus of salt-water pearl-bearing molluscs.

melee. Melee is a term used primarily to describe small (under .25 carat), round faceted diamonds. However, it is also applied to colored stones of the same size and shape.

melemine formaldehyde. A translucent to opaque synthetic **plastic,** used to imitate various colored gemstone. Hardness, 2½; specific gravity, 1.48; refractive index, 1.54 to 1.60.

mellow amber. A name for **gedanite.**

melon cut. A style of fashioning a bead or a cabochon stone; an elongated form with equidistant longitudinal depressions or meridians separating convex sections as in a cantaloupe.

melt. Often used to mean a paste or enamel in the liquid state before it hardens.

melting snow jade. Descriptive term for a white to grayish color grade of jadeite with opaque patches traversed by translucent streaks.

menilite (men'i-lite or men-ill'ite). Opaque, grayish or brownish banded common opal. An ornamental stone.

mercury vapor lamp. A light source derived from an electrical discharge through mercury vapor. Valuable as a source of **ultraviolet** light and also for distinctive spectrum in the visible region. (Shipley, Jr.)

Merguian Pearl. Pearl from Mergui Archipelago, on eastern shore of Bay of Bengal. Similar in quality to **Philippine pearl.**

Mesa Grande tourmaline. Tourmaline from pegmatite ledge near Mesa Grande, San Diego Co., Calif. Much of fine quality was formerly mined there together with pink beryl.

Meshed turquoise. Turquoise from Meshed, Iran (Persia), the market for Persian turquoise.

metallic luster. Having the surface sheen of a metal; with a metal-like reflection.

metalloidal luster (met"al-oy'dal). Reflecting light, somewhat like a metal, but less than **metallic luster.**

metamict. When the crystal structure of a material has been broken down by the emanation of radioactive constituents, it is said to be metamict; e.g., low-property zircon, ekanite.

metamorphic (met"a-more'fik). Of. pertaining to, produced by, or exhibiting **metamorphism.**

metamorphism. The change in chemical composition or in the structure of a rock or mineral by heat, pressure, and other natural agents.

meteoric glass. See **moldavite.**

meteorite. A mass of stone or metal that has fallen to the earth from outer space.

methylene iodide. (CH_2I_2). A highly refractive (R.I. 1.74) and heavy (S.G. 3.32) liquid used for specific gravity determination and as a contact fluid for the refractometer. For the latter use, it is usually saturated with sulphur (S) and tetraiodoethylene (C_2I_4) to attain an R.I. of 1.815 (Shipley Jr.).

metric carat. See **carat.**

metric grain. See **grain.**

mewdwins. Same as **medwins.**

Mex. Abbr. used in this book for Mexican language, and for Mexico.

"Mexican agate." Banded calcite or aragonite.

"Mexican amber." Fossil resin from Mexico, related to "San Domingo amber" (Schlossmacher). See also **bacalite.**

Mexican amethyst. Amethyst of a distinctive reddish purple color from Guanajuato, Mexico. (Eppler).

Mexican emerald. One which is or has been owned in Mexico, probably mined in what is today

Colombia.

"Mexican jade." A misnomer for green-dyed onyx marble (massive **calcite**).

"Mexican onyx." A misnomer for **onyx marble** (banded massive calcite).

Mexican opal. (1) Any opal from Mexico. (2) A term commonly used for **fire opal** and **water opal**, since this country is the principal source of these two varieties.

Mexican pearl. A term which is not used in the trade but which seems to have been added to pearl nomenclature by an incorrect interpretation of Schlossmacher's definition and description of the **occidental pearl**. The term could be used in a geographic sense to mean any pearl from east or west coast of Mexico including **La Paz pearl** and pearl from Gulfs of Campeche and Mexico. The suggestion that the term apply to pearls from Gulf of Mexico only seems illogical as the word Mexican is generally accepted as referring to the nation, and not the Gulf.

Mexican turquoise. (1) A name commonly used in some nations for light blue to greenish-blue and bluish-green turquoise from New Mexico (U.S.A.) (2) Blue turquoise with a brown matrix, from Baja, Calif., Mexico.

Mexican water opal. Term applied to translucent to almost transparent opal variety from Mexico with vivid play of color; yellowish by transmitted light. (Anderson)

Mg. Abbr. for the element magnesium.

mica (mike'a). A group of minerals notable for their easy cleavage, yielding thin flakes (laminae); low in hardness and of gemological importance only as inclusions. See **fuchsite; lepidolite.**

micaceous (mei-kae'shee-us). Composed of thin plates or scales, or, like mica, capable of being easily split into thin sheets.

micarta. A plastic similar to **bakelite.**

mica schist. Schist composed largely of mica.

microcline (my'kroe-kline). Green, pink, pale yellow or white mineral of **feldspar** group. Tri; $K.Al.Si_3O_8$. H. 6-6.5; S.G. 2.5-2.6; R.I. 1.52-1.53. Only gem or ornamental variety is **amazonite.**

micrometer. A device for obtaining accurate linear measurements of small distances. Usually reads to .001 inch or .01 millimeter. The most universally used is the *screw micrometer*, in which the motion is measured by means of an accurate threaded plunger working in a tapped hole. Other types are the *dial micrometer*, in which motion is transmitted through a gear train to a pointer revolving around a dial, and the *optical micrometer* in which measurements are made directly through a lens system which magnifies the object to be measured Shipley, Jr.).

micrometer caliper. Less correctly millimeter caliper gauge. See **caliper; gauge.**

"microphotograph." Incorrect designation for **photomicrograph.**

microscope. An optical instrument which affords high magnification of minute objects such as inclusions in gems. A *monocular micro-*

scope employs a single eye-piece or ocular. A *binocular microscope* is equipped with two oculars. In the Greenough type, two complete lens systems are used, giving true stereoscopic vision. A *polarizing microscope* is equipped with polarizing attachments providing polarized light, and is a combination of microscope and polariscope. With proper attachments and accessories, it may be used to determine **optic character.** See also **polariscope.** A *petrographic* or *petrological microscope* is a polarizing microscope especially designed for use with prepared **thin sections** of minerals or rocks. A *gemological* or *gem-testing microscope* is a polarizing microscope equipped with universal immersion stage and other accessories, the entire equipment especially designed for the testing of fashioned gemstones, particularly those set in mountings. A *pearl testing microscope* is a microscope equipped with special accessories for pearl identification especially with an **endoscopic stage** and a **pearl illuminator.**

microscopic. Pertaining to the **microscope,** or visible only by its aid; minute.

microscopy (my-kros'ko-pi). The art of observing and investigating objects under the **microscope.**

midge stone. Same as **gnat stone.**

Midnight Star. An unusual 117-carat purple star sapphire in Morgan Collection, Am. Mus. of Natural Hist.

milk opal. A translucent, milky-appearing variety of common opal. Rarely exhibits play of color.

milky quartz. A translucent to nearly opaque white variety of crystalline quartz. When containing small particles of gold is known as **gold quartz.**

millimeter. One thousandth of a meter (.03937 inch).

millimeter screw micrometer. A precision caliper gauge which measures the over-all dimensions of unmounted fashioned gems more accurately but less conveniently than dial gauges. See **Leveridge gauge.**

mimicry. Imitations of crystal forms of higher symmetry by those of lower grade of symmetry, usually the result of twinning.

Minas Geraes (meen'as jay-rice'). A state northeast of Rio, Brazil; highly productive of gems.

Minas Geraes emerald. Emerald from this state which is usually darker than **Bahia emerald.**

minas novas (Port.). See **pingos d'agoa.**

Minas Novas chrysoberyl. Yellowish chrysoberyl from Minas Novas district, Minas Geraes, Brazil. Usually lacking in transparency (Smith).

mineral. An inorganic substance occurring in nature with a characteristic chemical composition and usually possessng a definite crystal structure, which is sometimes expressed in external geometrical form or outlines. (Kraus)

mineralogy. The science of minerals.

mineral species. See **species.**

mineral turquoise. Term occasionally used to distinguish turquoise from odontolite.

mine run. Unassorted product of

a mine, but term is also used to mean the medium or low grades of anything, such as gemstones.

mine salting. See **salting.**

minimum deviation. The position of a prism in relation to a beam of light where the beam is passing through symmetrically, and, as a corollary, with minimum deviation. By measuring the prism angle (A) and the angle of minimum deviation (D), refractive index may be determined from the formula:

$$n = \frac{\sin \frac{1}{2} (A+D)}{\sin \frac{1}{2} A}$$

misnomer. An incorrect name, often but not always misleading as to the true nature of the subject named. In this book, titles of definitions within quotation marks are misleading, or tend to be misleading, as to the actual nature or value of the subject in quotes.

mixed cut. A combination of brilliant cut above the girdle with usually 32 facets, sometimes more but rarely less, and often a larger and higher table, and step-cut below with the same number of facets. Often used for colored stones, especially fancy sapphires, to improve color and retain brilliancy. Variation of a mixed cut with an emerald-cut crown sometimes used for zircons.

mixte (French). A semigenuine doublet.

Mn. Abbr. for manganese.

Mo. Abbr. for the element molybdenum.

mocha pebble. Same as **mocha stone.**

mocha stone. (1) White, gray or yellowish, translucent crypto-crystalline **quartz** with brown to red iron-bearing, or black manganese-bearing, **dendritic** inclusions to which can be assigned fanciful forms. (Schlossmacher) From many localities, especially the Northwest States of the U. S. A. Same as **landscape agate, tree agate,** etc., but not same as moss agate. (2) In Britain and U. S. A. distinction is rarely made, except gemologically, between mocha stone and **moss agate.** Originally named for city of Mocha; capitalized form Mocha stone is still sometimes used. Also spelled *mochastone.*

modern cut or **moderne cut** (moe-daern'). Any modification or combination of table cut, step cut and brilliant used especially in connection with diamond. Includes baguette, triangle, keystone, half moon, and others.

Moe or **Moe's gauge.** A caliper gauge with accompanying tables, for estimating weight of brilliant cut diamonds.

Mogok Stone Tract. A gem-bearing district north of Mandalay; home of the Burma ruby mines; also yielding sapphires, spinels, tourmalines, zircons, and some less important gems.

Mogul dynasty. See **Great Mogul.**

"Mohave moonstone." Translucent, lilac-tinted chalcedony from the Mohave Desert, California. (Merrill). Mohave is the Indian spelling; **Mojave** is the Spanish spelling.

Mohs scale (moze). The most commonly used scale of relative hardness of minerals—diamond 10, corundum 9, topaz 8, quartz 7, orthoclase feldspar 6, apatite 5, fluorite 4, calcite 3, gypsum 2, talc 1. Divisions are not equal, minerals representing various hardnesses having been chosen arbitrarily by the mineralogist F. Mohs. The difference between 9 and 8 is considerably greater than between the lower numbers, and between 9 and 10 is greater than between 9 and 1.

"Mojave moonstone" (moè-ha'vee). A gray translucent chalcedony (Pough). See **Mohave moonstone.**

Mokkastein (German). Mocha stone.

moldavite (mole'-dah-vite). A translucent to transparent, medium- to dark-green, yellowish-green, brownish-green, grayish-green to green **natural glass,** thought to be of meteoric origin. It is a **tektite.** Chemical composition, 60% to 70% silica, about 10% alumina, plus alkalis and various oxides; crystal system, amorphous; hardness, 5 to 5½; specific gravity, 2.34 to 2.46; refractive index, 1.48 to 1.52. Moldavite usually occurs in flat or rounded shapes smaller than a man's fist, and always exhibits a wrinkled and scarred exterior. Sources: Moldau River, Czechoslovakia, where it was first found in 1787 and after which it was named. Other tektite sources are Libyan Desert, Texas, Western Australia and the East Indies.

molded cameo. A cameo produced by casting in a mold such materials as ceramics, metals, glass, plastics, or sealing wax. See **Wedgwood.**

molecule. The smallest unit of a substance in which the chemical properties of that substance are entirely retained; may consist of one or more elements and therefore of more than one atom.

mollusc (mol'usk). A soft-bodied non-segmented invertebrate animal which typically possesses a hard shell. This shell may be univalve as in the snail, or bivalve, as in the oyster, cockle and mussel. Also spelled mollusk.

momme. The Japanese unit of weight for cultured pearls: equal to 3.75 grams, 75 pearl grains or 18.75 carats.

mondogoe. Bent or folded pearls (Boutan). Probably same as **madanku.**

monel metal. An alloy of nickel (about 75%), copper (about 23.5%), and iron (about 1.5%). Sometimes used for imitations of **hematite** cameos.

money stone. A local name in Pennsylvania for **rutile** (Merrill).

Mono. Abbreviation used in this book for **monoclinic system.**

monochromatic (mon"oe-kroe-mat'ik). Having or consisting of, one color only.

monochromatic light. (1) A term commonly used to described light from a single, limited region of the spectrum, hence light of a single color (Shipley, Jr.). (2) In its strictest but seldom-used sense, light which corresponds to one wave length only.

monochromator. A device for producing monochromatic light. Usually applied to a form of spectroscope which can be adjusted to transmit light from any desired region of the spectrum, but may also be applied to any source of monochromatic light (e.g. to a sodium vapor lamp). (Shipley, Jr.).

monoclinic mineral or **stone.** Mineral or stone of the **monoclinic system.**

monoclinic system (mon"oe-klin'ik). A crystallographic system; has three axes, two of which are unequal in length but at right angles to one another, the third also of unequal length and not at right angles to the plane of the other two. See also **crystal systems.**

monocular microscope. See **microscope.**

monster pearl. Same as **paragon pearl.**

Montana agate. Moss agate, or **mocha stone,** from the gravel beds of the Yellowstone River, extending approximately 250 miles from Billings to Sydney, Montana. Much of the material is uniform, translucent, pale-gray chalcedony with black manganese-oxide inclusions resembling moss, trees, bushes, ferns and other imaginative scenes and objects. Other specimens consist of bands, clouds and streaks of bright brownish-orange or reddish-brown iron oxide suspended in transparent chalcedony. Occasionally, the black and colored inclusions occur together. Montana agate is among the finest in the world, and is much preferred in the jewelry trade. It is also called Yellowstone agate.

"Montana jet." Obsidian, from Yellowstone Park.

"Montana ruby." A misnomer for **pyrope** or **almandite garnet.**

Montana sapphire. (1) Sapphire principally from Yogo Gulch, Fergus Co., and from the gravels of the Missouri River, near Helena, Lewis & Clark Co., Montana. Fine-quality blue stones, similar to the Burma product, are produced at the Yogo locality, as well as some of a paler blue color and a small percentage of fancies, principally purple, violet and grayish green. The stones seldom exceed a size from which three- or four-carat gems can be cut. Material from the latter source is largely light blue or blue-green, often with a grayish cast. Pink, light green, purplish blue, purple, yellow, orange and other colors are also known. Colors are often zoned, and the crystals rarely exceed one-half inch. (2) As a trade grade, the term refers to sapphire, no matter where found, possessing a comparatively light grayish-blue body color called **electric blue** or **steel blue.** Stones of this grade have a slightly metallic-appearing luster.

"Mont Blanc ruby." Reddish quartz.

moonstone. (1) A term applied correctly only to **adularia** (precious moonstone), a semitranslucent to translucent **orthoclase feldspar** that exhibits **adularescence** (a floating, billowy, white or bluish light effect, seen in certain directions as the stone is turned). This optical phenomenon is caused by diffused light reflection from parallel intergrowths of orthoclase and albite feldspars, the latter having a slightly different refractive index from the main mass. Moonstone is found principally in Ceylon. It is one of the birthstones for June. (2) Incorrectly applied, with proper prefix, to the milky or girasol varieties of chalcedony, scapolite, corundum, etc. See **adularescence, chalcedony moonstone.**

moor's head. Name for a colorless or greenish tourmaline crystal with a black termination or end. From Elba.

Moosstein (German). Moss agate.

Morales Pearl. See **Oviedo Pearl.**

128

moralla or **morallion.** (1) Semi-crystallized material from Colombian emerald mines, similar in appearance to turquoise matrix, but green; (2) as a trade term it is sometimes used to mean any of the poorer grades of emeralds.

morganite. A light red-purple to light purplish red caesium-bearing variety of **beryl.** From Brazil, Madagascar, California. Same as rose beryl; vorobievite.

Morgenthau Topaz. A 1463, blue, pear-shaped topaz owned and displayed by the American Museum of Natural History, New York City, one of the largest faceted topaz's of this color in existence. It was presented to the Museum in 1920 by M. L. Morgenthau.

morion (moe'ri-on). Deep-black, almost opaque, smoky **quartz.**

morning dew jade. Fanciful term used by Chinese to describe a greenish jade sprinkled with glistening specks.

moro coral. Dark red, the finest color of **Japanese coral.**

moroxite (moe-rok'site). A blue to greenish-blue variety of apatite.

mosaic agate. Brecciated Mexican agate (Merrill).

mosquito amethyst. Amethyst containing tiny scaly or platy inclusions of **goethite.**

mosquito stone. Spanish name for quartz with tiny dark inclusions. A variety of **mocha stone.**

moss. Term used for fractures or fissures in gemstones which produce the appearance of moss, as in many emeralds.

moss agate. (1) Term used generally in U.S.A. for any translucent chalcedony (cryptocrystalline quartz) containing inclusions of any color arranged in moss, fern, leaf, or tree-like patterns. Little if any distinction is being made in U. S. A. or England between it and **mocha** stone. (2) In European countries and in gemology the term moss agate is generally confined to translucent chalcedony containing green inclusions of actinolite or other green minerals arranged in the patterns mentioned above.

moss opal. Milky opal with black moss-like (tree-like) inclusions.

moss stone. (1) Crystalline **quartz** containing inclusions of green, fibrous crystals, probably asbestos. (2) Another name for moss agate.

mossy stone. In gemology, a stone containing **moss**-like inclusions.

mother liquid or **liquor.** (1) *Gemological,* a magma, especially a deep-seated magma in which diamonds may have formed; (2) *Chemical,* the residual solution remaining after its contained substances have become crystallized or precipitated.

"mother-of-emerald." (1) Green fluorite; (2) prase.

mother-of-opal. Rock matrix containing minute disseminated specks of precious opal (Merrill).

mother-of-pearl. The iridescent lining of the shell of any pearl-bearing mollusc; usually of same color composition and general quality as the pearls produced by the particular mollusc. See **nacre.**

mother-of-pearl opal (or **agate**). Same as **cachalong.**

mother-of-ruby. Ruby matrix.

mother rock. See **matrix.**

mottled stone. One with irregularly placed spots or patches of color.

mountain crystal. Rock crystal.

Mountain Lily topaz. Blue topaz from mine of this name in San Diego Co., Calif., in which large fine blue topaz have been found.

mountain mahogany. Reddish obsidian.

mountain stone. A Chinese name for jade.

mounted stone. (1) Stone fixed in a setting as in jewelry. See **loose stone.** (2) Stone improved in color by backing with foil or enamel or sometimes with a thin coat of dye. (Kraus and Slawson).

mounting. Trade term for that portion of a piece of jewelry in which a gem or other object is to be set or has been set. Same as **setting.**

mousseline glass (French). A thin glass, which imitates patterns in lace; called also **muslin glass** (Standard).

mouth jade. A term used synonymously with **tomb jade,** although more specifically it refers to jade which had been placed, usually together with quicksilver, in the mouths of the dead.

mucket pearl. Any **fresh-water pearl** from the **Lampsilis ligamentinus** mussel, the so-called mucket clam, a mussel of the Mississippi Valley.

mud. A lapidary's term for a mixture of silicon carbide grit and water, used as an abrasive in sawing of **colored stones,** to which mixture is added a small amount of fine clay or flour in order to obtain greater viscosity.

mud lapping. See **lapping.**

mud pearl. Usually, a dark natural pearl with a center of coarse calcite instead of thin nacreous layers. See **blue pearl.**

mud saw. A disk of iron, steel or copper varying in diameter from eight to fifty inches, which, when fashioning colored stones, passes through a metal container partly filled with **mud.**

mulawa. Singhalese name for the layer of clay which frequently lies just below the **illam** and which indicates the bottom of the mine.

Muller's glass. Same as **hyalite.**

multiple. The price of pearls subject to the multiple of weight. (Cattelle).

multiple pearl. Any **double pearl, triple pearl** or pearl which is formed of more than three pearls united under one nacreous coating.

muntenite. A variety of amber from Olanesti, Rumania. (English)

Mursinka aquamarine. Light bluish green aquamarine from Mursinka, in Ural Mts.

Mursinka topaz. Light blue topaz from Mursinka, in Ural Mts. Same as **Siberian topaz.**

muscle pearl. Small irregular pearl found in the muscular tissue near its attachment to the shell.

muscovite. A species of the **mica** group. Common mica. Mono. H. 2-2.25; S.G. 2.7-3.1; R.I. 1.55/-1.59-1.56/1.60. **Fuchsite** is a variety. See **agalmatolite.**

museum gem collections. Collections of special note are: *U.S.A.,* Am. Mus. of Natural Hist. (includes Morgan Collection); Metropolitan Museum of Art (Bish-

DICTIONARY OF GEMS AND GEMOLOGY

op Collection of Jade, Egyptian jewelry, etc.); New York; Harvard Mineralogical Museum, Cambridge; New England Mus. of Natural Hist., Boston; The Academy of Natural Sciences, Philadelphia; Chicago Natural History Museum (formerly Field Mus. of Nat. History); U. S. Nat'l. Mus. (Smithsonian Institution), Washington. *England.* British Museum (Natural History), London; Geological Museum, South Kensington, London.

France. Jardin des Plantes (including a Morgan Collection), Paris. *Germany.* Grünes Gewölbe, Dresden.

muslin glass. Same as **mousseline.**

mussel. A variety of bivalve mollusc of which certain varieties of both fresh and salt water produce pearls. See **Mytilidae; Unio.**

mussel-egg. Name given to freshwater pearls by Tennesseans.

mussel pearl. Pearl from a true salt-water mussel **Mytilus** as distinguished from pearl from so-called hammer mussel **Malleus.** Usually dark and possessing little, if any, luster, although Boutan mentions that it can sometimes be classed as a bluish **seed pearl.** See **Mytilus pearl.**

mussite. Same as **diopside.**

mutton fat jade. Descriptive term used by Chinese for a clear white nephrite resembling mutton fat.

"mutzchen diamonds." Rock crystal.

Muzo emerald. Colombian emerald from the ancient Muzo mine, about 75 miles N.N.W. of Bogota, which produces the finest known emeralds.

mya yay. In Burma, a trade name for the most precious variety of jadeite, translucent with a uniform grass-green color.

myrickite. (1) A name used for whitish or greyish chalcedony, opal, or massive quartz marked by or intergrown with pink or reddish inclusions of cinnabar, the color of which tends to become brownish. The opal variety is also known as **opalite.** From California, Arizona, Nevada, Oregon, and Washington.

Mytilidae. The family of sea mussels gemologically important only as producers of seed pearls. See **Mytilus pearls.**

Mytilus pearls. Pearls from family **Mytilidae.** Rarely lustrous, and if not, are known as "druggists' pearls."

131

N

n. In optics and mineralogy, the symbol for refractive index. Same as **R.I.** Also often used to indicate the **mean refractive index.**

Na. Abbr. for the element sodium.

nácar (Span.). Nacre.

nacker. Same as **nacre.**

nacre (nay'ker). The iridescent substance, principally **aragonite,** of which **pearl** and **mother-of-pearl** consist.

nacreous (nae'kree-us). Possessing a coating of nacre, or the appearance thereof.

nacrescope. A pearl illuminator. An instrument containing a strong light through which the nature of the nucleus of a pearl can sometimes be observed. Differs from **pearloscope** in that the effect of the passage of light through the whole pearl is observed. Can be used as an accessory of the gemological microscope. See **pearl illuminator; pearloscope.**

N. A. G. Abbr. for National Association of Goldsmiths (of Great Britain and Ireland), the commercial association of the British jewelry industry.

naoratna or **nararatna.** The nine-gem jewel of the Hindus which, like the **panchratna,** was a ceremonial offering to a Hindu temple.

narwhal ivory. A rather coarse ivory from the long, spiral tusk of the small Arctic whale known as the narwhal, or "unicorn" *(Mondon Monoceros),* so called because it usually has only one tusk. Hard-

ness, 2½; specific gravity, 1.90 to 2.00; refractive index, 1.55 to 1.57.

Nassau pearl. A name for **conch pearl.**

natal stones. Same as **birthstones.**

National Wholesale Jewelers' Association. This is a trade organization composed of firms that (1) buy and maintain stocks of jewelry and related goods, jewelers' supplies or related material; (2) sell primarily to the retailer for resale to the consumer; and (3) render a general distribution service to the retail jewelry trade. Its objectives are to foster and promote a feeling of good will and friendship among its members, and on broad and equitable lines to advance the welfare of the jewelry trade in the United States; and to establish harmonious relations among manufacturer, wholesaler and retailer. Headquarters: 1900 Arch St., Philadelphia, Pennsylvania 19103.

natrolite. A colorless or white, also reddish yellowish to greenish mineral sometimes fashioned into small ornaments, writing utensils, etc. in Germany, especially that combining tones of yellow from southern Württemberg. Ortho. $Na_2Al_2Si_3O_{10}$. H. 5-5.5; S.G. 2.2-2.3; R.I. 1.48/1.49; Bi. 0.013.

natural glass. Vitreous amorphous substances occurring in nature which have apparently solidified too quickly to crystallize. See **obsidian; tektite.**

natural pearl. A pearl which originates naturally in a mollusc as distinguished from a cultured pearl or imitation pearl.

natural stone. A stone which occurs in nature; as distinguished from a man-made substitute such as reconstructed, synthetic, assembled, or imitation stone.

navette (cut) (nav-vet'). French meaning little boat. Same as *marquise*. In U.S.A. *navette* or *boat shape* are names preferred in colored stone trade, *marquise* in diamond trade.

.needles. Slender needle-like crystals. Occur often as inclusions of rutile, actinolite, etc., in some gemstones. See also **fiber.**

needle stone. Sagenitic quartz.

nefretita. (Span.) Nephrite.

negative crystal. An angular cavity within a crystal or fashioned gemstone, the outline of which coincides with a possible crystal form of the mineral in which it occurs. Example: hexagonal forms in quartz, usually doubly terminated.

negative mineral or **stone.** A crystal exhibiting negative double refraction. See also **positive mineral** or **stone; optic sign.**

nephelite or **nepheline.** (nef'e-lite). A rock-forming mineral. Hex. $NaAlSiO_4$. Elaeolite is variously listed as another name for it or for a translucent gray, bright green, or brown to brownish red variety, of which the more desirable green is sometimes cut as a gem or ornamental stone. Usually full of small inclusions. Elaeolite often produces a cat's-eye or girasol effect when cut cabochon and has H. 5.5-6 S.G. 2.6. From Norway, Russia, Arkansas, and other sources.

nephrita (Span.). Nephrite.

nephrite (nef'-rite). An exceptionally tough, translucent to opaque member of the tremolite-actinolite series of the **amphibole** group, the less rare and valuable of the two kinds of **jade** minerals. It usually occurs in green of low intensity ("spinach jade"), gray, white, blue-green, yellow, black and red-brown colors. Chemical composition, a hydrous silicate of calcium and magnesium $(CaMg_5(OH)_2 (Si_4O_{11})_2)$; crystal system, monoclinic (but always a compact and massive, fibrous crystalline aggregate); hardness, 6 to $6\frac{1}{2}$; specific gravity, 2.90 to 3.00; refractive index, 1.606-1.632 (a single broad reading near 1.61 is most common); birefringence, .026. From Siberia, New Zealand, Wyoming, Calif., Alaska, China and other localities. See **jade, jadeite.**

"Nerchinsk aquamarine." Aquamarine-colored topaz from Nerchinsk, Siberia.

Nerchinsk beryl. Aquamarine, chrysolite beryl and morganite from Nerchinsk district, Transbaikal, Siberia.

Nerchinsk rubellite. Rubellite from near Nerchinsk in Transbaikal, Siberia.

neurita (Span.). Nephrite. (Eppler)

neutral gray. Gray which is devoid of any tinge of any hue. It may be of any **tone** from almost white to almost black.

"Nevada turquoise." Variscite.

Nevada turquoise. Turquoise from Nevada, the state of U.S.A. which produces the greatest quantity of this gemstone.

New Caledonia jade. Nephrite from Ouen Island, New Caledonia.

"New Guinea cat's-eye." Same as **"shell cat's-eye."**

New Guinea jade. Nephrite from

Humboldt Bay district, New Guinea.

New Mine sapphire. (1) A trade term applied to intense blue sapphire of velvety appearance during several years after the discovery, in 1926, of these stones at Bo Ploi, Siam. (2) A term which was also for a time used for **Montana sapphires,** mined by the New Mine Sapphire Syndicate, which were not of as fine blue as **Yogo sapphires.**

new rock. An abbreviation of **new rock turquoise.**

new rock turquoise. (1) Old Persian term for inferior turquoise or for turquoise matrix. (2) Term sometimes used in America for turquoise which does not retain its color very well. (3) A French and German term for **odontolite.**

Newton scale. A type of specific gravity scale.

"New Zealand greenstone." Serpentine; although originally the term meant nephrite.

New Zealand jade. Same as **nephrite;** from New Zealand.

Niagara spar. Term applied locally in Niagara Falls, N. Y., and vicinity, to fibrous gypsum imported through Canada from England. (Kraus and Slawson) Fibrous calcite, originally found in veins in limestone near Niagara Falls, Ont., was perhaps the original satin spar. See **satin spar.**

nicks. Very small fractures along the girdle or facet junction of a cut stone; more common in synthetic or glass reproductions than in the natural stones. See also **pit.**

Nicol. In microscopy and in mineral-ogy this word is almost always used to mean **Nicol prism.**

The term *between crossed Nicols* refers to the position of two Nicol prisms which are set so that the second does not transmit the light transmitted by the first, unless a doubly refractive substance be inserted between them. Some authorities capitalize the word when used in this manner; others do not.

nicolo (nik'oe-loe). Onyx with a black or brown base and a bluish-white top layer.

Nicol prism. (nik'ul) A calcite prism sawed through and recemented in such a fashion as to pass only the extraordinary ray of the two doubly refracted rays, thus producing polarized light. See **polarizing prism.**

niggerhead pearl. A **fresh-water pearl** from *Quadrula ebena,* a mussel of the Mississippi Valley, popularly known as the niggerhead "clam."

"night emerald." Same as **"evening emerald."**

nigrine. A black variety of iron-rich rutile which when polished resembles black diamond in brilliancy.

nilasa. Burmese term for mixed, inferior sapphires.

nilion. Name used by the Greeks for a stone thought to have been (1) grayish to honey-brown jasper or (2) nephrite.

nilt. Burmese term for large sapphires.

"nixonoid." A type of celluloid.

"nobbies." A local Australian name for a characteristic form of black opal. They are probably pseudomorphous.

noble metals. Same as **precious**

metals.

noble stone. Approximately same as precious stone. Noble opal is precious opal; noble topaz is precious topaz, etc. See **Edelstein**.

nodule (nod'ule). Small shapeless knot or lump of mineral or rock sometimes enclosing a foreign body in the center.

noncrystalline. Same as **amorphous**.

noodling. Local Australian term meaning to search the opal mine tailings or dumps for gem minerals.

Nophek. Fourth stone in the Breastplate of the High Priest. Translated as "carbunclus" and probably a garnet. Stone engraved "Judah."

norbide. An artificial abrasive used in fashioning gems. B_4C.

Nordica Pearl. A fine 175 gr. **abalone pearl** of greenish hue; part of the famous necklace of **colored pearls** which belonged to Madame Nordica.

normal. A word used in geometry to mean perpendicular. The normal is the direction perpendicular to (at right angles to) the surface of an object, such as the table of a stone. A direction or line which is said to be normal to such a table is perpendicular to it.

Norwegian amber. **Baltic amber**, from the coast of Norway.

noselite or nosean. One of the sodalite group of minerals, which group includes lazurite. Properties closely resemble those of haüynite, sodalite, and **lazurite**.

noumeite. Same as **garnierite**.

novaculite. A fine-grained siliceous rock used for whetstones. Found near Hot Springs, Ark., and sometimes fashioned as a **curio stone**.

nucleus. (1) The mother-of-pearl bead implanted in a mollusc to produce a cultured pearl. Uusally, it represents the major part of the diameter of the pearl. (2) The positively charged center portion of any atom.

nugget. Rounded, irregular lump, especially of a metal.

Numeite or Numeaite. German name for **noumeite**.

Nunkirchen jasper. Light grey to yellow or brownish red jasper from Nunkirchen, near **Idar-Oberstein**, Germany. Dyed and sold as "**Swiss lapis.**"

O

O. Abbreviation for the element oxygen.

objective. The system of lenses in a microscope which furnishes the initial magnification of the gem stone or other object. The image formed by the objective is picked up and further magnified by the **ocular.**

oblique system. Same as **monoclinic system.**

oblong hexagon cut. See **hexagon cut.**

obsidian (ahb-sid'-e-an). A transparent to opaque, black, brown, yellow, red, gray, slightly greenish or bluish **volcanic glass** (a rock). An ornamental stone; seldom cut as a gem. A number of varieties are distinguished: **banded obsidian** (irregular, agatelike bands), **onyx obsidian** (straight parallel bands), **flowering obsidian** (white patches of crystallized silica in the black groundmass), and **Apache tears** (small, rounded, irregularly shaped pieces, usually transparent to translucent and light to dark brown). Some material exhibits a sheen in certain directions, caused by minute, highly reflective inclusions. Chemical composition, 60% to 75% silica and 10% alumina, plus alkalis and various oxides; crystal system, amorphous; hardness, 5 to 5½; specific gravity, 2.30 to 2.60; refractive index, 1.48 to 1.51. Sources: widely distributed. See **natural glass, tektite.**

"**obsidian cat's-eye.**" Obsidian possessing **schiller.** Never chatoyant.

occidental. A prefix used (1) sometimes literally, i.e., to distinguish gemstones found in other parts of the world from those found in the Orient; (2) often to indicate inferior varieties or qualities as distinguished from the better qualities; and (3) frequently in misrepresenting a substitute as being the genuine gem it resembles; for example, "**occidental turquoise.**" See also **oriental.**

occidental agate. Agate poorly marked and not very translucent (Bauer).

occidental amethyst (obsolete). Genuine amethyst as distinguished from "**oriental amethyst.**"

occidental carnelian. Rarely used term for all but quite translucent carnelian. See **oriental carnelian.**

occidental cat's-eye. Quartz cat's-eye. See **oriental cat's-eye.**

occidental chalcedony. Rarely used term for all but quite translucent white or gray chalcedony. See **oriental chalcedony.**

occidental pearl. Defined by Schlossmacher as any pearl from Atlantic or Pacific Coast of Central America and apparently also Mexico, Venezuela, Colombia, Ecuador, and Peru. Described by him as larger, but less well shaped and duller than **oriental pearl.** However, the term is not used in American trade which classifies pearls of this general description as **Venezuelan pearl,** and of other description as **La Paz pearl.** See also **oriental pearl.**

"**occidental topaz.**" Citrine as distinguished from "**oriental topaz**" and from **precious topaz.**

"**occidental turquoise.**" Odontolite.

occurrence. The manner in which gem-minerals are found in the earth's crust.

ocean-spray. Satin spar (gypsum).

ocherous or **ochreous** (oe'ker-us). Earthy and usually red, yellow, or brown in color.

octahedral (ok"ta-hee'dral). Referring to or resembling an octahedron.

octahedrite. Same as **anatase.**

octahedron (ok"ta-hee'dron). A crystal form in the cubic system having the appearance of two four-sided pyramids united base to base.

octavo. A Brazilian gem weight, 17½ carats.

ocular. The system of lenses comprising the eye-piece or eye-lens of an instrument, as of a **microscope.**

oculus mundi (Latin). Eye of the World. A name for **hydrophane** which exhibits play of color.

Odem. First stone in the Breastplate of the High Priest; probably a carnelian, although Josephus translates as sardonyx. Engraved with name of Reuben.

odontolite (oh-don'-toe-lite). A translucent to opaque, deep-blue to greenish-blue fossil bone or tooth, colored by the iron-phosphate mineral **vivianite;** rarely colored green by copper. It is also called "bone turquois," and is sometimes used as a substitute for this mineral. Hardness, 5; specific gravity, 3.00 to 3.20; refractive index, 1.57 to 1.63. Principal sources: France and Siberia.

odor test. One made by heating, breathing upon, rubbing, or striking a mineral. Rarely of value in gem identification except in distinguishing amber from its substitutes.

oeil de boeuf (Fr., "bull's-eye" or "ox-eye"). **Labradorite.**

"oil pearl." Same as **Antilles pearl.**

oil stones (So. African). The agates found with alluvial diamonds.

oisanite. Same as **delphinite.**

ojo de gato (Span.). Cat's-eye.

old English cut. Same as **single cut.**

old-mine cut. (1) An early form of the **brilliant cut** with a nearly square girdle outline. (2) Incorrectly applied to a somewhat more modern style of brilliant cut that also has a much higher crown and table than the modern brilliant cut, but whose girdle outline is circular or approximately circular — a style of cutting that is more properly called a **lumpy stone** or an **old-European cut.**

old rock. An abbreviation of **old rock turquoise.**

old rock turquoise. (1) Old Persian term for fine quality turquoise; (2) French and German term for turquoise as distinguished from odontolite; (3) term used in American Indian country of Arizona and New Mexico for compact deep-blue turquoise which holds its color better than **new rock turquoise.**

oligoclose (ahl'-ih-go-klace). A transparent to translucent, gray, reddish, greenish, bluish or yellowish species of the **plagioclase** series of the **feldspar** group, of which **oligoclase moonstone, sunstone** and **aventurine feldspar** are varieties. Crystal system, triclinic; hardness, 6 to 7; specific gravity, 2.64; refractive index, 1.53-1.54; birefringence, .008; dispersion, .012.

oligoclase moonstone. A white to greyish adularescent variety of oligoclase. From North Carolina. (Schlossmacher).

olive. A popular trade name for a bead elongated parallel to its drill hole and hence shaped like an olive, but often much more slender. May be faceted or unfaceted.

olivet. African trade name for coral, imitation pearl, or a tube-shaped white glass bead, prized by natives.

"olivine" or "olivene." Incorrect jewelry trade name for demantoid. See olivine.

olivine (ahl'-ih-veen). The mineralogists name for peridot.

once. The square of the weight of a pearl, used in calculating the value. Also known as the "dollar base." See base price.

onegite. Light amethyst - colored sagenitic quartz. From Lake Onega, north of Leningrad.

"one-year pearl." A term that has been used for a cultured pearl on which exceptionally few layers of nacre have been deposited on the mother-of-pearl bead, regardless of the length of time it remained in the mollusc.

onicolo. Same as nicolo.

onychite. An ornamental alabaster or calcite (stalagmite) with yellow or brown veins, carved by the ancients into vases, etc. (Standard).

onyx. (1) One of the many varieties of chalcedony. Same as banded agate except that the alternately colored bands of onyx are always straight and parallel. Stones most common are black and white or gray, black and red to brownish red, white and red to brownish red, but those banded only with grays or gray and white are more specifically known as onyx agate. Stone cameos are carved principally from onyx. The term onyx used except as a qualifying adjective for other than parallel banded multi-colored chalcedony is incorrect. See "onyx"; carnelian onyx; sardonyx. (2) Qualifying adjective meaning parallel banded as in the term onyx marble.

"onyx alabaster." Misnomer for Parallel-banded calcite. See onyx marble.

onyx marble. A translucent compact variety of calcite generally deposited as stalagmites; with parallel bands usually irregular, curved or bent. Colors usually white, often grayish, brownish or reddish. Dyes easily and is marketed in several natural and dyed colors in many parts of the world under incorrect names, including "onyx," "Brazilian onyx," "Mexican onyx," "Mexican jade," Gibraltar stone, "Egyptian alabaster," and "oriental alabaster."

onyx obsidian. Parallel-banded obsidian.

onyx opal. Common opal with straight parallel markings.

oolitic (oe"ue-lit'ik). Containing or consisting of small rounded particles, suggesting fish roe, a texture possessed by some minerals.

opacity (oe-pas'i-ti). State of being opaque.

opaco (Span.). Opaque.

opal. A noncrystalline, transparent to opaque hydrous silica, occurring in nearly all colors. Opal with a black, white, gray or colorless (or sometimes orange to red) body may exhibit **play of color,** an optical phenomenon consisting of a variety of vivid, prismatic colors. Black or dark-gray specimens with an abundance of intense, attractively distributed and well-shaped color patches are the most valuable and sought-after kinds of opal. Material with orange, red, yellow or brown body colors, with or without play of color, is called **fire opal.** **Water opal** is colorless and transparent with play of color. Common opal, which never exhibits play of color, is found in a wide variety of colors and patterns, little of which is suitable for gem use. The play of color in dense-white opal, which may be masked by the material's translucency, can be made more apparent by "cooking" in a sugar solution and treating it with sulphuric acid, which carbonizes the sugar and produces a black background. Very low-property white opal from Mexico is impregnated with a black plastic to provide an effective substitute for black opal. **Doublets** are made by cementing a thin layer of opal to a thicker piece of nongem opal or other substance of similar appearance, using a black adhesive, to lend strength to the whole. A less common style consists of a thin piece of opal or opal chips cemented into a shallow depression in a piece of black chalcedony, the black border contrasting sharply with the opal center. An **opal triplet** consists of a base of common opal, chalcedony or other material, a thin layer of gem-quality opal and a top of colorless quartz. It resembles the opal doublet, except for the quartz top, which adds durability and prevents

scratching of the softer opal. Chemical composition, silica with 3% to 10% water ($SiO_2.nH_2O$); crystal system, amorphous; hardness, 5 to $5\frac{1}{2}$; specific gravity, 1.42 to 2.23; refractive index, 1.37 to 1.47 (usually 1.450). Important sources: Australia, Mexico, Czechoslovakia, Nevada. Opal is one of the birthstones for October. See **Australian opal, Mexican opal, fire opal.**

opala (Port.). Opal.

opal-agate. Banded opal having alternate layers of opal and chalcedony.

opal cat's-eye. The rarest variety of **harlequin** opal. It exhibits a chatoyant band, usually green, but also other colors.

opal dirt. Opal-bearing layers of soft clay-like material, or clayey layers of soft material, or clayey sand, underlying sandstone in most Australian deposits.

opal doublet. A thin layer of precious opal cemented to another substance of similar appearance, such as glass, chalcedony or inferior opal, using a black adhesive. A less common style consists of a thin piece of opal cemented into a shallow depression in a piece of black chalcedony. It provides an unusually attractive stone, since the black border contrasts sharply with the opal center. In cheaper stones of this kind, opal chips are cemented into the depression.

opalescence (oe' 'pal-es'ens). The milky or pearly appearance of some common opal. Not to be confused with the **play of color,** exhibited by precious opal. See also **girasol.**

opalescent cat's-eye. A confusing term sometimes applied to **chrysoberyl cat's-eye.**

"opalescent chrysolite." (1) Greenish chrysoberyl or corundum, exhibiting opalescence. (2) Chrysoberyl cat's-eye (a rare usage).

opalescent sapphire. Girasol sapphire.

"opal glass." Milky-white, sometimes yellowish variation of **crown glass** containing additions of fluorine, etc. S.G. 2.07 and up; R.I. 1.44. Used for imitations of some translucent gems and rarely, when etched with acid, for pearls, but not for precious opal. See also **fire opal glass.**

opaline (oe'pal-in or -ine). (1) Opal matrix; (2) pale blue to bluish-white opalescent or girasol corundum; (3) a brecciated impure opal replacement of serpentine (English).

opaline feldspar. Labradorite.

opalite. Term used for impure, colored varieties of common opal. See also **myrickite.**

opalized. Converted into opal.

opalized wood. Fossilized substance in which common opal, or more rarely, precious opal, has replaced wood. A variety of **silicified wood.**

opal jasper. Same as **jaspopal.**

opal matrix. Opal with portions of matrix included in the fashioned gem. See **opaline.**

opal mother. A dark opal matrix from Hungary.

opalo de fuego (Spanish). Fire opal.

"opal onyx." Misnomer for onyx opal.

opal pipe. Australian term for any long narrow cavity filled by opal.

opal triplet. An opal doublet of the usual type to which is cemented a convex-concave cap of rock crystal over the top of the opal to increase durability. The stones, which originated in Australia, are marketed under the name **Triplex Opals.**

opaque. Transmitting no light; opposite of **transparent.**

opera length. A pearl necklace 28 to 30 inches in length.

operculum (Latin). See **"shell cat's-eye."**

ophites. Serpentine marble, porphyry or talc, valued by the Egyptians. (Pliny)

ophthalmius. A medieval name for opal.

optical anomaly. An irregularity in optical properties or unusual phenomenon such as **anomalous double refraction** in a diamond or other singly refractive mineral. Observable in most synthetic spinel, but rarely seen in a genuine spinel. See **strain.**

optical calcite. Colorless transparent calcite which, because of its unusually high birefringence is used in the polarizing microscope and the **dichroscope.**

optical character. Same as **optic character.**

optically negative (stone). See **optic sign.**

optically positive (stone). See **optic sign.**

optical micrometer. See **micrometer.**

optical phenomenon or **phenomena.** See **phenomenon.**

optical properties. The effects of a substance upon light. **Refractive index** (R.I.), **double refrac-**

tion, (and its strength, **birefringence**), **dispersion, pleochroism** and **color** are gemologically the most important optical properties.

optical system. A group of lenses so arranged that the desired optical result is secured.

optic axes. Plural of **optic axis.**

optic axial angle. The acute angle between the two **optic axes** of a **biaxial** mineral. Usually given as 2V, which is the apparent value with the mineral not immersed.

optic axis. In any anisotropic (doubly refractive) mineral, a direction in which no double refraction occurs.

optic character. Refers generally to the optical properties of a gemstone, and especially to the number and position of optic axes, and the type of double refraction. (Shipley, Jr.). See **uniaxial, biaxial, optic sign.**

optics. The division of physics which covers the behavior of light.

optic sign. The type of double refraction in a mineral. In *uniaxial minerals* the material is positive when the extraordinary ray has a higher refractive index than the ordinary ray, negative when the ordinary ray has the greater index. In *biaxial minerals,* which have three basic optical directions, the refractive index of the intermediate or beta ray is the criterion; if its R.I. is nearer that of the low or alpha ray, it is said to be a *positive mineral* or *stone;* if it is nearer the high or gamma ray, it is said to be a *negative mineral* or *stone.*

orange. The **hue** midway between red and yellow; yellow-red.

orange-brown. In **color nomenclature system** of North American gemology, the color approximately midway between ꞌ(a) vivid orange and (b) the **tone** and intensity of brown which is almost black. Same as **brown-orange.**

orange-red. In North American gemology the **hue** midway between orange and red. Same as **red-orange.**

"orange topaz." Same as **"Spanish topaz."**

orange-yellow. In North American gemology the hue midway between orange and yellow. Same as **yellow-orange.**

orangy. A coined word, used in North American gemology to mean more nearly orange than any other hue, just as reddish means more nearly red than any other hue.

orangy brown. In North American gemology the color approximately midway between (a) orange-brown and (b) the tone and intensity of brown which is almost black. See **orangy.**

orangy red. In North American gemology the **hue** midway between orange-yellow and red. More red than yellow.

orangy yellow. In North American gemology the **hue** midway between orange-yellow and yellow. More yellow than orange.

orbicular. Round, circular. *Geology:* Containing minerals crystallized in rounded bodies with radial or concentric groups.

orbicular jasper. Jasper containing round or spherical inclusions, sprinkled or spotted here and there, usually of contrasting color to the body of the stone.

ordinary ray. In **uniaxial stones,** that ray of light which, like any ray in an isotropic stone, travels with the same velocity in any direction in the stone. See **extraordinary ray.**

ordinary refractive index. The R.I. of the **ordinary ray.**

oregonite. An **orbicular jasper,** found near Holland, Oregon. It is sometimes called **kindradite.** It is not to be confused with a nickel variety of nickel-iron arsenide, which is officially named oregonite.

"Oregon jade." (1) European misnomer for green jasper. (2) Misnomer for massive **grossularite** garnet found in Oregon, and indeed any almost any translucent to opaque green stone found in Oregon or California.

"Oregon moonstone." Same as **"chalcedony moonstone."**

organic gem materials. Naturally occurring substances whose origin is wholly or partly organic such as pearl, amber, coral and jet.

orient. The minute play of color on, or just below, the surface of a gem-quality pearl. It is caused by diffraction and interference of light from the irregular edges of the overlapping crystals or plates of aragonite that comprise the nacre of the pearl. See **overtone, pearl.**

oriental. Pertaining to the Orient, hence technically applicable only to gem materials originating there, but in general used as a trade prefix as (1) sometimes used to stress the genuineness, as **oriental turquoise;** (2) often used to indi-

cate the finer varieties of **gems** in more or less the same manner that the prefix *precious* or *noble* is used, as **oriental chalcedony;** and (3) as misnomer for fancy sapphires which were formerly described as **"oriental amethyst,"** "oriental emerald," etc.

oriental agate. Well-marked translucent agate. See **occidental agate.**

"oriental alabaster." Banded calcite or onyx marble. The alabaster of the ancients.

"oriental almandine." Purple-red sapphire.

"oriental amethyst." Violet to purple sapphire.

"oriental aquamarine." Pale bluish-green to greenish-blue corundum.

oriental baroque. Trade term for salt-water pearl of irregular form as distinguished from the fresh-water **slug** (pearl) which is also a **baroque.**

oriental carnelian. Deep bright red translucent carnelian.

"oriental cat's-eye." Girasol sapphire.

oriental cat's-eye. Same as **chrysoberyl cat's-eye.**

oriental chalcedony. Fine translucent gray or white chalcedony. The latter when cut cabochon is same as "chalcedony moonstone."

"oriental chrysoberyl." Yellowish-green sapphire.

"oriental chrysolite." Greenish-yellow chrysoberyl or sapphire.

"oriental emerald." Green sapphire.

oriental garnet. Almandine.

oriental girasol. Girasol sapphire.

"oriental hyacinth." Orange-red

sapphire.

oriental jasper. Bloodstone.

"oriental moonstone." Girasol corundum. See **oriental moonstone.**

oriental moonstone. Genuine moonstone as distinguished from "chalcedony moonstone."

"oriental onyx." Banded, mottled, or clouded **travertine.**

oriental opal. (1) Precious opal; (2) (obsolete), Hungarian opal formerly merchandised through oriental markets.

oriental pearl. (1) Any natural pearl from the *Pinctada* genus of saltwater bivalve molluscs. (2) More specifically, such a pearl fished in the Orient only. This usage is not general, however, since many pearls fished elsewhere are sold in India and are thereafter indistinguishable from those fished in the Orient proper. The Federal Trade Commission considers it an unfair trade practice to use the term to describe pearls not found in the Persian Gulf.

"oriental peridot." Olive-green sapphire.

oriental ruby. (1) Ruby from Burma or Thailand. (2) Sometimes used to distinguish genuine ruby from its substitutes, such as "spinel ruby."

oriental sapphire. American trade term for royal (slightly violet-tinted) blue sapphire. See **Burma sapphire.**

"oriental sunstone." Reddish or yellowish girasol corundum.

oriental sunstone (obsolete). Same as oriental girasol.

"oriental synthetic alexandrite." Same as "synthetic alexandrite."

"oriental topaz." Yellow corundum.

oriental turquoise. Genuine turquoise as distinguished from substitutes.

oriental vermeille. Red-brown corundum.

oriented stone. A stone so fashioned as to place the optic axis in a predetermined position, as for instance, in asteriated stones which should be so oriented as to place the axis normal to the top surface in order to achieve the best star. Most rubies should be cut with the axis normal to the table in order to exhibit the best color; most tourmalines with axis parallel to the table.

Orleans pastes. Reputedly fine imitations of gems in glass or enamel made about 1700 by a chemist, Homberg, who duplicated the collection, mostly intaglios, and cameos, of the Duke of Orleans, Regent of France. See also **Tassie paste.**

ormer. Same as **abalone.**

ornamental stone. A gemological classification which includes both those stones which have more or less beauty but which because they are insufficiently durable or beautiful or very easily obtained, are frequently fashioned into ornamental objects such as figures, ash trays, etc., and those which, when set in jewelry, are rarely mounted in gold or platinum; examples, **agate, onyx marble, rhodonite, rose quartz.** See **curio stone, decorative stone, gemstone, precious stone.**

orthite. Same as **allanite.**

ortho. Abbreviation used in this book for **orthorhombic system.**

orthoclase (or'-tho-klace). A transparent to translucent, colorless, gray, light-blue, bluish-gray, orange, brown, yellow or green species of the **feldspar** group, the principal variety of which is **adularia** (precious moonstone). The transparent light-yellow form does not exhibit adularescence and has little appeal as a gemstone. Chemical composition, potassium-aluminum silicate ($KAlSi_3O_8$); crystal system, monoclinic; hardness, 6 to $6\frac{1}{2}$; specific gravity, 2.56; refractive index, 1.518-1.526; birefringence, .005 to .009; dispersion, .012.

orthorhombic mineral or **stone.** Mineral or stone of the **orthorhombic system.**

orthorhombic system (ore"thoerom'bik). A crystallographic system; has three axes of unequal length, each perpendicular to the plane of the other two axes. See also **crystal systems.**

orthose. (1) Yellow orthoclase, sometimes yielding moonstone; (2) an obsolete name for the entire feldspar group of minerals.

oscillatory twinning. Repeated twinning in which the **lamellae** are in alternately reversed positions.

osseous amber (os'se-us). Same as **bone amber.**

Ostrea or **Ostrea edulis** (os'tree-a). The common edible oyster.

Ostridae. A family of bivalves which includes **Ostrea.**

ouachita stone. Same as **novaculite.**

oulopholite. A curio variety of gypsum found in the form of rosettes, flowers, vines, etc., in Mammoth Cave, Ky.

ounce pearl. (1) A low grade of pearl sold by the ounce. (2) A European name for seed pearl.

ouvarovite. Same as **uvarovite.**

oval cut. (1) A **brilliant** style of cutting in which the girdle outline is elliptical; i.e., a rounded oblong. Also called the **oval brilliant cut.** (2) An obsolete barrel-shaped style of cutting with a circular cross section and covered with triangular facets.

over-bleached pearl. Pearl which has been harmed by bleaching. See **bleached pearl.**

overtone. This is a term used first for natural pearls that had an additional tint modifying the rose coloration encountered when the nacreous layers were sufficiently thin and transparent to combine light diffraction and interference to create a lovely orient. Overlying the rosé cast the so-called fancy colors of green, blue, orange or purple gave an attractive overtone.

Oviedo Pearl. A 26-carat pearl purchased in Panama about 1520 at "650 times its weight in fine gold." Probably the same as the Morales or Pizarro Pearl. Thought to have been in Austrian crown before seizure of Austria by Hitler.

ovo doema. Brazilian term for water-worn quartz crystals (Pough).

owl-eye agate. An eye agate with only two "eyes," and those resembling the eyes of an owl.

ox-blood coral. Dark, rich, deep-red coral; very desirable.

oxeye. Labradorite with dark reddish change of color.

oxeye agate. An eye agate with only two "eyes," and those resembling the eyes of an ox in coloring. Same as **owl-eye agate.**

oxidation. A chemical union with oxygen.

oxide (ox'side or -sid). A compound of the element oxygen with another element or elements.

oyster pearl. A concretion found in common edible oyster (Ostrea edulis). Generally black, purple, or with a mixture of black and white, or purple and white. Almost invariably devoid of nacreous luster, possessing neither beauty nor value and hence not a **true pearl.**

ozarkite. White massive **thomsonite** from Arkansas.

P

P. Abbr. for phosphorus.

paar. (Ceylonese). The rock or hard-bottom oyster bed on Ceylon coast.

padmaradschah. Same as **padparadsha.**

padparadscha (pad"par-ad'sha). A rare light orangy-yellow to orange, variety of sapphire, more often encountered as synthetic sapphires of those colors.

pagoda. A coin used in India in the days of Tavernier. Value 8 shillings British.

painite. A deep garnet-red calcium borosilico aluminate, crystallizing in the hexagonal crystal system. First identified as a new mineral in 1957, when a single crystal was found near Mogok, Upper Burma, by A. C. D. Pain, the British gemologist. Hardness, 7½; specific gravity, 4.01; refractive index, 1.787-1.816.

painted boulders. Sandstone-quartzite stones coated or impregnated with opal. See **opal.**

painted opal. Transparent to translucent opal on which the back is painted black to improve the appearance of the stone.

painted stone. See **coated stone.**

Pai Yü. Chinese name for either white jadeite or white nephrite. Alternate spelling of Pao Yü.

Pala beryl, kunzite or **tourmaline.** Stones from Pala district of San Diego Co., Calif., many of fine quality.

Palau pearl. Cultured pearl from the Palau Islands in the Carolines, South Pacific. It is grown in limited quantity in the *Pinctada Margaritifera* mollusc.

pale. In the color nomenclature system of North American gemology a tone approximately the same as very light. Very pale is still lighter.

palladium (pal-lae'di-um) One of the **platinum metals.**

pampel. Same as **pampille.**

pampille (cut). A drop-shape closely related to the briolette but with circular (or polygonal) cross-section and usually more elongated. Covered with rows of facets of differing shapes and sizes, which become smaller as they approach the lower point of the stone.

Panama pearl. Same as **La Paz pearl.**

panchratna. A ceremonial jewel offering to a Hindu temple, composed of gold, diamond, sapphire, ruby and pearl. Like the **naoratna** the jewel is sold when no longer considered worthy and is eagerly purchased by devout Hindus (Kunz).

Pandora Opal. A famous 590-carat white opal found at Lightning Ridge, New South Wales, Australia, in 1929. Before cutting, it measured 4 x 2 x 1 inches and weighed 711 carats. It is described as a good-quality stone with a blood-red color pattern, interwoven with flashes of bronze, gold and blue. The *Pandora* is an opalized portion of the blade bone of a plesiosarus, an extinct sea reptile. Today, it is said to be owned privately in the United States.

pane. A star facet.

panella (Brazilian). A miner's term for **druse.**

146

panning. Primitive method of washing minerals from alluvial gravel by use of a pan.

pantha (Indian). White and translucent jadeite.

Pao Yü. Alternate spelling of **Pai Yü.**

Papua Gulf pearl. Pearl from Gulf of Papua, New Guinea. Not quite as white as **Australian pearl.**

paradise jasper. A local trade name for a variegated red jasper from Morgan Hill, Calif.

paragon pearls. Round pearls of exceptional size, few if any of which are **fine pearls.**

parent rock. In geology the rock formation which originally held, and may still hold, a mineral or ore, fragments of which have been carried elsewhere, as in a placer. (Standard)

Paris pearl. An imitation pearl, made partly from **essence d'orient.**

paronigars. Skilled workmen who string Bombay pearls

parti-colored stones. (1) Transparent stones with zones of different color such as pink and green zones often seen in tourmaline. (2) Also, technically, stones such as the sapphires of green color that are produced by blending very thin zones of yellow alternating with zones of blue.

parting. Separation of a mineral along planes of twinning, as opposed to true cleavage which occurs along crystallographic planes.

parure (pa"rur'). A French word meaning a set of jewels, such as a parure of emeralds, consisting of rings, bracelets, earrings, brooch, etc.

Passau pearl. Term for fresh-water pearl found in Central Europe, marketed through Passau, Bavaria.

paste. Name for glass when used as imitation of gems.

pastoral ring. Bishop's ring.

pate de riz (French, meaning rice paste). Glass which was or is made as an imitation of nephrite (Bauer-Spencer).

Pathakkamala. An Indian historical jewel set with precious gems. The central stone is an emerald one and one-half inches in diameter and weighs sixty rati. *(The Gemmologist).*

pate goung. The Indian name for the *Pinctada Vulgaris* species of salt-water pearl-bearing mollusc, which yields a type of Persian Gulf pearl.

Patricia Emerald. A 632-carat emerald crystal of fine color, owned and displayed by the American Museum of Natural History, New York City. It was found in the Chivor Mine, Colombia.

paulite. Same as **hypersthene.**

paved or pave' (pa'vae'). The style of setting small stones as close together as possible in areas, as distinguished from **channel setting.**

pavilion. *In North America and Britain,* the portion of a fashioned stone below the girdle. *On European continent,* the part above the girdle, the portion below being known as the culasse.

pavilion facets. The main facets on the pavilion of any cut stone. In the brilliant cut, the eight main large five-sided facets; although some diamond cutters further distinguish four of these by the name of quoin or bottom corner facets.

Pb. Abbr. for lead.

Peace Ruby. A ruby found in the Burma mines in 1919. It weighed 42 carats in the rough and sold for £20,000. The present whereabouts of this stone is unknown.

peacock opal. Opal whose play of color resembles that of a peacock's feathers: blue, green and purple or any two of these colors. See **opal.**

peacock stone. Banded malachite cut to exhibit an eye.

pear cut. Any style of cutting resembling a pear, or more loosely the outline of one, such as a **pendeloque.**

pear drop or **pear eye.** A pear-shaped **drop pearl.**

pearl. A calcareous concretion consisting of layers of **nacre,** which is made up of tiny crystals of aragonite bound together by **conchiolin,** a horny organic material, most of which have been concentrically deposited about a central point, or nucleus. In most cases, the nucleus is thought to have been the location of a parasite or other organic matter that the mollusc covered with the substances mentioned above, with which it also forms its own shell. Conchiolin predominates in the outer portion of the shell, aragonite in the mother-of-pearl lining and in pearls that occur in certain molluscs, notably in the salt-water genus known variously as *Pinctada, Margaritifera, Meleagrina* or *Pteria,* and the fresh-water genus *Unio.* The layers in round pearls, which form free within the **mantle,** are spherical and concentric. Many pearls are not round and others are attached to the shell. Gemologically, a **true pearl** is composed of predominately nacreous layers and forms unattached to the shell. **Fine pearls** are those true pearls that possess all the qualifications of a gemstone and are limited largely to **oriental** and **fresh-water** pearls. Chemical composition, aragonite and/or calcite ($CaCO_3$), water and conchiolin; crystal structure, an aggregate composed largely of minute orthorhombic crystals of aragonite and sometimes of hexagonal calcite crystals; hardness, $2\frac{1}{2}$ to $4\frac{1}{2}$; specific gravity, 2.66 to 2.78; refractive index, 1.53-1.69; birefringence, .156. Pearl is one of the birthstones for June. Sources: Persian Gulf, Ceylon, Australia, islands of the South Seas, Panama and Mexico. Fresh-water sources: the tributaries of the Mississippi River, Scotland, China and almost any river in a temperate climate. See **cultured pearl, blister pearl, cyst pearl.**

pearl compass. In determinative gemology, an apparatus for discriminating between genuine and cultured pearls. A pearl is hung between the poles of a powerful electromagnet. A cultured pearl tends to rotate and orient itself according to the structure of its core, while a genuine pearl tends to remain stationary.

pearl corundum. Corundum with bronzy iridescent luster.

pearl diver. One who dives for pearl molluscs.

pearl doctor. (1) One proficient in the preparation of **doctored pearls.** (2) A term also loosely used to mean one who peels pearls. See **peeling.**

pearl doublet. See **cultured blister pearl.**

pearl drop. The trade term for an irregularly shaped or imitation pearl mounted with an attached ring for use on pendants, earrings, etc.

pearl endoscope. See **endoscope.**

pearl essence. See **essence d'orient.**

pearl fluorescence detector. Usually a lead-lined, light-tight viewing box in which a pearl is activated by X rays. Persian Gulf pearls do not fluoresce. A few Australian pearls, all Japanese cultured pearls so far tested, and all fresh-water pearls do fluoresce.

pearl fluoroscope. See **fluoroscope.**

pearl gauge. A scale arranged as to various diameters and the corresponding estimated weights of fine spherical pearls.

pearl grain. The unit of pearl weights equal to ¼ metric carat.

pearl illuminator. A device which employs a light for the illumination of a pearl. It may illuminate the exterior for observation (a) of the entire pearl as in the **nacrescope** or (b) of the drill hole as in a **pearloscope;** or it may illuminate the drill hole as in the type of **endoscope** which employs a hollow needle with two mirrors.

pearling. The business of pearl fishing.

pearlite. Same as **perlite.**

pearl luster. The brightness of the reflection on the peak of the rounded surface of a pearl or cultured pearl. In general, the higher the luster, the more valuable the pearl. It varies from dull to highly glossy, depending on the nature of the layers and the degree of translucency. It should not be confused with **orient.**

pearl miscroscope. A microscope

equipped with a pearl-testing **stage.** Same as **pearloscope.** See **microscope.**

pearl mussel. Popular name for the Unio.

Pearl of Asia. A 605-carat baroque pearl, shaped somewhat like an elk's tooth but more cylindrical. It is claimed to have been valued at one time at more than $200,000. In 1918, it was bought as an investment by the Foreign Missions of Paris. It is of historic as well as biological interest because it belonged to the Emperor of China in the 16th century.

pearloscope. A name which has been used to include the various pearl-testing devices which employ a **microscope** and a **pearl-testing stage.**

pearl oyster. A popular but misleading name for the pearl-producing molluscs, as none of the *Ostridae* family, including the edible variety, bear fine pearls. See **Margaritifera; Ostridae.**

pearl peeler or **peeling.** See **peeler; peeling.**

pearl price calculator. A chart designed to obtain quickly, from weight, the **base price** of two or more pearls.

pearl radiogram. The record on a photographic film or plate of X rays transmitted through a pearl; an "X-ray photograph" of a pearl.

pearl sac. The tissue which forms about the irritating agent which starts the nucleus of a pearl. In cultured pearls this tissue is cut from one mollusc, the mother-of-pearl. sphere inserted in it, and then it is placed in an incision in another mollusc. In natural pearls it begins as an indentation in the mantle, eventually joins at the neck and secretes the nacre which forms the pearl.

pearl-shooting. Artificial coloring or dyeing of pearls.

pearl spar. Variety of dolomite with a pearly luster.

pearlstone. Same as **perlite.**

pearl-testing stage. See **stage; pearloscope.**

pearl tongs. Tweezers with concave hemispheres on each prong designed to fit and hold a spherical pearl.

pearly. Resembling the surface appearance of the pearl.

pearly luster. The combination of luster and of body appearance caused by internal structure, seen in moonstone, or pearl. See **sheen.**

pear pearl. A term often used for any **drop pearl,** but more especially for pear-shaped pearl.

pears. Pear-shaped pearls.

pear-shape (cut). Same as **pendeloque.**

pebble. (1) A rounded stone, especially a waterworn stone; (2) said in dictionaries to mean also transparent colorless quartz.

pebble crystal. A waterworn or similarly rounded crystal.

pebble ware. A variety of **Wedgwood** ware with a variegated body of different colored clays intermingled, called according to pattern, agate, Egyptian pebble, granite, lapis lazuli, porphyry, serpentine, verde antique, etc. (Standard)

Pechopal (German). Pitchopal.

peddi. Singhalese name for **basket.**

pedra de estrelada (Port.). Asteria.

pedra fina (Port.). Gemstone.

pedra preciosa (Port.). Precious stone.

pedra verde. (Port.). Nephrite.

peeler. A pearl with an imperfect skin, the removal of which might improve the pearl. Also a person who peels pearls. See **peeling.**

peeling. Removing outer layer or layers of a pearl in the hope that under layer will be of better quality.

peesal. Same as **pisal.**

peganite. Variscite from Saxony.

pegmatite. Coarsely grained, igneous rock mass, usually in form of a dike, which during its slow solidification contained rare gas or vapors, which aided in forming especially large and well-formed crystals, of which aquamarine, spodumene, topaz, tourmaline, and transparent quartz are gemologically important.

pegmatitic. Of, or pertaining to pegmatite.

Peiping jade or **Pekin jade.** (1) Any jade from Peiping, one of China's three largest jade markets, although little jadeite is cut or sold there. (2) Usually nephrite.

pelhamine. A variety of light gray-green **precious serpentine** from Pelham, Mass. (Eppler)

pelle d'angelo (Italian). Name for a rose-red coral.

Pellegrina Pearl. Misomer for **La Pellegrina Pearl.**

pencil stone. Same as **agalmatolite.**

pendant cut. A term used loosely as a synonym for **drop cut.**

pendeloque (pan"d'loke'). A pear-shaped modification of the round brilliant cutting often used for a pendant. Pear-shaped briolettes were formerly called pendeloques and the two styles are still often confused. See **briolette.**

penetration twin. A twin crystal in which the two or more parts appear to interpenetrate one another. The parts have some definite angular relationship to one another with respect to the axis of twinning. Examples: orthoclase and fluorite.

pentagon cut. Any of several variations of the step cut, having five straight sides.

pentagon facets. A British term for quoin and pavilion facets.

peredell topaz. Light green to yellowish green topaz.

Peregrina Pearl. Misnomer for **La Peregrina Pearl.**

perfect stone. A trade term, used principally for diamonds, referring usually to absence of inclusions or faulty structure within the stone, although some merchants have used it to refer to **make,** absence of exterior blemishes, and absence of undesirable colors. Federal Trade Commission defines as absence of blemishes or internal imperfections under magnification of ten power. American Gem Society prohibits the use of the term by its members and recommends use of the term *flawless* to mean absence of internal flaws. Less frequently used for colored stones in which small inclusions· or structural faults are less undesirable, and in fact, sometimes desirable.

perfection color. Finest color of that particular variety of gem.

perforated beads. Beads carved through to an irregular design.

peridot (pear'-ih-doe). A transparent to translucent mineral species, occurring in medium to dark tones of slightly yellowish green (the finest), light yellow-green to greenish yellow, and dark yellow-green to brownish green to almost brown. Peridot is known to mineralogists as **chrysolite** (the light tones) or olivine. Many jewelers have long referred to demantoid garnet as "olivine." Chemical composition, a silicate of magnesium and iron $(MgFe)_2SiO_4)$; crystal system, orthorhombic; hardness, $6\frac{1}{2}$ to 7; specific gravity, 3.32 to 3.35; refractive index, 1.654-1.690; birefringence, .036; dispersion, .020. Principal sources: Island of Zebirget, or St. John's, in the Red Sea; Burma; Arizona and New Mexico.

peridotite. A very basic igneous rock, consisting chiefly of olivine and pyroxene.

"peridot of Ceylon." Same as **"Ceylon peridot."**

perigem (per'i-jem). Trade-marked name for light yellow-green synthetic spinel.

perimorph. A mineral of one species enclosing one of another species (Webster). See **endomorph.**

periostracum (per″i-os'tra-kum). The outermost horny conchiolin layer of the shell of a mollusc.

peristerite (peh-riss'-ter-ite). A moonstonelike variety of sodium-rich **plagioclase feldspar** (albite). It has a white, cream, tan or brownish-pink body color and displays a variety of iridescent reflections. Sources: Ontario and Quebec, Canada, and Madagascar.

perla (Span.). Pearl.

perle coq. French term for a hollow pearl.

perle fine (French). Same as fine pearl.

perles au nacre. Same type as "perles des Indies."

"perles des Indies." Imitation pearls which were made from pulverized nacre of mother-of pearl.

perlite (pur-lite). (1) Obsidian with a concentric shelly structure, probably produced by contraction in cooling. (2) A gray obsidian. See also **spherule.**

perlometer. The manufacturer's trade name for his model of a pearloscope.

perola (Port.). Pearl.

Persian Gulf pearl. At present, the best quality of **oriental** pearl, noted for its fine color, shape and orient and seldom exceeding 12 grains in weight. It is principally from the vicinity of Bahrein Island in the Persian Gulf, where the host mollusc is *Pinctada Vulgaris.* The term is also deceivingly applied to imitation pearl. See **Pinctada.**

Persian lapis. A term still sometimes used for the fine quality ▪Afghanistan lapis from Badakshan, once Persian territory.

Persian turquoise. (1) A trade name for the finest quality turquoise, intense, light blue in color, which in early times came from Persia (now Iran) although some may have been mined in Turkestan or Tibet. (2) More specifically, turquoise from various present-day mines in Iran.

perspex. A polymerized acrylic ester plastic. S.G. 1.18; R.I. 1.50.

(Anderson). Same as **diakon.**

Peruvian emerald. A term applied to genuine emerald from South America taken to Spain during and after the conquest of Peru, which then included present-day Colombia. See **Colombian emerald.**

pesal. Same as **pisal.**

peso especificio (Span.). Specific gravity.

petal pearls. Flattened, leaf-like pearls.

Petoskey stone. Coral, principally the species known as *Hexagonaria,* variety *Prismatophyilum,* replaced by calcite. The distinctive pattern shown by one of these stones resembles a series of closely spaced hexagonal (six-sided) tiles, the centers of which contain numerous webs that radiate outward. Each of these individual segments measures about $\frac{1}{4}$ to $\frac{3}{4}$ inch in diameter. Other fossil coral results in different patterns; e.g., the species known as *Favosites* produces a honeycomb effect. Sources: various counties in Michigan.

petrifaction (pet"ri-fak'shun). Process of changing organic material into stone by replacement. The original structure is sometimes retained.

petrified asbestos. A name for either **tiger eye, hawk's-eye,** or **quartz cat's-eye.**

petrified wood. Fossilized wood in which the cells have been entirely replaced by crystallized silica and hence converted into quartz or opal, or (2), less often by other substance. It is usually easy to identify as it reveals, more or less, the original structural pattern of the wood. See **petrifaction; agatized**

wood; opalized wood; silicified wood.

petrographic or **petrological microscope.** See **microscope.**

petrosilex. (1) An old name for extremely fine crystalline porphyries and quartz and for those finely crystalline aggregates we now know to be devitrified glasses. (2) Hornstone (Schlossmacher).

Pezometer. Trade name for a German diamond weight calculator constructed by Wilhelm Rau, on same principle as **Moe gauge.**

phanerocrystalline. Having all crystalline grains large enough to be seen with the unaided eye as distinguished from **cryptocrystalline.**

phantasy pearl. An 18th Century name for **blister pearl.**

phantoms. In a transparent crystal, visible layers, of slightly different tone or hue, which once were the faces of the crystal, and on which during its growth particles of some different substance or substances, usually a mineral, were deposited in one or more adjacent atomic (growth) planes. producing an outline of the faces of the former crystal, parallel to the faces or to the **possible crystal faces** of the present crystal. Several phantoms may occur in the same crystal at different intervals. The differently colored zones in transparent tourmaline, sapphire, etc., are sometimes classified as phantoms but are usually more regularly spaced, more strongly colored and more often caused by differing coloring oxides.

Phassachate (German). A lead-colored agate.

phenakite (fen'-ah-kite). A transparent to translucent, colorless, white, gray or very pale blue, yellow, brown or pink mineral species, rarely cut as a gemstone. Chemical composition, beryllium silicate (Be_2SiO_4); crystal system, hexagonal; hardness, $7\frac{1}{2}$ to 8; specific gravity, 2.96; refractive index, 1.654-1.670; birefringence,.016; dispersion, .015. Sources: Russia, Brazil, Tanzania, Mexico, Colorado and elsewhere.

phenocrystalline. Same as **phanerocrystalline.**

phenomenal gem. A gemstone exhibiting an optical phenomenon. See **phenomenon.**

phenomenon. In gemology, an optical effect in visible light occurring in certain, but not in all, specimens of a species. See **adularescence; asterism; chatoyancy; fluorescence** (in ultra-violet light) **; girasol; laboradorescence; orient; play of color; schiller.**

phenyldi-iodoarsine. $C_6H_5AsI_2$. A highly refractive liquid (R.I. 1.85) used for making optical contact between stone and dense glass of refractometer, and as an immersion fluid (R. Webster).

Philip II Pearl. A Venezuelan pearl. Same as **La Peregrina.**

Philippine pearl. Pearl from various islands of the Philippine Archipelago and adjacent islands. In quality, Philippine **white pearl** is better than **Australian pearl** and inferior to **Madras pearl** or **Bombay pearl.**

phosphorescence. A continuance, after the removal of the exciting radiations, of **fluorescence.**

photometer. An instrument for measuring the intensity of light, or for comparing intensities from two sources.

photomicrograph. A photograph of the greatly magnified image of an object.

Photoscope. An instrument patented and manufactured by the Gemological Institute of America. It is used with the Polaroid Automatic Land Camera with automatic exposure control, a flexible light wire, and a binocular microscope to produce magnified black-and-white or color photographs of gems and gemstone inclusions.

Photostand. An instrument designed and manufactured by the Gemological Institute of America. It is used to produce ½x, 1x, or 1½x black-and-white or color photographs of gems and jewelry for selling, insurance, inventory or stock records.

physical properties. The **specific gravity, hardness, tenacity, cleavage, fracture** and other similar characteristics of a substance, and to a lesser extent, its optical properties.

picotite. Same as **chrome spinel.**

picrolite (pik'-ro-lite). A fibrous, dark-green, gray or brown variety of **serpentine.** See also **baltimorlite.**

piedra del sol (Span.) Sunstone.

piedra de madera. A Spanish name for jasper.

piedra de mes. Birthstone.

piedra de sangra (Span.). Hematite.

piedra de serra (Span.). Brazilian agate.

piedra de simava (Span.). Fire opal.

piedra dorado (Span.). A name for chrysolite.

piedra estrellada (Span.). Asteria.

piedra fina (Span). Gemstone.

piedra miel (Span.). Mellanite.

piedra moca. (Span.) Mocha stone.

piedra preciosa (Span.). Precious stone.

piedra sintético (Span.). Synthetic stone.

piedra verde (Span.). Nephrite.

pierre argentine (French, meaning *silvery stone.*) Moonstone.

pierre de lune (Fr.). Moonstone.

pierre étoilée (Fr.). Asteria.

pierre fausse (Fr.). Imitation stone.

pierre fine (Fr.). Precious stone.

pierre precieuse (Fr.). Precious stone.

pietra (Italian). Stone.

pietra albero (Italian). Tree stone. Same as **mocha stone.**

pietra dura (Italian). Ornamental stones, especially those inlayed in mosaic patterns in marble.

pietra precioso (Italian). Precious stone.

piece pearl. A name used in books by early authorities to mean a small pearl somewhat larger than **seed pearl.**

piedmontite. A brownish red variety of epidote from Piedmont, Italy.

piedra arbol (Span.). Mocha stone.

piedra de aguja (Span.). Sagenitic quartz.

piedra de calmuco. (Span.) A cloudy opal, usually a **cachalong.**

piedra de camela. Cinnamon stone.

piedra de grosella (Span.). Grossularite.

piedra de ijada (Span.). (Colic stone.) Original Spanish name for jade from which the words *jade* and *jadeite* have evolved in Spanish, English, and other languages.

piezoelectricity. The property possessed by certain crystals, such as quartz and tourmaline, of developing a charge of electricity when under pressure or tension. A piezoelectric effect is observed in some quartz which consists of alternate expansion and contraction producing oscillations useful in radio equipment.

pigeon blood agate. Local name for carnelian or red and white agate from Cisco, Utah.

pigeon blood ruby. Ruby of the finest color quality. Purplish red, likened to color of arterial blood of fresh-killed pigeon.

pigment (in gems). Term loosely used to mean the particles which impart color to gems; principally oxides.

pigtoe shell. The nucleus for most cultured pearls grown in Japan is the pigtoe clam shell from the Mississippi River and its tributaries. Several carloads are sold to Japanese growers annually.

Pike's Peak amazonite. Fine amazonite from Pike's Peak and its environs including Crystal Park, Crystal Peak, Devil's Head and other localities in Colorado.

pinacoidal. Relating to crystal forms with two planes parallel to two or more crystallographic axes.

pincette. A French name for tweezers.

pinchbeck. (1) An alloy of copper, zinc and tin used as imitation of gold. (2) Figuratively an imitation, especially a pretentious one.

Pinctada (Pink-tahd'-ah). The most important genus of salt - water pearl-bearing molluscs, a less popular name for which is *Margaritifera*. The major species of this genus are *P. Maxima*, *P. Margaritifera*, *P. Vulgaris* and *P. Martensii*.

pinfire opal. Opal in which the patches of play of color are very small and close together and usually less regularly spaced than the color patches in harlequin opal. The small pinpoints can be of any color, but red is considered the most desirable.

pingoo. Burmese term for silky ruby with or without star (Gems & Gemology).

pingoo-choo. Burmese term for best quality star rubies.

pingos d'agoa (Portuguese meaning drop of water). Brazilian term for colorless water-worn pebbles (Bauer).

pink beryl. Same as **morganite.**

pinked topaz. Pink topaz artificially colored by heating yellow or brown varieties. See **heated stone.**

pinking. Heating topaz to change its color to pink.

"pink moonstone." Pink girasol **scapolite.**

pink sapphire. Pale to light red corundum as distinguished from full red or dark red which is ruby. As yet there is no standard of determining the dividing line between these, the more highly transparent stones of light to full color being often classed as sapphire while more often a much paler stone is called Ceylon ruby.

pink topaz. Topaz either naturally pink or artificially colored pink by heating yellow or brown varieties. See **pinked topaz.**

Pinna (Pin'-ah). A pearl from *Pinna Nobilis*, a species of the genus of marine bivalve mollusc known as *Pinna*, or **wing shell.** It is usually reddish, orangy or rose tinted, lacks orient, and has a more crystalline structure and is more translucent than that produced by the *Pinctada* genus. The *Pinna* pearl is found in very small quantites, primarily in the Mediterrean Sea, and has very little commercial importance.

pin-point opal. Same as **pin-fire opal.**

Pintadina. The pearl oyster. (Standard)

pintas. A Mexican name for surface indications of opal-producing areas.

pipe opal. A local Australian name for precious opal found in tubular channels (originally steam vents) in sandstone.

piropo (Span. and Italian). Pyrope.

piruzeh (Persian). Turquoise.

pisal. Ceylonese trade grade for a deformed pearl or cluster of small misshapen pearls, of poor color and of little value. (Kunz.).

pisolitic (pie"soe-lit'ik or piz"oe-lit'ik). Composed of or containing rounded masses about the size of peas.

pissophane. Wax-impregnated hydrophane (Schlossmacher). See **pyrophane.**

pistacite (pis'ta-site). Epidote.

pit. Trade term for a small fracture in the flat surface of a facet of a gem, or along the junction of two facets.

pit amber. A name for mined amber in contrast to sea amber.

pitch garnet (German Pechgranat). Very dark yellow andradite.

pitch lap. A metal or other rigid lap whose surface has been covered with pitch, useful in obtaining better polish on soft gemstones.

pitch opal. A yellowish to brownish common opal with a pitchy luster.

pitch stone. Obsidian with pitchlike luster. Gray, yellow, red or brown, containing more water and harder (5½-6) than most obsidian (Eppler).

pitchy luster. Resembling the luster of a fresh surface of pitch.

Pitdah. Second stone in Breastplate of the High Priest, called topazius. However, "topazius" of the ancients signified a stone of greenish hue, chrysolite, or peridot. The derivation of the Hebrew Pitdah is "yellow" and may refer to our topaz. Engraved with the name Simeon.

pitted. Containing pits.

Pi Yü. Chinese name for the vegetable green nephrites, although some jadeites of those hues are sometimes included. See **spinach jade; Fei Ts'ui; Pao Yü.**

Pizarro pearl. See **Oviedo pearl.**

Pl. Abbreviation for pleochroism.

placer (plas'er or pla-ser'). Alluvial or glacial deposit in which minerals are found. Usually an accumulation of sand and gravel containing gold, gem material, or other minerals of value.

Placuna pearl. A pearl from the *placuna* or window glass shell with a micaceous luster. Is sold in the Orient, usually for medicinal purposes (Kunz).

plagioclase. The series or group of feldspar minerals, including **albite, oligoclase** and **labradorite.**

plain cut. A form without facets; cabochon, for example (Pough).

plane of symmetry. If a plane could be passed through a crystal and divide the two portions such that one is a mirror image of the other, it is called a plane of symmetry.

plaque. There are many variations of this form of cutting. The distinguishing characteristic is two parallel surfaces, usually flat, with a relatively narrow space between. Some have a beveled edge, although this is not an essential characteristic. If the area between the two parallel surfaces is quite thick, the stone is usually called a **tablet.**

plasma (plaz'ma). Green semi-translucent, almost opaque, cryptocrystalline **quartz,** sometimes with white or yellowish spots; with red spots it is **bloodstone.**

plaster stone. Gypsum.

plastic. A natural or, more frequently, a synthetic material which can be shaped when soft and hardened afterwards. Sometimes transparent or translucent, as **bakelite,** or **lucite.** Occasionally fashioned as imitation gems, especially those with resinous luster like that of amber.

plate cut. A style of cutting in which many opaque ring stones are fashioned. Consists of large, flat, parallel top and back; sides may be beveled or stepped.

plates. Laminated layers in a mineral; broad, relatively thin masses.

platinum (plat'i-num). (1) A metallic element. (2) A very heavy, very pale gray, soft metal of the **platinum metals,** more costly than gold. See **iridio-platinum.**

platinum metals, the. The precious metals known as the platinum group: platinum, iridium, palladium, ruthenium, rhodium, and osmium. The first two are used as principal, and the next three as minor constituents of alloys used for mountings or settings of gems.

Plato, or Plato-Sandberg, effect. A method of distinguishing flawless synthetic corundum without visible striae from flawless natural corundum. The optic-axis direction is first located by use of the **polariscope,** and then the unknown is examined between crossed Polaroids under about 20x to 30x while immersed in methylene iodide. When a synthetic corundum is examined parallel to an optic-axis direction under these conditions, two sets of lines at 60° to one another resembling repeated-twining lines, identify it. Natural material, except that from Tanzania, shows no similar effect. The method was developed by Sandberg of the Swiss Jewel Factory and confirmed by Dr. W. Plato, a German professor of inorganic chemistry.

platy. Consisting of, or readily splitting into, **plates.**

play of color. An optical phenomenon consisting of a variety of prismatic colors, seen in rapid succession as a cabochon-cut gem is moved about, as in **opal.** A widely accepted theory proposes that play of color is caused by diffraction of light by innumerable, regularly arranged, optically transparent spherical particles of amorphous silica and from the spaces, or voids, between these particles. The spheres, and hence the voids, are arranged regularly in three dimensions (face-centered cubic), so that the whole arrangement makes a three-dimensional diffraction grating. The important feature is that the spacing of voids is the same as that of the spheres, and when this is about that of the wavelength of visible light, diffraction occurs. The angle through which the light is diffracted varies continuously with wavelength, so that different colors appear at different angles, thus producing play of color. Only pure spectral colors can arise from this process. This theory of the internal structure of precious opal was proved in the mid-1960's by research with the electron microscope. See **opal.**

pleochroic colors. The colors observable in a **pleochroic gem.**

pleochroic gem or **stone.** One which exhibits **pleochroism.**

pleochroic halo. In gemology, a cloudy inclusion in some gems apparently caused by inclusions of radioactive minerals and generally surrounding such inclusions. Sometimes concentric, sometimes radial.

pleochroism (ple-och'ro-izm). The property of most doubly refractive colored minerals of exhibiting either two or more different **colors** when viewed in different directions by transmitted light, the doubly refracted rays traveling in different directions having been absorbed differently by the mineral. Rarely distinguished by the eye except as one blended color, unless viewed through an instrument such as a polarizing microscope, polariscope, or dichroscope. The

comparative strength of pleochroism is expressed as *strong, distinct* or *weak.* See **dichroism; trichroism.**

pleocroismo (Span.). Pleochroism.

pleomorphism (plee"oe-more'fizm). Same as **polymorphism.**

pleonaste (plee'oe-nast). Black spinel.

plexiglass. A trade name for transparent methyl-methacrylate plastic. S.G. 1.19; R.I. 1.49.

plume agate. Highly translucent to almost opaque, grayish, creamy-white, milk-white, pinkish or yellowish **chalcedony,** containing black, red, brownish-red or orange, coarse to fine plumelike inclusions. The two most noted localities for this agate variety are Brewster Co., Texas (the Woodward Ranch, near Alpine), and Crook Co., Oregon (The Carey Ranch, near Prineville). See **agate.**

plumose. Feather-like.

pocket. A cavity in rock, often filled with minerals.

point. Term used in the jewelry trade to mean one hundredth of a carat. A sapphire weighing .52 carat is said to be a fifty-two point sapphire or a fifty-two pointer.

point agate. Same as **point chalcedony.**

point chalcedony. Pough lists as w h i t e or gray chalcedony flecked with tiny spots of iron oxide, the whole surface assuming a uniform soft red color.

pointed hexagon cut. See **hexagon cut.**

point source (of light). A single point from which light emanates, such as the sun, the filament of an electric lamp or other superheated metal, etc. The term is often extended to include as well the reflections of such point sources as seen in mirrors, or the facets of gemstones. Some objects are designed to reflect multiple images of a point source, and each of such images is also popularly known as a point source.

polariscope. An optical instrument consisting basically of two polarizers with a means of rotating a specimen between them. The polarizer through which light enters is called the polarizer, that through which observations are made is called the analyzer. A polariscope is used to ascertain whether a substance possesses **single refraction** or **double refraction**.

polarity (of crystals). The property of having differing types of termination at the two ends of a prismatic crystal. May be reflected in pyroelectric properties, conduction of electric current, etc.

polarized light. Light of which the vibrations have been limited to parallel planes, as contrasted with ordinary light, which vibrates in all planes at right angles to its direction.

polarizer. A device employed to produce polarized light: Nicol prism, polaroid sheet, tourmaline plate, glass reflecting plates, etc.

polarizing microscope. See **microscope.**

polarizing prism. Any prism so constructed as to produce polarized light; usually made of sawn and recemented calcite. (R. M. Shipley, Jr.) See also **Nicol prism.**

Polaroid. A trademarked name for a plastic sheet in which innumerable, tiny, highly dichroic crystals of *herpathite* (quinine idosulphate) are held in common orientation. Light transmitted through it becomes polarized.

polish. A smooth surface, usually produced by friction or abrasion.

polished girdle. See **girdle.**

polishing. The act of producing a polish, especially on the facets of a gemstone.

polka-dot agate. Local name for translucent, almost colorless, chalcedony, with yellow, red, or brown circular dots. From Oregon.

pollucite. A rare, transparent, colorless gem mineral of interest to collectors only. Iso. $H_2Cs_4Al_4(SiO_3)_9$; H. 6.5; S.G. 2.9; R.I. 1.52. Disp. 0.012. From Australia, Sweden, Maine and other sources.

polychroite. Same as **iolite.**

polymorphism. The occurrence of a chemical substance in two or more crystal forms possessing different atomic structure, and therefore different properties. Carbon crystallizing as diamond (isometric) and graphite (rhombohedral) is called *dimorphous*; TiO_2, crystallizing as rutile, brookite, and octahedrite is *trimorphous*. These as well as others such as SiO_2, crystallizing in a greater number of forms are *polymorphous* or *pleomorphous*.

polysynthetic twin or **twinning.** See **twin; twinning.**

Polystyrene. A trademarked name for a synthetic **plastic** (polyvinyl benzene) that has been used to produce gemstone imitations by the injection-molding process. Specific gravity, 1.05; refractive index, 1.59.

"pomegranate ruby." In India, a misnomer for red spinel.

pom-pom agate. A **sagenitic** agate in which yellow to orange inclusions are arranged in patterns resembling pom-poms, or chrysanthemums. Principally from Brewster Co., Texas. See **agate**.

popo (West African). Green jasper.

poppy stone. Red orbicular jasper popular with mineral collectors for cutting cabochon. From California.

porcelain. A hard, translucent clayware body that is occasionally used for the production of some opaque imitation gemstones. It is seldom cut and polished; usually it is molded and glazed with a glassy coating. The specific gravity is approximately 2.30.

porcelainite. Hard baked or partly metamorphosed clay or shales found on floors or roofs of burned-out coal mines.

"porcelain jasper." Red or green **porcelainite**.

porcelain opal. Milky white opal more opaque than **milk opal**.

porous stones. Those crystalline or cryptocrystalline aggregates which permit the entrance of solutions such as dyes between particles. See **stained stone**.

porphyritic obsidian. Obsidian resembling **porphyry** in appearance.

porphyry (por'fi-ri). A fine-grained rock containing embedded crystals of much larger size. Polished sections produce a distinctive mottled design.

porphyry ware. A variety of **Wedgwood** colored and marked to resemble porphyry.

Port. Abbr. used in this book for Portuguese.

portrait stone. A flat style of cutting, with parallel table and base, that permits one to see through to any object over which it is placed.

positive mineral or **stone.** A doubly refractive mineral or stone in which the index of refraction for the extraordinary ray is greater than for the ordinary ray, the former being refracted nearer to the normal than the latter, as in quartz. See also **negative mineral**.

positive double refraction. See **optic sign**.

positive stone. See **optic sign**.

possible crystal face. A face which, because of the known crystal system to which a mineral belongs, might be, or have been, present on a crystal, but which may not now be existent on it.

potato stone. A potato-like geode of quartz, having a central cavity lined with crystals.

potch. Australian miners' term for an opal which may be colorful, but without fine play of color.

potstone. Soapstone (impure talc).

prase (praze). Translucent, light-grayish yellow-green **chalcedony**. Also sometimes applied to **crystalline quartz** containing a multitude of green, hairlike crystals of **actinolite**.

prase malachite. Grayish chalcedony the color of which is caused by thick sprinklings of inclusions of malachite. From Arizona and other copper-producing states.

prase opal. Same as **prasopal.**

prasio (Span.). Prase.

prasius. Prase.

prasopal. Green **common opal** colored by chrome. From Australia, Hungary, Brazil (Eppler). See also **crysopal.**

precious cat's-eye. Chrysoberyl cat's-eye.

precious coral. Coral of reddish hues and tones distinguished from common coral and **black coral.**

precious jade. True jadeite or nephrite, more often the former.

precious metals. Metals which are more beautiful, rare, easily worked, and resistant to corrosion than most other metals, and which also have durability desirable in jewelry, coinage and the arts. **Gold, silver,** and the **platinum metals.**

precious moonstone. Adularia. See **moonstone.**

precious olivine. Peridot.

precious opal. A classification which includes opal with **play of color** and also, according to most authorities, **fire opal.** See **common opal, semiopal.**

precious serpentine. Translucent oily-green to light-green to greenish-yellow serpentine

precious stones. As contrasted with so-called semiprecious stones, include the more important and comparatively more valuable gems such as diamond, ruby, sapphire, and emerald. However, in a strict sense all genuine gem materials are precious. See **semiprecious stones.**

precious topaz. (1) Term still applied, by some jewelers, to genuine topaz to distinguish it from topaz-colored quartz, known as "jewelers' topaz". (2) Incorrect term for yellow-to-brown sapphire.

precipitate. The solid produced (generally in powdery or minutely crystalline form) when chemical reaction produces an insoluble compound.

preform. A commercially shaped blank of gem material for lapidary work. Its use saves the preliminary work of cutting.

prehnite (prane'ite or pren'ite). A translucent green-to-yellowish green, also white or grayish gem mineral of most interest to collectors. Cut cabochon and somewhat resembling jade, green varieties often fade. Ortho. $H_2 Ca_2Al_2(SiO_4)_3$; H. 6-6½; S.G. 2.8-2.9; R.I. 1.62/1.65; Bi. 0.030. From France, New Jersey, and Lake Superior district.

pressed amber. An amber substitute produced by consolidating fragments of amber under pressure, usually with linseed or other oil as a binder. Also called reconstructed amber.

pressed cameo. Similar to **molded** cameo, but pressed.

pressed copal. Made like pressed amber, from fragments of copal.

pressed glass. Glass objects formed by forcing glass heated to a viscous state into moulds. Process used to produce the cheapest sort of imitation gemstone.

Pride of Australia. A black opal found in the Lightning Ridge district, New South Wales, Australia, in 1915. After cutting, it weighed 225.75 carats and had a predominance of green play of color, with lesser amounts of orange. The present ownership of this stone is unknown.

primary colors. A term which may

refer either to three primary hues, red, yellow and blue, or to six primary hues, red, orange, yellow, green, blue and violet. See **spectrum**.

primary deposit. A deposit of minerals *in situ;* i.e., where they were formed, as distinguished from **secondary deposit**.

princess length. A pearl necklace 18 inches in length.

prism. (1) *(Optics)* Transparent medium contained between plane facets, usually inclined to each other. (2) *(Crystallography)* A form having all its faces, with the exception of bases, parallel to one axis.

prismatic (priz-mat'ik). (1) *(Optics)* Resembling the colors formed by the refraction of light through a prism. (2) *(Crystallography)* Having elongation in one direction, commonly parallel to one of the crystallographic axes; also parallel to the faces of a crystal, as prismatic cleavage.

prismatic layer. A layer, in pearl or mother-of-pearl, composed of minute crystals of aragonite arranged with their principal axes perpendicular to the surface of the layer.

"prismatic moonstone." Clouded chalcedony.

"prismatic quartz." Iolite.

prismatic spectroscope. See **spectroscope**.

prism, polarizing. See **polarizing prism**.

proper proportion (of a cut gemstone). In a transparent stone, the proportion of the mass above and below the girdle, as well as the angles of the facets in relation to the girdle, which will produce the greatest brilliancy

from the particular species. These proportions vary with the R. I. of the gem species. A table of proper proportions of various stones appears on Page 84 of Kraus and Slawson's *Gems and Gem Materials*, 3rd edition.

properties. Term loosely used to mean the **physical properties** and **optical properties** of a gemstone or its substitute.

proportion (of a cut gemstone). See **proper proportion**.

Proportionscope. A diamond-grading instrument designed and manufactured by the Gemological Institute of America. It combines lenses and movable mirrors to project the silhouette of a diamond on a screen. Diagrams and scales on the screen, as well as a "zoom" range, enable the instrument to analyze the proportions of a round brilliant-cut diamond, as well as some fancy cuts. It is also useful for determining the recutting of old-miners and damaged stones.

protons (proétons). The name for the particles or electrical charges which make up the nucleus of an atom. See **electrons**.

Prussian amber. Succinite from Prussia, See also **Baltic amber**.

pseudo. False.

pseudochrysolite. Moldavite.

pseudocrocidolite. Quartz pseudomorphous after crocidolite; tiger-eye and hawk's-eye.

pseudodiamond. Quartz crystal.

pseudoemerald. Malachite.

pseudohexagonal, pseudotetragon-

al, etc. Having false and misleading resemblance to crystals of the hexagonal, tetragonal system, etc.

pseudojade. False jade. Term like many others with the prefix *pseudo-* referring to almost any similarly appearing substitute of the stone.

pseudojadeite. Name given especially to a jade-like mineral from a jadeite quarry at Tawmaw, Upper Burma. S.G. 2.577; classed as albite.

pseudomalachite. A hydrous phosphate of copper occurring ordinarily in massive forms of bright green color resembling malachite.

pseudomorph. A mineral having the characteristic crystal form of another species (the original material composing it having been altered or replaced but retaining the form of the original species.) Thus tiger eye (quartz) is pseudomorph of the mineral crocidolite and is no longer crocidolite, but quartz. It is said to be pseudomorphic or pseudomorphous after crocidolite.

pseudomorphic or **pseudomorphous.** See **pseudomorph.**

pseudophite (sue'-do-fite). A compact, massive, greenish mineral of the chlorite group resembling serpentine, sometimes miscalled "Styrian jade." Sources: Hungary, Moravia and Griqualand West, Africa.

pseudosuccinito. Amber from Equilleres, Basses-Alpes, France. R.I. 1.085.

psilomelane chalcedony (si-lom'-e-lane). Black-banded chalcedony heavily impregnated with psilomelane (a black manganese oxide). It is occasionally cut into cabochons and is popular as a tumbling material. From Mexico.

Pteriidae. Same as **Aviculidae** or **Malleidae.**

pudding stone. A conglomerate in which the pebbles are rounded and cemented together by a finer-grained mineral. See also **breccia.**

pudding stone jade. Nodules of nephrite cemented together by a darker olive-green variety of nephrite.

"pudding stone jasper." A pudding stone of quartz pebbles cemented by chalcedony. Cut as a curio stone in Lake Superior district.

punamu. Maori name for axe stone or **nephrite.**

purple-of-the-veins jade. A fanciful descriptive term applied by Chinese to a stone which, if jade, must be extremely rare.

purplish red. In color nomenclature **system** of North American gemology, a hue between **red** and **violetish red** but nearer the latter.

purpurin. Same as **hematinon.**

putty powder. Same as tin oxide.

pycnometer or **pyknometer.** Same as **specific gravity bottle.**

pyralin. A variety of celluloid.

pyralmandite. A contraction of pyrope and almandite for garnets of intermediate composition.

pyramid. A crystal form. See **pyramidal.**

pyramidal. Possessing the form of or pertaining to the **pyramid;** a crystal form the faces of which commonly intersect three crystallographic axes.

"pyramidal garnet." Idocrase.

pyrite. Same as iron pyrites. A metallic, pale brassy yellow mineral, widely sold as marcasite which it slightly resembles; also often occurring as flecks (inclusions) in lapis lazuli and popularly called "fool's gold." Iso. FeS_2; H. 6-6½; S.G. 4.8-5.2. From many localities.

pyritohedron. See **dodecahedron.**

pyroelectricity. An electric charge produced in certain substances by heating, as in tourmaline.

"pyroemerald." Green fluorite.

pyrometer. An instrument for measuring high temperature used in production of **heated stones.** Such instruments are used in heating gemstones accurately to alter their color.

pyrope (pi'-rope). The transparent, dark, very slightly brownish red to intense pure-red species of the **garnet** group. It has long been described and sold by such misleading names as "Arizona ruby" and "Cape ruby." Chemical composition, magnesium-aluminum silicate $(Mg_3Al_2(SiO_4)_3)$; crystal system, isometric; hardness, 7; specific gravity, 3.62 to 3.87; refractive index range, 1.72 to 1.75; birefringence, none; dispersion, .027. Sources: Czechoslovakia, South Africa, N.M., Ariz., Rhodesia, Ceylon, Burma and elsewhere.

pyrophane. Wax-impregnated hydrophane (Bauer-Spencer).

pyrophyllite (pi-ro-fil'-ite). A massive, white, gray, grayish-white, greenish, brownish-green or yellowish mineral species, talclike in appearance. It is used for slate pencils and carvings and includes part of what is known as **agalmatolite.** Chemical composition, a hydrous aluminum silicate (H_2Al_2-$(SiO_3)_4$); crystal system, orthorhombic (foliated, radiated lamellar or somewhat fibrous; also granular to compact or cryptocrystalline); hardness, 1 to 2; specific gravity, 2.80 to 2.90; refractive index, 1.552-1.600. Sources: N.C., Ga., Calif. and elsewhere.

pyroxene (pie'rok-seen or peer'-ox-ene). In mineralogy, a group of minerals which includes **diopside, enstatite, hypersthene, jadeite,** and **spodumene.** They all contain silica in combination with other elements.

Q

quahog pearl. Pearl from the quahog *(Venus mercenaria)*; a salt water clam. From Atlantic coast of North America. Same as **clam pearl.**

quartz (kworts). The most common and widely distributed mineral. It includes many varieties of gemstones and ornamental stones of many colors, combinations of colors and degrees of transparency, some crystalline and some cryptocrystalline (the subspecies **chalcedony**). Among the well-known varieties are **amethyst, citrine, agate, aventurine, bloodstone, tiger's-eye** and many others. Chemical composition, silicon dioxide (SiO_2); crystal system, hexagonal (some varieties massive); hardness, 7; specific gravity, 2.65 to 2.66; refractive index, 1.544-1.553; birefringence, .009; dispersion, .013.

quartz cat's-eye. Translucent to semitransparent chatoyant quartz, usually grayish green to gray-green to greenish yellow, although it may also be white, gray-brown, brownish, green or black. The presence of a multitude of minute, parallel inclusions arranged throughout the stone at right angles to the "pupil" of the eye and parallel to the base of the stone are responsible for the chatoyancy. The finest stones exhibit a narrow, well-defined eye that rivals chrysoberyl in beauty and perfection. It is also called **occidental cat's-eye,** to distinguish it from chrysoberyl, which is known correctly as **oriental cat's-eye.** Misnomers are "Bavarian" and "Hungarian cat's-eye." The best-quality material is found in the Ceylon gem gravels; poorer stones come from Hof and other locations in Bavaria.

quartz glass. (1) Transparent fused rock crystal, better known as *fused quartz*; (2) a term sometimes applied, often deceptively, to any glass, which, being made from sand, is principally quartz.

quartz rock. Same as **quartzite.**

"quartz topaz." A frequently used incorrect name for citrine. See **topaz quartz.**

quartzite. (1) A **metamorphic** rock produced by the recrystallization of a sandstone under heat and pressure, consisting of a granular, interlocking mass of disoriented quartz crystals with irregular boundaries. When this kind of quartzite exhibits bright or strongly colored reflections from inclusions of tiny platelets or flakes of another mineral, it is called **aventurine quartz.** (2) Sandstone cemented by solution-deposited silica.

Queen Elizabeth Pearls. A name sometimes applied to the four drop pearls, suspended from the intersections of the arches of the Imperial State Crown of Great Britain, which pearls, according to tradition, belonged to Queen Elizabeth (Younghusband). Elizabeth was one of the world's greatest collectors of pearls.

Queen of Pearls. See **La Reine des Perles.**

Queen Pearl. The most famous American **fresh-water** pearl. Found in Notch Brook near. Paterson,

New Jersey, in 1857, it was pinkish and weighed 93 grains. It was purchased by Tiffany & Co., and was sold to a French gem dealer, who sold it to someone who gave it to Empress Eugénie. She, in turn, left it to a Philadelphia friend, and it is now in the Evans Collection belonging to the University of Pennsylvania.

Queensland opal. Australian opal with light yellowish color. From Queensland.

Queensland sapphire. Sapphire from near Anakie, Queensland, Australia, which is usually the dark blue of the typical **Australian sapphire.** Often green, sometimes yellow, pink or purplish. Rarely lighter and more desirable blue. Many bluish star sapphires also have been found here.

Queenstownite. Same as **Darwin glass.**

queluzita (Brazilian). Spessartite.

Queretaro (ka-ray'tah-ro). Mexican state and city, 100 miles northeast of Mexico City, known as principal locality for **Mexican opal.**

quicksilver jade. A descriptive term of the Chinese for an unusual variety of **jade.**

quilate (Spanish and Portuguese). Carat.

quincite or **quinzite.** (1) A rose-colored common opal. (2) A variety of sepiolite associated with it but spelled *quincite* only.

R

radiated. Having fibers, columns, scales, or plates diverging from a point.

radiograph. Term used for X-ray photos of pearls which indicate the nature of their interior structure. See **X rays.**

radio opal. Common opal of a smoky color caused by organic inclusions or impurities (Merrill).

rainbow agate or **chalcedony.** Iridescent agate.

"rainbow obsidian." An American Indian name for iridescent obsidian. From Lake County, Oregon.

rainbow quartz. Same as **iris quartz.**

rain stone. Pebbles of waterworn quartz.

Ramona beryl, hessonite and **tourmaline.** From Ramona gem mines, 10 miles S.E. of Mesa Grande, San Diego County, Calif.

raspberry spar. Rhodochrosite; also incorrect name for pink tourmaline.

rati. See **rutee.**

ratna. In Singhalese, a gem.

ratti (rut'ee). See **rutee.**

Rayner refractometer. A gemological refractometer employing a fixed prism of dense glass or, rarely, a prism of diamond. Suitable for use in the hand. See **Smith Refractometer, Tully Refractometer, Erb & Gray Refractometer, Duplex Refractometer.**

"reconstituted turquoise." A turquoise substitute made by consolidating into cabochon shapes a blue powder that may or may not contain turquoise as a constituent.

reconstructed amber. Same as **pressed amber.**

"reconstructed emerald." A term which has been applied to various imitations of emerald, including glass, doublets and especially **smaragdolin.** Emerald was never successfully reproduced as a reconstructed stone.

reconstructed ruby and sapphire. Terms often mistakenly used for **synthetic** ruby and sapphire.

reconstructed stones. Stones made by fusing together small particles of the genuine stone. They differ from **synthetic stones.**

reconstructed turquoise. (1) Reconstructed stone made from small particles of turquoise (Schlossmacher). (2) Incorrect term for a turquoise substitute made of powdered ivory, cemented and stained.

Red Admiral Opal. A black opal, weighing 40 to 50 carats in the rough, found in the Lightning Ridge district, New South Wales, Australia, in 1920. The stone's pattern, consisting of a vivid mixture of many colors, red predominating, resembles that of a wing of a British butterfly called the red admiral; hence, the alternate name, *Butterfly Stone.* The finished weight of the stone is not known, nor is its present location.

red-brown. In color nomenclature system of North American gemology, the color approximately midway between vivid red and the tone and **intensity** of brown which is almost black. Same as **brown-orange.**

reddish brown. In color nomenclature system of North American gemology, a color which is approximately midway between (a) **red-brown** and (b) the tone and intensity of brown which is almost black.

reddish orange. In North American gemology, the hue midway between red-orange and orange; hence more orange than red.

reddish violet. In North American gemology, the hue midway between red-violet (purple) and violet.

reddish yellow. A hue which would correspond roughly with **orange-yellow.**

red flame opal. Opal that exhibits pronounced streak or streaks of red.

redmanol. Name of a phenol resin molding composition and varnish somewhat similar to bakelite.

red-orange. In North American gemology the **hue** midway between red and orange. Same as **orange-red.**

red-purple. Same hue as **reddish violet.**

red-ring test. This is a very simple means of detecting a garnet-and-glass doublet, if a stone is of a color other than red. If the stone is placed table down on a piece of white paper, a red ring close to the girdle, produced by the garnet crown, will appear.

"red schorl." Rutile.

Red Sea pearl. (1) A pearl from the waters of the Red Sea, principally from its southern end, and marketed mostly through Bombay. It is from the *Pinctada Vulgaris* mollusc. (2) An incorrect term that has been used for **coral** fashioned as a bead.

red top moss agate. Mocha stone with red stain at base of the black dendritic inclusions.

red-violet. In North American gemology the **hue** midway between red and violet. The same hue as purple.

red-yellow. The same **hue** as orange, which is midway between red and yellow.

reflected light. Light that has been reflected from any surface; hence, any light not traveling directly from the sun, or lamp, or other source. See **reflection, transmitted light.**

reflection. The returning or deflection of light which strikes a surface.

reflection or **reflecting goniometer.** See **goniometer.**

reflectometer. Same as **total reflectometer.**

refraction. Bending of light rays. The deflection from a straight path suffered by a ray of light as it passes obliquely from one medium into another in which the velocity of the ray is different, as from air into water, or from air or water into a gem mineral. See **R.I. refractive index; D.R.; double refraction.**

refractive. Having the power to refract.

refractive index (pl. indices). The ratio of the sine of the **angle of incidence** to the sine of the **angle of refraction.** A measure of the amount a light ray is bent as it enters or leaves a given substance, expressed by numerals that indicate the comparative bending power of different substances such as gems. The index (R.I.) of a vacuum is 1.00, of water, 1.33, fluorite 1.43, methelyne iodide 1.742, rhodolite garnet 1.76. Different specimens of the same species usually show slightly different R.I.'s and the range of differences is indicated thus: Pyrope 1.74-1.75. Furthermore, the R.I. of any doubly refractive mineral varies, and it is customary to indicate the highest and lowest values, which in this book are indicated thus: Quartz, R.I. 1.54/1.55. In addition, since different specimens usually show slightly different R.I.'s, the range of such differences is indicated thus: Corundum, R. I. 1.76/1.77-1.77/1.78. See **refraction; index of refraction; double refraction; mean refractive index; R.I.**

refractometer (ree" frak tom' e-ter). Any optical instrument used for measuring the **refractive index** of any solid or fluid substance. Refractometers used for gemology are almost universally based upon the measurement of the variation of the critical angle in a hemisphere or prism of highly refractive glass; such variation is produced by placing the specimen to be tested in contact with the reflecting surface of the dense glass prism or hemisphere. An instrument of this type is also known as a *total reflectometer.* Gemological refractometers usually read R.I. of either mounted or unmounted stones, directly on an enclosed scale. By use of **monochromatic light** and by revolving the stone on the hemisphere (or by revolving the glass and stone together) the highest and lowest **R.I.** of many stones may be obtained, as well as the **birefringence.** See **Rayner, Tully, Erb & Gray,** and **Smith refractometer.**

refrangibility. The capacity of being refracted. See **refraction.**

refrangible (ree-fran'ji-bl). Capable of being refracted, as rays of light. See **refraction.**

Regent Pearl. Same as **La Régente Pearl.**

Registered Jeweler. A title awarded by the American Gem Society to qualified retail jewelers. After membership in the Society is attained, the title is secured by successful completion of comprehensive proctored examinations based on prescribed training and examinations in diamonds and colored stones. See **American Gem Society, Certified Gemologist.**

regular system. Same as **isometric system.**

reniform. Kidney-shaped.

repeated twin or **twinning.** See **twin** or **twinning.**

reproduction. A term used to include **reconstructed stones, synthetic stones,** and, less accurately, **cultured pearls,** in a manner similar in its application to the use of the word for the finer copies of original works of art. Imitation stones are not reproductions as they differ structurally or chemically from the stones they imitate. See also **imitations; synthetic stone.**

resin (rez'in). A solid to semisolid, transparent to opaque organic substance (from plants). Usually yellow to brown in color, but resins—especially the synthetic products—may occur in almost any color. See **fossil resin.**

resinoid. Same as **bakelite.**

resin opal. Honey-yellow, to ochreous-yellow variety of common opal with a resinous luster.

169

resinous luster. Luster like that of natural yellow resins.

Retail Jewelers of America, Inc. The Retail Jewelers of America is a national trade association that was formed in 1957 upon merger of American National Retail Jewelers' Association and the National Jewelers' Association. The purpose of the organization is to promote the general welfare, standing and prosperity of the retail jewelry industry. Forty-two state jewelers' associations are affiliated with the RJA; membership in a state association automatically establishes membership in the RJA, and vice versa, thus creating a national team for retail jewelers. The organization sponsors and manages an annual National Jewelry Trade Show in New York City. Headquarters: 1025 Vermont Ave., NW, Washington, D.C. 20005.

Retger's salt. Thallium silver nitrate which, when melted at 75° C. to a yellow liquid, has S.G. of 4.6; lower S.G. if diluted. A **heavy liquid.**

reticulated (ree-tik′ue-late″ed). Having slender crystals or fibers crossing like the meshes of a net.

retinalite. A variety of massive pale greenish yellow **precious serpentine.**

retinite. A fossil resin.

rhinestone. (1) Historically, rock crystal. (2) *In the jewelry trade, of U.S.A.*, the commonest usage is for foil back imitations of diamond but term is sometimes used for other colored foil backs and occasionally for colorless glass.

rhinoceros horn. The horn of the rhinoceros (family *Rhinocerotidae)*

has been used for ivory in China. It consists of a mass of closely packed hairs or horny fibers growing from the skin of the animal. It may attain a foot in length. The material has a low hardness and a specific gravity of 1.29. Source: Africa and Asia.

rhodizite (ro′-dih-zite). A transparent, light-yellow, light yellowish-green, colorless or, rarely, light-red mineral species. Rhodizite is very rare and is only seldom cut for collectors. Chemical composition, a potassium-aluminum borate ($KAl_2B_3O_8$); crystal system, isometric; hardness, 8; specific gravity, 3.40; refractive index, 1.69. Sources: Russia and Malagasy Republic.

rhodochrosite (ro-doe-kro′-site). A transparent to semitranslucent, pale to deep rose-red, brown, yellowish, greenish or gray mineral species, often attractively banded in various tones of pink. It is desirable for cabochons, slabs and ornamental articles. Infrequently seen are transparent, light to medium orange-red crystals, which are occasionally cut for collectors. It is also called **Inca rose** and **rosinca.** Chemical composition, manganese carbonate ($MnCO_3$); crystal system, hexagonal (crystals rare; usually granular, massive stalactitic formations and crusts); hardness, $3\frac{1}{2}$ to $4\frac{1}{2}$; specific gravity, 3.45 to 3.60; refractive index, 1.600-1.820; birefringence, .220. Sources: Argentina, Saxony, Rumania, Colorado, Montana and elsewhere.

rhodoid. An artificial resin (cellulose acetate) used to imitate amber S.G. about 1.28; R.I. about 1.49. (Anderson).

rhodolite (ro'-do-lite). A rare, brilliant, transparent, purplish-red to violetish-red to slightly brownish-red species of the **garnet** group. It represents a combination of **pyrope** and **almandite** and is characterized by a lighter tone and a higher degree of transparency than either of these two garnets. Crystal system, isometric; hardness, 7 to 7½; specific gravity, 3.74 to 3.94; refractive index, 1.74 to 1.77 (usually 1.76); birefringence, none; dispersion, .026. Sources: Ceylon and N.C. Garnet is the birthstone for January, and it is correct to use rhodolite or any other member of the garnet group for this purpose.

rhodonite (roe'doe-nite). A translucent to opaque, pink or rose, to red-brown ornamental mineral. Rose-colored is used principally in Russia, for brooches, beads, buttons, Easter eggs, etc. Tri. $MnSiO_3$; H. 5.5-6.5; S.G. 3.4-3.7. R.I. 1.71/1.73-1.73/1.74. Bi. 0.011 to Bi. 0.013. From Siberia, New Jersey, and elsewhere.

rhomb (rom or romb). In crystallography, a form bounded by three parallel pairs of lozenge-shaped faces.

rhombic (rom'bik). Four-sided; each side of equal length but not at right angles to each other as a rhombic facet.

rhombic dodecahedron. See **dodecahedron.**

rhombic facet. See **rhombic.**

rhombohedral system (rom' 'boehede'ral). A division of the hexagonal system. See also **crystal systems.**

rhomboid. A **parallelogram** in which there are no right angles and the adjoining sides are of unequal length.

rhomboidal. Shaped like a **rhomboid,** as a rhomboidal facet.

"rhyolite glass." Obsidian.

R.I. Abbreviation for **refractive index.**

riband agate. A variety of banded agate with especially wide bands that are planar or uniformly curved.

riband jasper. Banded jasper with ribbon-like stripes of alternating colors. See **Egyptian jasper.**

ribbon agate. Same as **riband agate.**

ribbon jasper. Same as **riband jasper.**

rice jade. Descriptive name used by the Chinese for a particular quality of jade.

rice stone. Steatite the color of unpolished rice.

Richelieu pearl. A brand of imitation pearl.

ricolite. A green banded serpentine.

ring agate. Agate with concentric rings but with less distinct color contrasts than **eye agate.**

ring-around. Term applied by American fishermen to a pearl having a discolored ring around it.

ring stone. (1) Any stone usable in a finger ring. (2) A trade term for any facetted stone with crown consisting of large table.

ripe pearl. A rarely used term for pearl which is nacreous and of good luster, in contrast to unripe pearl, which is of inferior nacre or luster. See **unripe pearl.**

river agate. Pebble of mocha stone or moss agate from a stream bed.

river pearl. A fresh-water pearl.

river sapphire. Light-colored sapphire from Montana.

R. J. Abbreviation for **Registered Jeweler, A.G.S.**

roasting. Heating at a low red heat with a strongly oxidizing blow-pipe flame, for the purpose of driving off sulphur, arsenic, etc.

robold pearl. A trade term for a pearl which is not quite round.

rock. Any mineral or aggregate of minerals comprising an important part of the earth's crust. A rock may consist of a single component, such as marble, or be an assemblage of two or more, such as granite.

rock amber. Same as **block amber.**

rock crystal. Clear, colorless quartz.

rock glass. Obsidian.

rockhound. An amateur gem, mineral and rock collector, who may also be a lapidary.

"rock ruby." Red pyrope garnet.

rock turquoise. Turquoise matrix with scattered specks of turquoise.

"Rocky Mountain ruby." Garnet.

rod. A thin cylindrical form of flame-fusion synthetic corundum or spinel.

Roebling Black Opal. A 355.19-carat black-opal cabochon from Virgin Valley, Humbolt Co., Nevada. It is on display at the Smithsonian Institution, Washington, D.C.

Roebling Opal. An opal in the U. S. Nat'l. Museum (Smithsonian Institution) said to be the largest mass of precious opal known, weight 2610 c. (Foshag). From Virgin Valley, Nevada. See **Roebling Black Opal.**

Roentgen or **Röntgen ray.** Same as **X ray.**

rogueite. A local trade name for greenish jasper from gravels of Rogue River, Oregon.

Rohrbach's solution. Solution of barium mercury iodide in water. S.G. 3.58. A heavy liquid.

rolled pebbles. Pebbles which have been worn by transportation in water to a comparatively smooth and round shape.

Romanian amber. Same as **Rumanian amber.**

romanite. Same as **rumanite.**

Roman pearl. A sphere of opalescent glass with interior coated with **essence d'orient** and then filled with wax.

romanzovite (roe'manz-oe-vite). Dark brown **grossularite** garnet; from Finland (Schlossmacher).

rondel. Same as **rondelle.**

rondelle (ron-del'). A thin disk of gemstone, metal or other substance pierced through the center for use between beads in necklaces. Its edges are usually facetted, but if not its shape is that of the **lentil.**

rosaline (roe'za-lin). Thulite.

rosa pallido coral (Italian). Pale red coral.

rosa vijo coral (Italian). Vivid red coral.

rose agate. Local name for a grey and rose banded agate from Brewster County, Texas.

rose beryl. Same as **morganite.**

rose cut. A style of cutting, the bottom of which is wide, flat and unfacetted, and the top of which is somewhat dome-shaped, is covered with facets, and terminates in a point. Now confined to small stones.

rose garnet. (1) A name for **rhodolite.** (2) A trade name for an ornamental stone containing rosolite, vesuvianite and wollastonite from Xaloctoc, Mexico. (3) A trade name for a **rose-cut garnet.**

roseki. Term used by Japanese for agalmatolite or figure stone (Webster).

"rose kunzite." Pink synthetic sapphire or spinel.

roselite (roe′ze-lite). Name correctly applied to a triclinic non-gem mineral, and sometimes incorrectly to a pink garnet. See **rosolite.**

"rose moonstone." Pink scapolite.

rose opal. Same as **quincite.**

rose pearl. Pink, iridescent, fresh-water baroque **pearl.**

rosé pearl. A trade term for a pearl with a pinkish **orient,** although it is often used to refer to a pink body color.

rose quartz. The semitransparent to translucent, pink, rose-red to pale-rose variety of **crystalline quartz.** It exists almost exclusively in the massive form; individual crystals of sufficient size to be identified as such are rare. Analine dyes are sometimes used to produce darker or more uniform colors, but such material, as well as the naturally colored, has a tendency to fade. Cabochon-cut stones may exhibit asterism. Sources: Brazil, Madagascar, India, Russia and elsewhere. See **star quartz.**

rose topaz. Light rose to lilac colored topaz. See **pink topaz.**

rosette. Same as **rose cut.**

rosin (ros′in). A variant of resin.

rosinca. Trade name for banded rhodochrosite from Argentina.

rosolite. A rose-pink grossularite garnet from Xalostoc, Mexico. Same as **landerite.**

Rospogli, Rospoli, or **Ruspoli sapphire.** A 135-carat, flawless, brownish sapphire in Museum of Jardin des Plantes, Paris.

Rosser Reeves Star Ruby. A fine-quality, 138.70-carat star ruby, the largest gem of this kind in existence. It is on permanent display at the Smithsonian Institution.

rosso coral (Italian). Red coral.

rosso scuro coral (Italian). Dark red coral.

rosterite. Rose-red beryl.

rothoffite. Yellow to brownish andradite garnet.

rottenstone. An abrasive powder; principally silica from decomposed limestone. Used in final polishing of colored stones. See **tripoli.**

rouge (roozh). Formerly prepared by reducing hematite to fine powder. Now a red amorphous powder consisting of ferric oxide; used for polishing metals.

rough. Trade term for any gem mineral which has not yet been cut and polished.

rough gem or **gem mineral.** One which has not been cut and polished.

roumanite. Same as **rumanite.**

royalite. Trade-marked name of a purplish red glass.

royal topaz. Blue topaz.

rozircon (roe″zur-kon′ or roe-zir kon). Trade-marked name of a pink synthetic spinel.

rubace. See **rubasse.**

rubasse (roo-bos'). Quartz colored red by numerous small scales or flecks of hematite or oxide of iron. From Brazil, and other sources. Imitated under same name, or name *rubace*, by red stained crackled quartz.

rubellite (roo'bel-ite). Red tourmaline.

rubicelle (roo bi-sel). Yellow to orange-red spinel.

Rubin (German). Ruby.

rubino-di-rocca (Italian). Red garnet of violet tinge.

rubis (French). Ruby.

rubolite. A variety of red **common opal.**

ruby. (1) The red variety of **corundum.** Intense, medium to medium-dark purplish red (so-called pigeon's blood) is best, intense red is fine, and dark red is less desirable. Star ruby is rare. In the jewelry industry, the finest purplish-red stones, principally from Burma, are known as **Burma,** or **oriental, rubies;** less valuable, darker red, principally from Thailand, as **Siam** rubies; and light red, from Ceylon and elsewhere, as **Ceylon ruby** or pink sapphire. (2) A color designation meaning bright red to violetish red, as in **ruby glass, ruby spinel,** etc.

ruby balas. Balas ruby.

"ruby cat's-eye." Term applied to girasol ruby with a **chatoyant effect.** Although a true cat's-eye is theoretically possible in a ruby, as well as in any gem species yielding asterias, a well defined single band of light occurs rarely. See also **girasol.**

ruby glass. Bright red glass.

ruby juice. Transparent red lacquer sometimes used for coating pavilion of stones. See **lacquer back.**

ruby matrix. (1) Any rock embedded with red corundum; (2) especially that which consists of **smaragdite** and red corundum found in Clay Co., N. C., and sometimes cut cabochon.

"ruby sapphire." A term sometimes used for **almandine sapphire** or **amethystine sapphire.**

ruby spinel. Ruby-colored or red spinel.

ruby tin. Red **cassiterite.**

ruin agate. Agate with markings which resemble. the outlines of ruins.

ruin marble. Calcite with markings of iron oxide resembling ruins.

Rumanian amber. Same as **rumanite.**

rumanite (roo'man-ite). Yellow-brown to red, also black amber, containing cracks. Workable, and rarer than **succinite.** Rarely yellow, sometimes black. Fluorescent varieties are even more frequent than in simetite and are sometimes greenish or bluish.

Russian alexandrite. Alexandrite from Urals which occurs in smaller sizes than **Ceylon alexandrite.** Also more bluish (Smith).

Russian amethyst. See **Siberian amethyst.**

"Russian chrysolite." Same as **"Uralian chrysolite."**

"Russian crystal." Colorless selenite.

Russian emerald. Emerald from the Starka, Takovaya and other tributaries of the Bolschoi Reft in the Urals, Siberia, generally of inferior quality to **Colombian emerald.** See **Takovaya.**

174

Russian jasper. Red flecked jasper. (Eppler)

Russian jet. Jet from Irkutsk, Siberia.

Russian lapis. (1) Trade term for lapis lazuli, from the Russian Badakshan near the border of Afghanistan, or for **Afghanistan lapis** exported through Russia. (2) A term which can be accurately applied to an inferior quality of lapis lazuli from Lake Baikal, in Siberia.

Russian topaz. Same as **Siberian topaz.**

rutee or **ruttee** (Anglo-Indian). A pea-like scarlet seed of the licorice, used as a weight; about 1.75 grains troy. Same as rati or ratti; see also **tank.**

rutilated quartz. Same as **sagenitic quartz.** See **rutile.**

rutile (roo'teel or roo'til). A transparent-to-opaque, brownish-red-to-black mineral of higher R.I. than diamond. Sometimes cut for collectors. Important as acicular inclusions in many gem stones Tetr. TiO_2; H. $6-6\frac{1}{2}$; S.G. 4.2-4.3; R.I. 2.62/2.90; Bi. 0.287. From Italy, Switzerland, North Carolina, and other sources.

rutile, synthetic. Transparent rutile has been synthetically produced commercially since 1948. It has been fashioned and marketed as gemstones under various names including Titania, Miridis, "Rainbow Diamond," Kenya Gem, Zaba Gem, Sapphirized Titania. Colors include yellow to very pale yellow, greenish blue to bluish green, and other hues. Tetr. H. 6-7; S.G. 4.26. R.I. 2.616-2.903; Bi. .287; Disp. Several times that of diamond.

rutilio. (Span.) Rutile

S

S. Abbr. for the element sulphur.

sabalite. Same as **trainite.**

"sacred turquoise." Pale-blue **smithonite.**

saffronite or **safronite.** A little-used coined word recommended by 1933 B. I. B. O. A. conference to supplant topaz as then used by jewelers to mean citrine or **topaz quartz.**

safirina (Port.). Misnomer for blue spinel or quartz.

sagathai. Burmese term applied to ½ carat rubies.

sagenite (saj'-eh-nite). Chalcedony or quartz containing numerous needlelike crystals of other minerals, such as rutile or tourmaline, is called **sagenite** or **sagenitic** quartz.

sagenitic quartz. Term used for transparent colorless or nearly colorless quartz containing needle-like crystals of rutile, actinolite, goethite, tourmaline or other mineral, regardless of the manner in which the crystals are arranged. See **sagenite; rutilated quartz.**

Saint Edward's Sapphire. Fine blue sapphire reputedly worn by King Edward about 1042. Recut as a rose and now in diamond-paved cross which surmounts the British Imperial State Crown.

Saint Stephen's stone. Translucent whitish or greyish chalcedony sprinkled with small red spots.

sakal (Egyptian). Amber.

"Salamanca topaz." Citrine from Cordova; not from Salamanca. Same as **"Hinjosa topaz."**

salam stone. (1) Term used in the Orient for **sapphire.** (2) Variety of transparent pale red or blue sapphire found chiefly in Ceylon.

salis gem (Obsolete). Moonstone.

salting. Scattering upon the surface or digging into the ground, gems or particles of gold or other rich ore to make a mine or reputed mine appear rich.

salt-water pearl. Any pearl from any salt-water mollusc, including *Pinctada, Mytilidae, Pinna* and *Haliotidae.*

samadiam pearl. Ceylonese trade grade for a pearl of reddish hue, pear shaped, but dull. (Kunz)

sammatti. Singhalese name for master of a pearl fishing boat.

sammyi. Alternate Burmese name for **byon.**

samotsvet. An ancient Russian word for a natural colored stone.

sandalwood jade. A descriptive term used in China for a particular variety of jade.

Sandawana emerald. Emerald from the Sandawana Valley, Rhodesia, Africa. It is usually of very small size but often of exceptionally fine color. See **emerald.**

sanding. The operation in fashioning gemstones during which deep scratches left by grinding are removed by garnet paper, emery cloth or silicon-carbide paper.

"San Domingo amber." A **fossil resin** from San Domingo, West Indies. A variety of retinite. Transparent and rarely if ever cloudy. Yellow to brownish. Typically with blue fluorescence.

sandstone. A rock consisting of old beds of sands or very small rounded gravels or both, bound together by natural cement which is usually of light hue.

sandstone opal. A contraction of **sandstone boulder opal.** A variety of boulder opal in which thin layers of opal occur between layers of sandstone and soft clay.

sandy sard. Sard dotted with darker spots.

Sang-i-yeshan. Bowenite from northwestern China.

sanguinaria. A Spanish name for (1) heliotrope; (2) hematite. See **piedra de sangra.**

sanidine. A colorless or white to yellowish or greyish variety of **orthoclase,** of which the transparent colorless to yellowish varieties are often cut for collectors.

"saphir d' eau." (French, water sapphire.) Iolite.

saponite. A very soft white, greenish, bluish or reddish mineral; S.G. 2.2-2.3; R.I. 1.48-1.52. From Scotland, Ontario, Minn., Mich., and other sources. See **soapstone.**

sappare. Translucent cyanite.

sapphire (saf'-ire). Any gem **corundum** other than ruby. In the jewelry industry, the word generally means **blue sapphire;** other colors are known as pink sapphire, purple sapphire, yellow sapphire, etc. These, as a group, are distinguished from blue as **fancy sapphires.** Sources: best-quality blue from Kashmir, India; fine blue from Burma, Thailand and Montana; lighter blue from Ceylon; and other colors principally from Ceylon, Australia and Montana. It is the birthstone for September.

sapphire cat's-eye. Term often applied to **girasol sapphire** with a chatoyant effect. Although a true cat's-eye is theoretically possible in sapphire, a well-defined single streak of light occurs rarely. See **"ruby cat's-eye."**

sapphire glass. Sapphire-blue glass. One variety of unknown composition has exceptional hardness up to 6¾.

sapphire spar. Cyanite with opalescence or girasol effect.

sapphire spinel. Sapphire-colored spinel. An unrecommended term; derivation similar to that of **ruby spinel.**

"sapphirin" or **"sapphirine."** Names used for (1) blue quartz or chalcedony; or (2) blue spinel; or (3) a blue cobalt glass. Sapphirine is also the correct name of a mineral of no gem interest.

sapphire quartz. (1) A translucent, coarse-grained quartz aggregate, colored blue by included fibers of silicified crocidolite that, unlike hawk's-eye, are not in parallel arrangement. Also called **azure quartz** or **siderite.** (2) In the western United States, this term is used for light sapphire-blue **chalcedony.**

sappir. A foreign word Hebraicised. Almost every authority is agreed that the modern lapis lazuli is the stone described under that name. Fifth stone in the Breastplate of the High Priest. Old versions of Bible translate as *sapphirus* or *sapphiri*, but most probably a lapis lazuli. Engraved with the name Issachar.

sard. The translucent brown to reddish-brown variety of **chalcedony.** It is similar to **carnelian** but the colors are less intense; i.e., more brownish and somewhat darker.

sard agate. Banded agate similar to sardonyx in coloring except bands are not straight and parallel.

Sarder (German). Sard.

sardium. A name for **sard** which has been artificially colored brown.

sardoine (Fr.) Sard.

sardónice (Span.). Sardonyx.

sardonyx (sar'don-iks). Chalcedony (agate) with straight parallel bands or layers of reddish-brown to brown alternating with other colors. Name is used incorrectly for (a) carnelian and, (b) more often, for **sard** or **carnelian onyx.**

sard stone. Name variously applied to (1) sard; (2) sardonyx.

satelite. A trade name for fibrous **serpentine** from Tulare County, California, with slightly **chatoyant effect.**

satin spar. (1) Translucent fibrous, silky white **gypsum.** When cut cabochon, has a pearly **chatoyant effect.** From England, Russia and other sources. (2) less correctly **aragonite** (calcite) of the same description which is more accurately called calcite satin spar. See **Niagara spar.**

satin stone. Same as **satin spar.**

saussurite. A jade substitute. A compact altered feldspar consisting chiefly of **zoisite.** Greenish or white. H. 6-7; S.G. 3.2-3.3; R.I. 1.70/1.70. From Switzerland, Lake Superior and elsewhere.

sautoir, or lariat. A string of approximately equal-size pearls measuring between 31 and 47 inches in length. Also called a **rope.**

sawing. In fashioning, this process of grinding a narrow slit through a gemstone is usually accomplished by a metal disc charged with an abrasive. Phosphor bronze charged with diamond is used for diamonds and other valuable gemstones, sheet iron and diamond for less valuable ones, and the **mud-saw** for inexpensive ones.

"Saxon or **Saxony chrysolite."** Pale greenish-yellow topaz.

"Saxon" or **"Saxony topaz."** (1) Incorrect term for citrine. (2) Correct term for genuine yellow topaz from Saxony, although rarely used in U.S.A.

Sb. Abbr. for the element antimony.

scale. (1) The portion of a weighing instrument which holds the object to be weighed. (2) The weighing instrument or balance itself, as the **Berman balance.** (3) A series or group of lines or graduations placed on some substance. (4) In *descriptive mineralogy*, same as a plate or **tabular crystal.**

scaly. In mineralogy consisting of scales or **tabular crystals.**

scapolite. A group of minerals consisting of meionite, wernerite, mizzonite, and marialite. In gemology no distinction is made between them, all being called scapolite. Gem varieties are very rare and are transparent to translucent; yellow, pink, blue or violet. The last three produce well-defined cat's-eyes (rare). Tetr. H. 6.5; S.G. 2.6-2.7; R.I. 1.54/1.55-1.55/1.57; Bi. 0.016-0.022; Disp. 0.016. From Brazil and Madagascar (yellow only) and Burma (all gem colors).

scarab. A gemstone or other substance fashioned into a conventionalized representation of a *Scarabaeus* beetle which, especially *Scarabaeus sacer*, was worshipped by ancient Egyptians as a symbol of fertility and resurrection. Fashioned by them in minerals, metals or ceramics, especially faience, with inscriptions on the base. Were used as talismans and ornaments and were buried with the dead. These and modern scarabs have been mounted in jewelry, especially finger rings. Their intaglio-cut bases are also used as seals. All modern seal rings are probably a development of the scarab and the **cylinder.**

scenic agate. Practically same as **landscape agate.**

scepter quartz. Quartz forming in a crystal resembling a scepter in shape.

Schettler Emerald. Emerald weighing 87.64 carats; cut in India. In Am. Mus. Natural Hist. N. Y.

schiller. A **phenonenom** related to **sheen.** An almost metallic iridescent shimmer seen just below the surface in certain directions in certain minerals as in bastite, bronzite, hypersthene, etc. Differs markedly in appearance from any other optical phenomenon except adularescence and aventurescence.

"schiller chrysolite." Misnomer for **chrysoberyl cat's-eye.**

schiller obsidian. Obsidian with schiller effect.

schiller quartz. Quartz cat's-eye.

schiller spar. Same as **bastite.**

schist (shist). A metamorphic rock with a highly developed parallel or foliated structure, along which it splits easily.

schmelze (glass). (1) Any one of the various kinds of decorative glass especially the variety that is colored red with a metallic salt, as copper or gold, and used to flash white glass (Standard). (2) A term which has been defined, apparently in error, as a particular kind of ancient glass which was green in color, but red by transmitted light, similar to **Solomon's gem.**

Schmuckstein (German). A term which distinguishes either "semiprecious" or ornamental stone from *Edelstein.*

Schnecken or **Schneckenstein topaz.** Genuine topaz. Same as **Saxon topaz.**

schnide. Bluish glassy common opal from Queensland.

schorl. (1) Black tourmaline; (2) An old name for the tourmaline species.

Schwefelkies (German). **Pyrite.**

"scientific brilliant." Term unsuccessfully coined for early synthetic colorless sapphire

"scientific emerald." (1) Originally a misleading trade name for emerald-colored beryllium glass. (2) Any green glass imitation of emerald.

scientific gem. Same as **scientific stone.**

"scientific ruby." Red glass.

"scientific sapphire." Blue glass.

scientific stones. A term correctly used for reconstructed or synthetic stones, but often used misleadingly for various imitations.

"scientific topaz." (1) A name for the first synthetic sapphires which were pale pink (2) Topaz-colored glass.

scintillation. Scintillation in gemstones can be defined broadly as an alternating display of reflections from the polished facets of a gemstone seen by the observer as either the illuminant, the gemstone or the observer is in motion — a flashing or twinkling of light from the facets. Comparative scintillation, or the degree of scintillation, is determined by (1) the number of facets on the stone that will reflect light to the eye as the stone is moved about (i.e., the number of individual reflections); (2) the quality of polish of the facets, since the more highly polished the facets, the brighter the reflections and hence the stronger the reflections from them; and (3) the brilliancy of the stone and thus the degree to which light is returned to the eye after refraction into the stone and back out through the crown.

scissors cut. A modification of the step cut which increases the **scintillation** of stones of lower **R.I.** such as quartz, beryl, topaz, tourmaline, etc., by breaking up the long running facets, next the girdle, into four triangular facets, and usually the corner facets into two or four facets of triangular or other shapes.

sclerometer. An instrument for determining the degree of hardness of a mineral by measuring the comparative pressure necessary to scratch it with a moving diamond point.

scoop stone. A name for amber dredged from Baltic Sea.

scorpion stone. Coral or jet.

"Scotch" pebble. One of several varieties of quartz, chiefly cairngorm.

"Scotch" or Scottish pearl. Freshwater pearl from Scotland.

"Scotch" or Scottish stone. Cairngorm.

"Scotch or Scottish topaz." Same as **topaz quartz.**

screw micrometer. See **micrometer.**

sea amber. Amber which has been scooped from the ocean or found on the beaches. Its surface is devoid of the incrustations natural to mined amber unless they have been artificially removed to imitate sea amber. See **scoop stone.**

seam. A thin vein; also a bed in stratified (layered) rocks, as a seam of coal.

seam opal. (1) Masses of common opal with bands of precious white opal from White Cliffs, New South Wales, Australia. (2) A name for **sandstone opal.** (3) A form of White Cliffs white opal found in thin, flat cakes, sometimes without adhering matrix. It sometimes consists of both common and precious opal.

sea pearl. Same as **salt-water pearl.**

seastone. Amber.

seaweed agate. A descriptive term for certain specimens of **mocha stone** or **moss agate.**

Seberget. Same as **Zeberged.**

secondary deposit. A deposit consisting of minerals (1) which have been altered or decomposed from minerals which occupied the same deposit, or (2) which have been transported from the place in which they were formed, as into an **alluvial deposit** (for instance, the secondary deposits of sapphires in gem gravels).

secondary twinning. Twinning produced subsequently to the original formation of a crystal, or crystalline mass, due to pressure, causing the inversion of the atomic pattern of the crystal structure in certain lamellae. The cause of parting.

sectile. Capable of being cut as into slices or shavings.

sedimentary rock. That formed by the consolidation of sediments deposited from the agent (water or air) that transported them; e.g., sandstone or shale.

sedimentation. The deposition of materials being transported by water.

seed pearl. A name for any **true pearl** of rounded irregular shape weighing less than ¼ **pearl grain.**

selective absorption. See **absorption.**

selective reflection. The reflection by a substance, such as an opaque gem, of light rays of only certain wave lengths, the others being absorbed. This cause of color in gems is a sort of selective **absorption.**

selenita (Span.). Moonstone (feldspar).

selenite (sel'e-nite). Colorless **gypsum** occurring in crystals or large cleavage masses. Used as an **ornamental stone,** especially in Russia.

selenites. (Obsolete) Moonstone.

semeline. Same as **spinthere.**

semence (Fr.). **Seed pearl.**

semibastard amber. Partly cloudy **bastard amber.**

semicarnelian. An old and undesirable name for yellow **carnelian.**

semicrystalline. Partly crystalline or partly amorphous.

semigenuine doublet or **triplet.** See **doublet, triplet.**

semiopal. Term loosely used for (1) common opal; (2) hydrophane; (3) any partially dehydrated common opal.

semiprecious. An indeterminate and misleading classification that includes all gemstones other than the so-called precious stones; i.e., diamond, ruby, emerald, sapphire and pearl. It does not recognize the fact that a poor-quality ruby may be far less costly than a fine specimen of jadeite, for example. **Gemstone** is a word that is being used with increasing frequency to include all fashioned gem materials. See also **precious stones, ornamental stones, decorative stone.**

semitranslucent. A degree of diaphaneity between translucent and opaque. P a s s e s l i g h t through edges of cabochons but very little through thicker parts.

semitransparent. A degree of diaphaneity between transparent and translucent. Objects may be seen, but imperfectly, through thick sections of semitransparent material, and quite clearly through thinner parts.

"semiturquoise." A term which has been used for soft pale blue turquoise or turquoise-like mineral.

sepiolite (seep'-e-oh-lite). The mineralogical name for **meerschaum.**

serpentine. A translucent-to-opaque mineral of many colors. Has been used for cameos, intaglios, and as an ornamental or decorative stone. Only greenish gemstone varieties of gemological importance, principally as jade substitutes. Mono. H_4 $Mg_3Si_2O_9$. H. 2½-4, or rarely to 6; S.G. 2.50-2.65; R.I. varies from 1.49-1.57. Source widely distributed. See **bowenite, williamsite, verde antique; precious serpentine.**

"serpentine cat's-eye." Same as **satelite.**

"serpentine jade." A term sometimes used for **bowenite.**

serpentine marble. Same as **verde antique.**

serpentine ware. A variety of Wedgwood; colored and marked to resemble **serpentine.**

Serra points. Term applied to loose amethyst crystals (detached from their geodes) in Southern Brazil. See **amethyst points.**

Serra stone. Agate from Serra do Mar (Mountains), in the state of Rio Grande do Sul, in Southern Brazil.

setting. Same as **mounting.** More specifically, only that portion of the mounting which actually holds a stone, as distinguished from the rest of the mounting to which the setting is attached, such as the shank of a ring.

S.G. Abbreviation for **specific gravity.**

shade. In color terminology (1) any dark tone of a **hue**; (2) incorrectly used as a synonym of **hue.**

shale. A fine-grained sedimentary rock, formed from beds of clay, mud or silt.

shamir. In Jewish legends a miraculous stone used in engraving the names of the twelve tribes on the stones of the High Priest's Breastplate. Thought to be corundum (emery).

Shanghai jade. Any jadeite or nephrite from Shanghai, China's largest jade market before World War II.

shank pearl. Same as **chank pearl.**

Shark's Bay pearl. Yellowish to yellow pearl from Shark's Bay, Western Australia. Sometime classed as **colored pearl.** It is produced by the mollusc known as *Pinctada Carcharium.*

sharp-cornered emerald cut. A 30-facet **square emerald** cut with but four equal sides, and therefore with a girdle outline which is square.

Shebo or **Shebho.** The eighth stone in the Breastplate of the High Priest. Translated as *achates* (agate). Probably a grey and white banded agate. Engraved with name Benjamin.

sheen. The effect of a mineral's body texture on its surface luster. For example, unpolished tiger's-eye has a silky appearance; after polishing, however, it loses this appearance on the surface, but the effect is still visible in the body of the stone.

shell (cutting). A cabochon with base or back hollowed out to lighten the color or to eliminate undesirable inclusions. A garnet so fashioned is called a garnet shell; a sard is called a sard shell.

shell agate. Agate containing silicified mollusc shells.

shell cameo. A cameo carved from shell with raised figure cut from white layers and the background cut away to the darker layers.

"shell cat's-eye." (1) The "trap door," or **operculum,** of the marine gastropod **Turbo Petholatus,** a sea snail. It is usually about one-half to one inch in diameter and is domed and oval or round, with round markings of yellowish to white and reddish to dark brown and green. It does not have either the long, narrow pupil of a gemstone cat's-eye or the movable effect of that "eye." Source: the waters north of Australia to Indochina. (2) A cabochon cut from a portion of a nacreous shell; usually dyed.

sherry topaz. (1) **Topaz** the color of sherry wine. (2) An incorrect name for **citrine** of the same color.

Shoham. The eleventh stone in the Breastplate of the High Priest. Usually translated as **onyx.** Engraved with the name of Gad.

shwelu. In India, a light green jadeite gemstone with spots and streaks.

Si. Abbr. for silicon.

"Siam or Siamese aquamarine." An incorrect but rarely used term for blue zircon or for greenish spinel.

Siam or Siamese ruby. (1) Any ruby from Siam. (2) Dark slightly brownish or orangy-red ruby, regardless of its source, as distinguished from true red to purplish red **Burma** or **oriental** ruby. (3) Misnomer for dark red **spinel.**

Siam or Siamese sapphire. Very dark-blue sapphire from Thailand (Siam). As an American trade grade, the term refers to a less-desirable sapphire than those from Kashmir or Burma. However, some very lovely sapphires are mined in Thailand.

Siam zircon. (1) Blue zircon, usually from Cambodia. Imported to Thailand (Siam) as brownish or grayish stones that are usually heat treated and fashioned in Bangkok before being exported. (2) Zircon from the less-important Thailand mines.

Siberian amethyst. A long-established trade grade that refers to the most desirable hues of amethyst, which range from deep purplish red to purple red.

Siberian aquamarine. Same as **Mursinka aquamarine.**

"Siberian chrysolite." Demantoid garnet.

Siberian emerald. Same as **Russian emerald.**

Siberian garnet. Almandine garnet.

Siberian jade. Nephrite from Siberia, fine almost emerald-green qualities being found in Lake Baikal region.

Siberian lapis. Lapis lazuli from south of Irkutsk, near Baikal. Seldom as fine color as other **Russian lapis,** or as Afghanistan lapis, but more translucent and with fewer pyrite inclusions.

"Siberian ruby." Rubellite from Urals.

Siberian topaz. A term used for (1) **Uralian topaz;** (2) colorless, bluish, or yellow to brown topaz from Trans-Baikal, in the region around Nerchinsk; and (3) blue, yellow or green topaz from Kamchatka.

Siberian tourmaline. Light violetish red (rubellite) to violet tourmaline from the Urals.

siberite. A purplish **rubellite.**

Sicilian amber. Simetite.

siderite (sid-er-ite). (1) A name for **sapphire quartz.** (2) More correctly the name of a mineral species of no gemological interest.

Siegstein (German, meaning "victory stone.") Has been applied to **star sapphire.**

Siegstone. Incorrectly coined word combining English and

German. See **Siegstein.**

silica. A white or colorless, extremely hard, crystalline silicon dioxide (SiO_2) found pure as quartz, in many rocks and sands, and combined with various other metallic oxides in all the silicate minerals, a group of minerals which yield many gem varieties.

silica glass. (1) An artificial glass made by fusing quartz in an oxy-hydrogen flame. Hardness, 5; specific gravity, 2.20; refractive index, 1.46. (2) A pale, yellowish-green **natural glass,** 98% silica, much more than in moldavite or obsidian. It was discovered in 1932 on the Libyan Desert, after meteorites had struck the sand.

silicate. Any material containing silicon and oxygen in the anion — usually in a multiple of SiO_4 in which the oxygen atom occupies tetrahedral positions with silicon at the center. These are combined with metals to form most of the rock-making minerals.

siliceous or **silicious.** Of, pertaining to, or containing **silica.**

"siliceous malachite." Green **chrysocolla.**

silicified (si-lis'i-fide). Converted into quartz or opal.

silicified wood. A term which includes all those varieties of **petrified wood** that have been converted into **silica.**

silicon carbide. An abrasive of importance in fashioning **colored stones;** powdered in a binder, or molded into fashioning wheels or tools.

silk. Microscopically small inclusions in ruby or sapphire; subsurface reflections which produce a whitish sheen resembling the sheen of silk fabric. Inclusions now generally conceded to be tiny needles of rutile, although some authorities still mention canals or negative crystals. See **pseudosilk.**

silky luster. A silklike sheen, a reflection from fibers in fibrous crystalline aggregates such as tiger eye. See also **chatoyancy.**

sillimanite. Same as **fibrolite.**

"sillimanite cat's-eye." Same as **"fibrolite cat's-eye."**

silt. A fine-grained, uncemented alluvial deposit.

silt pearl. See **mud pearl.**

"Silver Peak jade." Local Nevada term for **malachite.**

silver. A metallic element and precious metal.

silver stone. Moonstone.

"simaostone." Simav opal.

simav opal or **stone.** Opal from mine near city and sea of that name N. E. of Smyrna, Turkey. Colorless, milky or brownish; also yellow, orange or red varieties, some with same play of color as that in **fire opal.**

simetite (sim'e-tite). Amber from the waters off Sicily. Red to light orange yellow or brown, contains less succinic acid; usually darker than succinite. Also strong yellowish green or bluish sheen, due to fluorescence. Better known as Sicilian amber.

simili. A name for lead glass imitations of colorless gemstones.

"Simon stone." Simav opal.

simple cabochon. See **cabochon.**

simulated hematite. See **imitation hematite.**

simulated stone. Any substance fashioned as a gemstone which imitates it in appearance. An advertising term widely used in

U. S. A. but not often by better jewelry stores.

Singhalese cat's-eye, Singhalese garnet, etc. Same as **Ceylon cat's-eye, Ceylon garnet,** etc.

single bevel cut. A style with beveled sides, flat top and flat base, used for opaque stones.

single cabochon. Same as **simple cabochon.**

single circle goniometer. See **goniometer.**

single cut. A brilliant form of cut with but eighteen facets, eight bezel, eight pavilion, a table and a culet.

single refraction. When a ray of light enters a crystal of the isometric system, or an amorphous substance, it is refracted in the normal manner; this is single refraction in contradistinction to **double refraction.**

singly terminated crystals. See **termination.**

sinhalite. A transparent, light to dark greenish-brown, yellowish-brown or brown mineral species; also black. First identified and described as a new mineral in 1952, it was long thought to be brown peridot. Chemical composition, a magnesium-aluminum-iron borate $(Mg(Al,Fe)BO_4)$; crystal system, orthorhombic; hardness, 6 to 7; specific gravity, 3.47 to 3.50; refractive index, 1.667-1.705; birefringence, .038; dispersion, .017. Sources: Ceylon and Burma.

Sinkiang jade. Nephrite fom Sinkiang, Chinese Turkestan.

sinopal or **sinople.** An aventurescent quartz with inclusions of a red iron mineral. From Hungary.

sintered synthetic spinel. This lapis-lazuli substitute is made by heavily charging finely ground synthetic spinel with cobalt oxide and sintering the combination to the point of semifusion, at 2135°. It is recompacted by pressure, producing an opaque, intense, blue to violetish-blue material. The pyrite inclusions of genuine lapis-lazuli can be imitated by adding gold filings. It is made in flat plates about three millimeters thick and in spheres of several millimeters. The properties are near those of transparent synthetic spinel. See **synthetic spinel.**

"Sioux Falls jasper." A decorative brown jasper-like fine-grained quartz, from Sioux Falls, So. Dakota. Used for tables and interior architectural trim.

Siriam garnet. (1) Almandine garnet. Same as **Syriam garnet.** (2) Same as **grenat Siriam.**

sirippu pearl. Ceylonese trade grade for a pearl grooved with irregular wrinkle-like furrows.

skeleton crystals. Those with edges defined, but with faces not fully filled in, as crystals of ice on window panes.

skew facet. An old name for eight of the sixteen top break facets on the old style cushion-shaped diamond.

skiagram. A name sometimes used instead of **radiograph** for X-ray photograph of pearls.

skill facet. A name for certain top and bottom **break facets.** Now distinguished from other **break facets** only by diamond cutters. Term has also been incorrectly defined as being synonymous with **star facet.**

skin. As applied to pearls, the outer layer of nacre.

skinning. Same as **peeling.**

slitting. A term used for the sawing of **colored stones.** Usually accomplished with a thin soft metal wheel or disc which revolves vertically. The operation precedes **grinding.**

slitting wheel. The saw used in **slitting** colored stones.

slug (pearl). Trade term for very irregular distorted fresh-water **pearl** frequently composed of intergrown masses, groups or clusters of small pearls. Often without luster.

slush box. Container about the polishing wheel which collects the **mud** often used in **lapping.**

Smaragd (German). Emerald.

smaragdine (Rare). Of, or pertaining to **emerald.**

smaragdite (smar - ahgd' - dite). A massive, foliated, bright-green **amphibole.** Smaragdite is composed of actinolite, hornblende, diallage, red corundum and other minerals, which, because of its resultant great variation in hardness, makes it difficult to cut. It has been substituted for jade. An alternate name for the material is **edenite.**

smaragdmatrix. Emerald. Feldspar and quartz embedded with emerald.

smaragdolin. Trade name of a Viennese firm for a glass imitation of **emerald** which was usually beryl glass and was sold in boules shaped like those of synthetic corundum. H. 5-5.5; S.G. 3.3.-3.45; R.I. 1.62

smaragdus (Latin). Emerald; which name, in Latin, includes most green stones.

Smaryll. A trademarked name for a **triplet** consisting of a transparent, colorless beryl crown and a colorless, flawed-beryl pavilion, joined together by a green organic cement.

smeraldo (Italian). Emerald.

Smith refractometer. A very small gemological refractometer that employed a segment of a hemisphere of highly refractive glass in a nonrotating mount. It was suitable for use in the hand. See **Rayner Refractometer, Tully Refractometer, Erb & Gray Refractometer, Duplex Refractometer.**

smithsonite. A usually translucent to semitranslucent but rarely transparent mineral species, occurring in white or light tones of grayish green, greenish blue, green, blue, brown, yellow, pink or banded material. It is occasionally cut in the cabochon form. The better light-blue qualities sometimes resemble turquois and the apple-green colors are sometimes substituted for jade or chrysoprase. Chemical composition, zinc carbonate ($ZnCO_3$); crystal system, hexagonal (usually in compact, stalactitic or granular masses and is often associated with **hemimorphite,** a zinc silicate); hardness, 5 to 5½; specific gravity, 4.10 to 4.65; refractive index, 1.62-1.85; birefringence, .230. Sources: notable localities include Australia, Greece, Germany, Sardinia, Italy, Rhodesia, South-West Africa, Scotland, N.M., Mo., and Ark.

smoky opal. Smoky-brown common opal.

smoky quartz. Smoky greyish-brown to almost black crystalline quartz. Much of it, by heating, becomes yellow to yellow-brown **topaz quartz.** See **cairngorm, morion.**

"smoky topaz." Smoky quartz.

Sn. Abbr. for the element tin.

snowflake obsidian. Obsidian containing white patches of crystallized silica resembling snowflakes. Also called **flowering obsidian.** See **obsidian.**

soap-rock. Soapstone.

soapstone. Steatite. However, much agalmatolite is loosely called soapstone, as is also **saponite** which, however, is of no gemological interest.

Sobrisky opal. Opal from Lead Pipe Spring district, Death Valley, Calif.

soda-jadeite. Burma jadeite as distinguished from **diopside jadeite.**

sodalite. A semitransparent to semitranslucent, light- to dark-blue mineral species, often mottled or veined with nephelite, cancrinite and other minerals; also, white, gray and pink. It is frequently used as a substitute for **lapis-lazuli** ("Canadian lapis"), although it rarely contains the pyrite inclusions of lapis. Sodalite is popular for cabochons, tumbled gems and a variety of ornamental objects. Chemical composition, sodium-aluminum chlorosilicate ($Na_4Cl(AlSiO_4)_3$); crystal system, isometric (crystals rare; ordinarily found in compact, cleavable, nodular or disseminated masses); hardness, 5 to 6; specific gravity, 2.20 to 2.40; refractive index, near 1.48. Sources: Ontario and British Columbia, Canada, India, Bolivia, Brazil, Italy, Russia, Norway, Mont. and Me.

sodium light. Light emitted by the glowing vapor of sodium, consisting of two sets of light waves of slightly different wave lengths, and commonly considered to be a **monochromatic light.** Used with the **refractometer** to produce more well-defined readings than can be obtained with white light. Special **monochromators,** employing special electric bulbs and special filters, produce similar light consisting of but a few wave lengths, and such light is also popularly known as sodium light.

sodium vapor lamp. A light source derived from an electrical discharge through sodium vapor. Valuable as a source of monochromatic yellow (sodium or D-line) illumination, which when used as illumination in using the usual gemological **refractometer,** assists the efficiency of the instrument.

"soldered emerald." A name for any **emerald doublet,** but correctly for a fused one only.

soldier's stone. Amethyst.

"solid gold." Term once used incorrectly for gold or any alloy of gold of over 10 parts of gold. Based on the standard of pure gold, consisting of 24 parts. Thus 14 karat gold contains 14 parts of pure gold. See **alloy.**

solidification. The process of changing from a liquid or gas to a solid, as, for instance, the solidification of molten alumina to solid in the synthesis of corundum.

solitaire (French, *alone*). Used in English to mean a ring containing a single gem and often extended to mean a ring containing one important gem, with comparatively unimportant stones set in the shank (or finger band).

Solomon's gem. Probably paste which was green by **reflected light** and red in **transmitted light.** Said to have been made in Alexandria of the Roman world. See **Schmelze glass.**

Somondoco emerald. (1) In the trade, a term sometimes used for emerald from the Somondoco district, Colombia, and therefore for **Chivor emerald** which constitutes most of the emerald from the district. A few of these are fine quality. (2) More specifically, emerald from the Somondoco mine, which was mined by the Inca Indians, then hidden from the Spanish conquerors.

Sonstadt's solution. An amber-colored saturated solution of potassium mercuric iodide in water. S.G. 3.196 reducible by dilution in water; R.I. 1.733. A **heavy liquid.** Same as **Thoulet solution.**

"Soochow or Soochoo jade." Originally a combination of jade and quartz, but a term now used for serpentine, agalmatolite, dyed soapstone and similar jade substitutes.

soudé emerald. Same as **soldered emerald.**

source (of a gemstone). A term used in gemology to mean the geographical location in which a species or variety of gemstone is found or mined.

"South African jade." Same as **"Transvaal jade."**

"South African nephrite." Same as"**Transvaal nephrite."**

South African tourmaline. Same as **Transvaal tourmaline.**

South African turquoise. Turquoise **of** fine blue color found in limited quantity in Kimberly neighborhood.

Southern Cross Pearl. Same as **Great Southern Cross.**

South Sea pearl. A term which might refer to any pearl found in Oceania or Micronesia, but which is usually used only for **cultured pearl** from Palau or other islands held by Japan before World War II, to distinguish it from pearl cultured in Japan.

space lattice. See **lattice.**

spalmandite. A contraction of spessartite and almandite for garnets of intermediate composition.

Spaltbarkeit (German). Cleavage; cleavability.

Span. Abbr. used in this book for Spanish (language).

spandite. A contraction of spessartite-andradite applied to garnets; intermediate in chemical composition between spessartite and andradite.

Spanish amethyst. A term formerly used for fine purple amethysts of unknown origin, marketed through Spain.

Spanish citrine. Citrine from Spain, especially that called "Hinjosa topaz."

Spanish emerald. (1) South American emerald, which came into Europe through Spain during and after the conquest of Peru, was usually called Spanish emerald. Even today, a particularly beautiful emerald is sometimes referred to by this term in Europe. (2) In the American jewelry trade, a common misnomer for a greenglass imitation of emerald.

Spanish jet. Jet of good quality from Aragon and Oviedo, Spain.

"Spanish lazulite." Iolite.

"Spanish topaz." (1) A trade term broadly used for any orange to orange-red **citrine.** (2) More specifically, that citrine called **"Hinjosa topaz."** See also **"Madeira topaz."**

spar. In mineralogy, the equivalent of the German word "spath" meaning a crystalline mineral found in the fields, as feldspath (feldspar). Most of these spars are more or less vitreous, and easily cleavable as feldspar and fluorspar.

spat. Spat is the term used to refer to the young cultured-pearl-producing molluscs during their free-swimming period to the point at which they attach themselves to rocks and other solid objects. Special cages with darkened interiors are used to gather the swimming spat to anchor them.

species. A mineralogical division. All the varieties in any one species have the same basic properties such as refractive index, specific gravity, and hardness; but they may vary widely in form, color, and transparency. See **variety.**

specific gravity (abbr. S.G.). The ratio of the density of any substance to that of water at 4°c. S.G. of gems is usually obtained by **hydrostatic weighing.** See also **Berman balance.**

specific-gravity attachments. The accessories used in conjunction with a **diamond balance** for obtaining the specific gravity of gemstones by the **hydrostatic weighing** method. They consist of a beaker, beaker stand, wire stone basket and wire counterbalance.

specific gravity bottle or **pycnometer.** An especially made water bottle with a drilled glass stopper so marked that it can always contain a definite amount of water. Used for determining S.G. of liquid, powders and small fragments (and, rarely small loose stones) by **direct weighing method.**

specimen. (1) Term broadly used to refer to any single gem or piece of rough as distinguished from the entire variety or species. (2) More especially if it is representative of the class or exemplifies an unusual property.

Speckstein (German). **Steatite.**

spectacle stone (obsolete). Popular name for **selenite.**

spectra. Plural for spectrum.

spectral colors. Same as **spectrum colors** or **primary colors.**

spectrolite. A coined name for a multihued type of **labradorite** with a dark body color from southeastern Finland.

spectroscope. An optical instrument for forming and examining spectra, by the dispersion of light into its component wave lengths: (1) by diffraction through a **grating** (the diffraction spectroscope); or (2) by refraction through a **prism** (the prismatic spectroscope). Used in determinative gemology for observing the comparative absorption of different hues in different stones.

Spectroscope Unit. An instrument designed and manufactured by the Gemological Institute of America to provide the precise lighting necessary to maximize the usefulness of the spectroscope. The variable-intensity transmitted beam is passed through the prism to reduce heating in the specimen, an iris diaphragm controls and directs beam size, and a folding arm permits light to be reflected from above. The scale is lighted and three motions are possible on the spectroscope.

spectroscopy. (spek-tros' ko-py). The science pertaining to the use of the spectroscope and phenomena observed by it.

spectrum. A word which (1) as used generally and in fundamental gemology refers to the **visible spectrum.** (2) As used in physics or advanced gemology may refer to **electromagnetic spectrum**, or to that portion of it which includes the **infra-red** and **ultra-violet** as well as the invisible spectrum. See also **absorption spectrum; emission spectrum.**

spectrum, absorption. See **absorption.**

spectrum colors. The hues into which white light is separated upon passing through a prism. Six of these hues are easily distinguished by the eye: red, orange, yellow, green, blue and violet. See **visible spectrum.**

spectrum, emission. See **emission spectrum.**

specular hematite. The metallic dark grey to black variety of **hematite.**

specular iron. Same as **specular hematite.**

specular reflection. Reflection of light from the surface only, as distinguished from reflection of light from positions below the surface.

speculum. Medieval name for the crystal ball used in divination.

sperm-whale ivory. A coarse kind of ivory, resembling bone more than ivory, from the teeth of the sperm whale, or cachalot *(Physter Catodon)*. It is used occasionally for carving small ornamental objects. Hardness, 2¾; specific gravity, 1.90 to 2.00; refractive index, 1.55 to 1.57. Source: the warmer parts of all oceans.

spessartine. The French word, sometimes used in England, for **spessartite.**

spessartite (spess'-ar-tite). The transparent, yellow-orange to orangy-red, orangy-brown or reddish-brown species of the **garnet** group. Gem-quality material, which usually approaches an orange color, is quite rare. Chemical composition, manganese-aluminum silicate $(Mn_3Al_2(SiO_4)_3)$; crystal system, isometric; hardness, 7 to 7½; specific gravity, 4.12 to 4.18; refractive index, 1.79 to 1.82 (usually 1.81); birefringence, none; dispersion, .027. Sources: Ceylon, Brazil, Virginia, Malagasy Republic, East Africa, Calif., Nevada and Colo. Garnet is the birthstone for January, and it is correct to use spessartite or any other member of the garnet group for this purpose.

sphaerule, sphaerolite or **sphaerulite.** (1) Synonymous terms used in mineralogy to describe a radiating spherical group of minute acicular or prismatic crystals or **crystallites**; a spherical body having a radiated structure. Occur particularly in some vitreous volcanic rocks such as obsidian and/or perlite, also in agate (Wild), and in nephrite (Schlossmacher). (2) The word *sphaerulite* has also been suggested as a name for an **obsidian** containing sphaerulites of crystallites.

sphalerite. (sfal' or sfael'er-ite). A mineral closely approaching diamond in refractive index and atomic structure. When transparent and yellow to brownish yellow is sometimes cut as a gem and has higher dispersion than any other genuine gem.Too soft and easily cleaved for practical use in jewelry. Iso. ZnS; H. 3.5-4; S.G. 4.0-4.1; R.I. 2.37; Disp. 0.157. From Spain, Mexico and other sources. **Syn. Rutile** has higher dispersion.

sphene. A transparent-to-opaque rose red, yellow to green, brown, grey or black mineral of high refractive index. Gem varieties are transparent yellow to greenish and are in great demand by collectors for their brilliancy and exceptional fire. Mono. CaTiSiO$_5$; H. 5-5.5; S. G. 3.4-3.6; R.I. 1.88/1.99-1.91/2.05; Bi. 0.105-0.135. Disp. 0.52. Switzerland, Ceylon, Ontario, Quebec, New York, Pennsylvania and other sources. Its mineralogical name is *titanite*.

spherical aberration. See **aberration.**

spherulitic jasper. Jasper with inclusions of spherulites which are usually quartz. If they are of different color from the jasper it is usually an **orbicular jasper.**

Spiller amber. An obsolete name for **pressed amber.**

spinach jade. Dark green **nephrite.**

spinel (speh-nel'). A transparent to opaque, red to purplish-red, intense orange-red **(flame spinel),** light to dark orangy-red, light to dark slightly grayish-blue, greenish-blue, grayish-green, light to dark purple to violet, very dark green to black mineral species **(pleonaste** or **ceylonite).** The latter two colors find very little use as gemstones. A characteristic of spinel is its low-intensity ("grayed-out") colors. Chemical composition, a double oxide of magnesium and aluminum (MgAl$_2$O$_4$); crystal system, isometric; hardness, 8; specific gravity, 3.57 to 3.90; refractive index, 1.715 to 1.720 (rarely as high as 1.765); dispersion, .020. Principal sources: Burma and Ceylon. See **synthetic spinel, synthetic stone.**

"spinel ruby." Red spinel.

"spinel sapphire." Blue spinel.

spinel twin. Variety of **contact twin** which is typical of twin crystals of spinel and which consists of two identical but reversed portions of **octahedrons** joined on a plane which is parallel to a face of the octahedron.

spinthere. Greenish **sphene.**

splendent. Very bright by reflected light.

splintery fracture. Breakage which produces elongated splinter-like fragments.

split facet. Break or cross facet.

spodumene (spod'-u-meen). A transparent mineral species occurring in the **pyroxene** group. Its color varieties are pink to light violet **kunzite);** intense light to medium green to yellowish green **(hiddenite);** light yellow; greenish yellow or colorless; and, very rarely, light blue. Chemical composition, a lithium-aluminum silicate (LiAl(Si-

O$_3$)$_2$); crystal system, monoclinic; hardness, 6 to 7; specific gravity, 3.18; refractive index, 1.660-1.676; birefringence, .016; dispersion, .017. Sources: Calif., Brazil, Madagascar, N.C., Me., Conn. and Burma. See **kunzite, hiddenite.**

spread. Width of a stone at the girdle, especially if that width is so great, in proportion to the depth of the stone, that it markedly affects the possible beauty of the stone.

square. Term used in pearl trade for method of reckoning the cost of any pearl of any size at a lot price, by the square of price given, with the grain as a unit. See **base price.**

square cut. (1) Step cut with square outline and table. (2) A variation of this; a **fancy cut** with only four facets, or four facets and a culet, on the pavilion. (3) Any square stone.

square emerald cut. (1) Name often applied to any **emerald cut** in which the four longer sides of the table, of the culet and of the outline of the girdle are respectively of equal length; i.e., an octagon of four long, and four very short equal sides. (2) More specifically, an equal-sided **sharp-cornered emerald cut.**

square hexagon cut. See **hexagon cut.**

square method. A method of computing the value of pearls. See **base.**

stability. An aspect of durability, in addition to hardness and toughness, that refers to the ability of a gemstone to resist loss of color, dissolution by chemicals or other forms of deterioration. For example, pearl is damaged by weak acids, turquoise tends to become greenish when it absorbs skin oils and acids, and the color of kunzite tends to fade. However, most of the important gems are very stable.

Stachelbeerstein (German). Grossularite.

stage. The portion of a **microscope** on which the specimen is placed for observation. In a polarizing microscope used in pearl or gem-testing it rotates and is called a rotating stage. An *immersion stage* is a microscope stage which permits immersing the specimen. A *universal stage* or *universal motion stage* is a microscope stage which permits placement of the specimen in any desired position. Most universal stages are calibrated to permit measurement of the angle between any two positions. See **microscope.** A *universal immersion stage* is a microscope stage which affords universal motion of an immersed specimen. The stage is of the greatest value in gemological microscopy. An *endoscopic stage* is a microscope stage equipped with an *endoscope.* A *pearl testing stage,* if complete, is a microscope stage equipped with both a pearl endoscope and a **pearl illuminator.**

stained agate. See **stained stone.**

stained stone. A stone, the color of which has been altered (1) by dyeing with analine dyes, which fade or (2) by impregnation with a substance, like sugar, followed by either a chemical or heat treatment, which usually produce a permanent color. Cryptocrystalline quartz is especially adapted to staining, including agate, in which the bands become more pronounced.

stalactite. An inverted conical mineral formation, attached to the roof of a cave, formed by the percolation of mineral-bearing water.

stalagmite. A conical or cylindrical formation on the floor of a cave, produced t by the dripping of mineral-bearing water from the roof.

stalky. Consisting of slender columns, or long stout fibers (crystals).

standard brilliant. Term used to describe the usual 58 facet **brilliant cut** diamond with circular unpolished **girdle.** See **full cut brilliant.**

stantienite. A black fossil resin, rarely occurring in amber mines in East Prussia; of little or no gemological importance. Called black amber. See **true amber.**

star. (1) A rayed figure, normally of four to twelve rays, consisting of two or more intersecting bands of light, seen in an **epiasteria;** an optical phenomenon caused by reflected light from inclusions (or channels). Stars are usually four- or six-rayed, but three, five, seven, or nine-rayed stars occur, or are possible, due to absence of inclusions in a portion of the stone. (2) The stone itself; an epiasteria which must be cut cabochon to exhibit the light phenomenon. See **asteria; star stone.**

star agate. Agate exhibiting star-shaped figures.

star almandine sapphire. A correct name for purplish star sapphire which is usually misnamed "star ruby."

star amethystine sapphire. A correct name for violet star sapphire which is usually misnamed "star ruby."

"star beryl." A term which has been applied to **asteriated beryl.**

star chrysoberyl. A term applied to chrysoberyl specimens which have shown an indistinct unsymmetrical six-rayed star with two of the three streaks which make up the star closer to one another than either is to the third streak.

star cut. (1) A form of standard **brilliant cut** with 56 facets, table and culet, but with the lower break facets elongated until their points almost reach the culet; thus the pavilion facets roughly form a 16-rayed star. (2) A complicated brilliant form used for colored stones in which every portion but the table is covered with star (i.e., triangular) facets.

star diopside. Black, dark-greenish black, dark-brown to brown-black asteriated diopside showing a four-rayed star. Source: Nammakal, southern India. See **diopside.**

star doublet or **triplet.** Assembled stones which imitate star sapphire or ruby, consisting usually of (a) a cabochon top of some asteriated stone, usually decolorized rose quartz; (b) a thin mirror of sapphire or ruby color, sometimes indented with intersecting lines; and (usually) an unpolished domed back of some transparent-to-translucent substance which imitates the back of the genuine stone. Star sapphire has also been imitated by coating the back of decolorized rose quartz with a brilliant coloring substance. See **lacquer back;** also **starolite.**

star enstatite. Dark-brown asteriated enstatite showing a six-rayed star, usually poorly developed.

Source: southern India. See **enstatite**.

star facets. The triangular facets which immediately adjoin the table in a brilliant-cut stone.

star garnet (rare). Garnet displaying normally four-rayed or six-rayed, or both four-rayed and six-rayed epiasterism when cut cabochon. See **star**.

Starilian. A trademarked name for **strontium titanite**.

starlight. A distortion of the word **starlite**.

starlite. A name proposed by Kunz for blue zircon, but rarely used in U.S.A.

"star malachite." Chalcedony with inclusions of malachite arranged in the form of a star. A variety of **prase malachite**.

Star of Artaban. A 316 c. blue star sapphire in Smithsonian (U. S. National Museum), Washington.

Star of Asia. A 330-carat blue star sapphire in the Smithsonian Institution, Washington, D.C. It is said to be one of the finest of its kind in existence. From Burma.

Star of Destiny. The trademarked name for an **assembled stone** used to reproduce the appearance of star ruby and sapphire. It consists of a ceramic back, a synthetic corundum or spinel top, and a thin metallic film between the two. The star is caused by reflection of three sets of lines engraved on the base of the otherwise transparent top portion.

Star of India. A Ceylonese blue star sapphire of 563.35 c. Thought to be largest in world. Comparatively flawless, with well-defined star. In Am. Mus. of Nat. History, New York.

Star of the West. A 105 grain Australian pearl once sold for 6,500 pounds sterling.

starolite or **star-o-lite.** A manufacturer's trade name for a **star doublet** backed with a blue mirror.

star quartz. Asteriated rose quartz which often shows a star by transmitted light and sometimes by reflected light if cut cabochon. See also **starolite**.

star quartz doublet. A **star doublet** of asteriated quartz.

star ruby. A ruby epiasteria with normally six rays. The trade illogically but usually uses the same name for pink, purple or violet star sapphires. See **star; star amethystine sapphire; star almandine sapphire; syn. ruby**.

"star ruby sapphire." Pink, purple or violet star sapphires.

star sapphire. A sapphire **epiasteria** with normally six rays, rarely twelve. Bluish and gray are most frequent, although light purplish occurs often, and other colors rarely. See **star, syn. sapphire**.

star spinel (rare). Spinel displaying four-rayed or both four-rayed and six-rayed epiasterism on one stone. A seven-rayed epiasteria is in the collection of U. S. National Museum. See **star**.

star stone. (1) In general, any stone in which a rayed figure can be seen as in a **star sapphire, star agate, starolite**, or even in specimens of petrified wood in which (in its more transparent portions) numerous small star-like figures sometimes occur. (2) More correctly, an **asteria** only.

"star topaz." Yellow **star sapphire.**

"star zircon." See **"asteriated zircon "**

staurolite (sto'-roe-lite). The best-known variety of this mineral is the translucent to opaque, brown to black, interpenetrating twin-crystal type that occurs in the form of a 90- or 60-degree cross. Used without fashioning for amulets, charms and rosaries, these curio stones are variously called **fairy stone, cross stone, twin stone,** or **lapis crucifer.** Very rarely, transparent reddish-brown, yellowish-brown or brownish-black crystals occur. Chemical composition, a hydrous silicate of aluminum and iron ($HFeAl_5Si_2O_{13}$); crystal system, orthorhombic; hardness, 7 to $7\frac{1}{2}$; specific gravity, 3.65 to 3.75; refractive index, 1.736-1.746; birefringence, .010; dispersion, .021. Sources: Switzerland, Virginia, France, South-West Africa, Ga., Tenn., Me., N.H. and elsewhere.

stealite. Chiastolite.

steatite (stee-a-tite). A very soft and easily carved ornamental mineral (massive talc) sometimes used as an inferior substitute for jade. Brownish, greyish green, grey or almost white. Sometimes tinged with red. Ortho. or mono. (Dana) H. 1-2.5; S.G. 2.6-2.8; R.I. 1.54/1.59.

steinheilite. Cordierite.

stellate. Radiating so as to produce star-like forms.

step cut. A basic style of cutting in which all facets are four-sided and in steps or rows, both above, below and usually on the girdle; all parallel to girdle and therefore, except those on the corners, long and usually narrow. Two or three rows above and usually more below. Among many modifications are the **emerald cut, square cut, scissors cut.**

Stephen's stone. Same as **Saint Stephen's stone.**

stichtite (stick'-tite). An opaque, lilac to rose-colored mineral, often with veinings of serpentine. It is occasionally used for cabochons and carvings. Chemical composition, a hydrated magnesium - chromium-iron carbonate ($Mg_6Cr_2(OH)_{16}$-CO_34H_2O); crystal system, hexagonal (massive aggregates of platy micaceous crystals); hardness, $1\frac{1}{2}$ to 2; specific gravity, 2.15 to 2.22; refractive index, 1.518-1.545 (a single vague reading at about 1.53). Sources: Tasmania, the Transvaal, Morocco, Quebec and the Shetland Islands.

stilbite. A mineral which often forms cross-shaped twin crystals usable as ornaments. A substitute for **staurolite.** H. 3.5-4; S.G. 2.1-2.2.

stone. (1) Any small piece of rock or mineral. (2) In the gem trade the term usually implies a cut and polished mineral (or occasionally a rock, such as lapis lazuli or obsidian) or any artificial reproduction of, or substitute for it. See **gemstone.**

stone cameo. See **cameo.**

stone gauge. (1) A device for measuring gemstones, such as a **Leveridge gauge.** (2) A series of sizes, each of which is numbered, established as a standard and guide for ordering gemstones. (3) A card or plate with the various stone sizes shown as holes or printed shapes of appropriate dimensions for each size.

stone paper. A sheet of paper folded to form a pocket in which gemstones are contained. Usually, a durable paper stock is used. One or more sheets of similarly folded paper may be used to line and strengthen the outer paper. Weight, lot number and coded or uncoded prices are usually marked on the flap. Also called **diamond paper.**

strahlite. A name for **actinolite.**

strain. An irregularity in the usual orderly pattern of atoms in the crystal structure of a mineral, frequently caused in diamond by an inclusion of a tiny crystal or crystals of diamond or another mineral. Strain produces **anomalous double refraction** in diamond, garnet, spinel and other isometric (singly refractive) minerals.

strass. (1) **Flint glass** with high content of lead which results in relatively great S.G., R.I. and dispersion. It is the most common glass imitation of diamond. Also used to imitate other colored gemstones. See **paste.** (2) A term widely, but incorrectly used as a synonym of paste to mean any glass imitations of gems.

strata (plural of stratum). Layers. In geology, it usually refers to beds of sedimentary rock.

strawberry pearls. Large, pink, iridescent and lustrous baroques, fairly regular in shape, with the appearance of being thickly sanded under the nacre.

streak. The color of the powder of a mineral, which can be observed by drawing the mineral across a **streak plate,** a test of only occasional value in determinative gemology. See **hematite.**

streak plate. A piece of unglazed porcelain. See **streak.**

stria (stry'a). A line, especially one of a series of parallel lines as in groups of demarcation lines between differently colored layers seen in some genuine sapphires in which they are parallel and straight, and in synthetic sapphire in which they are parallel and curved. See **striations.**

striae (stry'ee). Plural of stria.

striated crystal. One with striae on the surface of a face or faces.

striations (strye-a'shuns). Striae, usually parallel, on the faces of crystals.

striped jasper. Same as **banded jasper.**

strontium titanate. A manufactured, transparent gem material that possesses a high degree of brilliancy and dispersion and little body color. It resembles a diamond in appearance, except for its excessive dispersion. Chemical composition, strontium titanium oxide ($SrTiO_3$); crystal system, isometric; hardness, 5 to $5\frac{1}{2}$; specific gravity, 5.13; refractive index, 2.409; birefringence, none; dispersion, .190. First produced by the Titanium Division of the Natural Lead Co., in 1955, it was distributed initially under the trade name *Starlian.* One present trade name is *Fabulite;* others are *Diagem, Wellington Stone,* etc.

Stuart Sapphire. A 104-carat blue sapphire set in the back of the

British Imperial State Crown. It measures 1½ x 1 inch.

"Styrian jade." Same as pseudophite.

subadamantine. Luster not as highly reflective as **adamantine,** but more so than **vitreous.**

submetallic luster. Like **metallic,** but somewhat dulled.

substitute. In gemology, any substance represented to be, or used to imitate, a more valuable or better known substance such as a genuine gemstone.

subtranslucent. Same as **semitranslucent.**

subtransparent. Same as **semitransparent.**

subvitreous. Having an imperfect vitreous luster.

succinite. (suk'sin-ite). The mineralogical term for an amber mined in East Prussia or recovered from the Baltic Sea. Yields succinic acid when heated. See **amber; Baltic amber.**

succinite garnet. Light yellow amber-colored andradite.

succinum. Ancient name for amber.

Sudaifee pearl. Pearl from the Sudaifee variety of the *Pinctada Vulgaris* mollusc of the Persian Gulf. It is often yellowish in color.

sulphur stone. Pyrite.

Sulu pearl. Fine quality **Philippine pearl** from the Sulu Archipelago, the portion of the Philippine Islands between Mindanao and Borneo. Usually reaches the trade as Manila pearl.

Sun God Opal. Same as **El Aguila Azteca Opal.**

sun opal. A fire opal.

sunstone. A translucent gray, white or colorless **albite** (or other) **feldspar** that exhibits a reddish or golden **adularescence** from minute, flaky inclusions of hematite arranged parallel to planes of repeated twinning. Fine sunstone resembles orthoclase moonstone, except that the billowy light is reddish or golden instead of bluish. Sources: Norway, India, Malagasy Republic, Calif. and Russia.

Suriam garnet. Same as **Syriam garnet.**

Sverdlovsk. A large city (formerly Ekaterinburg) in Ural Mts., Siberia. A mining, cutting and trade center of gemstones from the Urals. See **Takavaya; Russian emerald.**

Swedish amber. See **Baltic amber.**

sweetwater agate. Dark-gray translucent chalcedony nodules containing dendritic growths in star patterns. It is found in the Sweetwater River area of Fremont Co., Wyoming. See **agate.**

sweet-water pearl. Pearl from fresh water.

swirl marks. Curved lines within a **glass imitation** gem, resembling the appearance of a viscous, flowing liquid. This effect may be caused by an improper mixture of the materials that comprised the glass melt, or by a disturbance of the melt as it cooled. Also called **flow lines.**

"Swiss lapis." Chalcedony or jasper artificially dyed blue.

Symerald. A trademarked name for the synthetic-emerald overgrowth on beryl, made by the scientist Lechleitner for the firm of Sturmlecher of Vienna, Austria.

"synthetic alexandrite." Synthetic spinel or synthetic sapphire. See **synthetic stone. "Alexandrite."**

"synthetic aquamarine." Pale blue synthetic sapphire or synthetic spinel. Synthetic aquamarine is not yet made commercially.

synthetic corundum. A reproduction of the structure, composition and properties of corundum by man. Most commercial synthetic corundum is made by the **Verneuil** process; i.e., by melting alumina in an oxyhydrogen flame. It is also made by a flux-melt process by Kashan Laboratories and Carroll Chatham. It is produced in boules; in long, slender rods; and in many other shapes by the Verneuil method and in crystals by flux-melt or hydrothermal methods. Synthetic star ruby and sapphire of various colors are also made. It is detected most effectively by the nature of its inclusions, which differ from those of genuine corundum.

synthetic emerald. A synthetic reproduction of natural emerald, made by both flux-fusion and hydrothermal techniques. The properties of most types differed from their natural counterparts, but the structure and composition are those of natural emerald. Recent products are very close to natural emerald in properties. It is also made by coating prefaceted natural beryl with synthetic emerald. Inclusions in all types made to date differ from natural emerald.

"synthetic hematite." Manufacturers' misnomer for various metallic imitations of **hematite.**

synthetic ruby. Made commercially since 1891. Synthetic star first produced in 1947. See **synthetic corundum.**

synthetic rutile. A manufactured, transparent gem material that has been produced commercially since 1948 by the Linde Co. and the National Lead Co. It is noted for its high degree of dispersion, which is considerably higher than that of diamonds. Chemical composition, titanium dioxide (TiO_2); crystal system, tetragonal; hardness, 6 to $6\frac{1}{2}$; specific gravity, 4.25 to 4.28; refractive index, 2.616-2.903; birefringence, .287; dispersion, .330. Colors include pale yellow, brownish red and greenish blue to bluish green. It is sold under many trade names, including *Miridis, Kenya Gem, Tiania, Tiru Gem, Johannes Gem, Diamothyst* and a host of others.

synthetic sapphire. Blue first produced commercially in 1909; synthetic star in 1947. See **synthetic corundum.**

synthetic spinel. A manmade reproduction of natural spinel. It is made in many colors by the same method (the **Verneuil** process) as synthetic corundum and in similar forms, except that the boules usually exhibit four lateral faces at right angles to one another. It was produced accidentally, prior to 1909, during the search for a method of manufacturing blue synthetic corundum. The property values of synthetic spinel are appreciably higher than those normally encountered in similar colors of the natural material. Specific gravity, 3.61 to 3.66; refractive index, 1.725-1.728.

synthetic stone. A reproduction of a natural stone that has approximately the same physical, chemical and optical properties as the genuine stone it reproduces. Many gem materials have been synthesized as a laboratory experiment, but only corundum, emerald, spinel, rutile, garnet and strontium titanate have been made commercially and cut as stones for the trade.

Syriam garnet. An old name for almandine garnet.

"Syrian garnet." Incorrect name for **Syriam garnet.**

"synthetic turquoise." A misnomer for various amorphous imitations of turquoise, including **Vienna turquoise.**

T

taaffeite. A transparent, light reddish-violet to dark brownish-purple mineral species, first described in 1945 by Count Taaffe, an Irish gemologist, after whom the stone was named. It is extremely rare; only a few specimens are known to exist. Chemical composition, a magnesium-beryllium aluminate ($MgBeAl_4O_8$); crystal system, hexagonal; hardness, 8; specific gravity, 3.62; refractive index, 1.719-1.723; birefringence, .004; dispersion, .019. Source, Ceylon.

tabasheer or **"tabasheer opal."** Translucent to opaque, white to bluish-white amorphous silica; found in certain species of bamboo in India, Burma, and South America. Resembles **hydrophane.**

table. (1) *Gemological:* The horizontal flat surface (facet) on the crown of a faceted gemstone. (2) *Mining:* A concentrating machine which separates smaller crystals or portions of rock or crystals from larger portions.

table cut. (1) Probably the earliest style of fashioning diamonds, in which opposite points of an octahedron were ground down to squares to form a large culet and a larger table; the remaining portions of the eight octahedral faces were then polished. This style of cutting is still used for **calibre-cut** stones. (2) A term sometimes used loosely to describe any one of the variations of the **bevel cut,** provided it has the usual large table of that cut.

table cutter. A lapidist in a large shop who fashions only the tables of gemstones. Because the table is the largest facet and irregularities of polish are more apparent on it, the lap must be more skillfully handled than in polishing smaller stones.

tablet. *In mineralogy,* a **tabular crystal.**

tabular. In mineralogy, formed in broad flat crystals or masses, tablet-like.

tabular crystal. A broad flat crystal; a tablet-like crystal.

Tahiti pearl. (1) Any pearl from Tahiti. Like pearls from other islands in the South Seas, it may be white, yellowish, grayish or blackish. (2) A trade term for any white pearl with only a tinge of orient, often with a slightly grayish, metallic cast. It is found in the *Pinctada Margaritifera* mollusc.

tailings. The part of washed gem ground or of an ore concentrate which is thrown behind the tail of the washing apparatus to be washed again or to be thrown out.

taille en seize (Fr.). Faceting in sixteen facets, plus table and culet. Same as **single cut.**

Takovaya or **Takawaya.** A river in Ural Mts. near which emeralds were discovered about 50 miles northeast of **Sverdlovsk,** in the most important emerald-bearing district on the Eurasian continent. Beryl, alexandrite and phenacite are also found there. Also spelled *Takovaja.*

Takovaya alexandrite. Fine alexandrite found in association with Takovaya emerald.

talc. A very soft mineral. H_2Mg_2 $(SiO_3)_4$. Its only variety of gemological interest is **steatite.**

Talifu jadeite. A term referring to Talifu or Tay-hy-fu, Yunnam Province, China, a jadeite market, but not a source.

talisman. A charm, often a gemstone, which is supposed to produce unusual effects, such as protecting the wearer, or bringing him good luck, good fortune, etc.

Talisman of Charlemagne. A jewel composed of two large sapphires, cut en cabochon, and joined and surrounded by precious stones. These form a small box containing a cross. Was in cathedral at Aachen before World War II.

talladura (Span.). Cut (of a stone).

tallar (Span.). To cut gems.

tallow drop. A style of cutting precious stones in which the stone is domed on one or both sides. (Century dictionary). Same as **cabochon.**

tallow top. A cabochon stone with a low, convex surface.

taltalite. Green Brazilian tourmaline.

tama (Japanese). Jade. Same as **gigaku.**

Tammaw jade. Same as **Tawmaw jade.**

tangawaite or **tangiwaite.** Name for bowenite from New Zealand. Resembles **nephrite** in appearance.

tangiwai (Maori). Same as **tangawaite.**

tank. A Hindu unit of weight for pearls; 24 ratis or about 0.145 oz.

Tanzanite. A coined name for a recently discovered (1967) transparent blue variety of the hitherto undistinguished mineral **zoisite.** It is highly trichroic in a rich blue, deep red and greenish yellow. After mild heat treatment, this variety of zoisite usually assumes a lovely violetish-blue color comparable to that of the finest Kashmir sapphire. The name derives from its discovery and only known source in Tanzania. Refractive index, 1.691-1.704; specific gravity, 3.36; hardness, 6 to 7. See **zoisite.**

Tarshish. The tenth stone in the **Breastplate of the High Priest.** The Hebrew word *tarshish* means *a stone of Tarsus* from Tartessus, (a maritime country mentioned in the Old Testament, probably in Spain). Tartessus means "golden stone" sometimes translated as "chrysolite" which was probably the topaz of today. May have been citrine quartz or topaz quartz. Dr. Kunz suggests yellow jasper. Engraved with the name Naphtali.

Tasmanian alexandrite. Alexandrite of good quality from Tasmania.

Tasmanian topaz. Colorless to light blue topaz from Tasmania.

Tasmanian zircon. Yellow brown to dark red zircon from Tasmania, the former becoming colorless by heating.

Tassie paste. Glass which is lower in lead content than strass, used by James Tassie (1735-1799), a Scottish chemist who studied art and later produced impressions in his paste of most of the then-known famous antique intaglios and cameos, remarkable reproductions representing almost all colored stones.

Complete sets were made for collections. The paste was inferior for imitating diamonds. It contained about 49% silica, 34% lead monoxide, 10% potassium oxide, etc.

tataya. Burmese name for topaz.

Tauridan. Very light blue, almost colorless, topaz. Same as **Siberian topaz.**

Tavernier rule. A method of gem value calculation. Price increases by the square of weight of stones. Now obsolete.

Tawmaw (Tawma, Tammaw) jade. Jadeite from Tawmaw, in upper Burma, probably the most important jadeite source.

tawmawite. A chrome-rich variety of **epidote.** Yellow, dark-green to green, approaching emerald color. From Tawmaw, Upper Burma.

tecalco. See **tecali.**

·tecali. A name for **onyx marble.** From Tecali, Mexico, also spelled Tecati and Tecalco. See "**Mexican onyx;**" "**Mexican jade.**"

tecati. See **tecali.**

"Tecla emerald." A false **triplet.**

"Tecla pearls." Trade-marked name for both solid and wax-filled **imitation pearl** beads.

tektite. A natural siliceous glass, found as loose, rounded, pitted fragments in various parts of the world. Now thought to be of meteoric origin. (Spencer). Its only gem variety is **moldavite.**

template. In the jewelry field, a thin sheet of material, usually plastic, in which have been cut openings of many shapes and sizes for outlining cabochons on pieces of slabbed gem material. When a shape to produce the desired pattern from the rough has been chosen, it is marked on the slab with an aluminum or bronze pencil and serves as a guide for further work. Many templates have openings of standard millimeter sizes; stones cut accurately to fit the openings will also fit ready-made jewelry mountings calling for these sizes.

templet. Same as **bezel facet.**

tenacity. Same as **toughness.**

termination. In mineralogy, the end of a crystal and especially the natural crystal faces on that end as distinguished from a broken or polished end. A crystal is said to be *singly terminated* if natural faces occur on only one end as in **attached crystal;** *doubly terminated* if they occur on both ends as in **disseminated crystals.**

terminology. The technical or special words or terms used in any science, art, industry, trade, etc. See **nomenclature.**

test stone. Basanite. Used for testing streak of precious metals.

tetr. Abbr. used in this book for **tetragonal system.**

tetrabromoethane. Same as **acetylene tetrabromide.**

tetragonal mineral or **stone.** Mineral or stone of the **tetragonal system.**

tetragonal system. In crystallography, a system which has three axes, two of equal length perpendicular to one another, the third of a different length, perpendicular to the plane of the other two. Same as isometric system except that crystals are longer or shorter than their width. Zircon and rutile are the only important gem minerals of this system. See also **crystal systems.**

tetrahedral. Pertaining to the tetrahedron, a four-sided form of of the cubic system.

Thailand. Same as Siam.

Texas agate. Jasp-agate from gem gravels of Pecos River, Texas.

thallite. Same as **delphinite.**

thallium glass. A flint glass which contains thallium. S.G. up to 5.4. Highly refractive and dispersive; occasionally used especially to imitate gems of high dispersion.

thermo-luminescence. A variety of **luminescence** produced, as in chlorophane, by heat (infra-red) rays.

Thetis hair stone. Crystalline quartz containing inclusions of green fibrous crystals which may be tangled or wound into a ball and are hornblende (Schlossmacher), or actinolite or asbestos (Bauer). See **moss stone, Venus hair stone, sagenitic quartz.**

thin section. In mineralogy, a thin slice of a mineral, usually prepared for examination under a microscope of high magnification by cementing to a thin transparent glass plate or slide.

thiruvana. Singhalese word for a rocky gravel of whitish color finding of which indicates the presence of gem-bearing ground.

thomsonite. A translucent to opaque **curio stone,** popular in Lake Superior district where it occurs as water-worn pebbles, or more rarely in amygdules. Mottled or banded; sometimes **orbicular.** White, gray, brownish, reddish, yellowish, greenish. Cut cabochon. Ortho. $2(Ca,Na_2)Al_2(SiO_4)_2.5H_2O$. H. 5-5.5; S.G.

2.3-2.4 (Kraus); R.I. varies from 1.51 to 1.54. See **comptonite, lintonite, ozarkite.**

thool. Ceylonese pearl trade term for seed pearl. Same as **tul.**

Thoulet solution. (thue-lae) Same as **Sonstadt's solution.**

three-phase inclusion. An inclusion in a gemstone consisting of a liquid or negative inclusion which in turn encloses (a) a gas or air bubble or bubbles, and (b) a small mineral crystal or crystals. Distinguishable under gemological microscope in some stones, especially some emeralds.

thulite (thue'lite). (1) An ornamental and decorative stone. The light red to light purplish red (rose) variety of **zoisite.** (2) Also the name for a variety of saponite of no gemological interest.

thumb marks. In gemology, the rhythmic or rippled markings or fractured surfaces of crystalline quartz which contains **twinning laminae.**

Thursday Island pearl. Australian pearl fished in neighborhood of Thursday Island in the Torres Strait, between Australia and New Guinea.

Ti. Abbr. for the element titanium.

Tibet stone. Mixture of aventurine quartz and quartz porphyry which may be of various colors. Has been cut as **ornamental** or **curio stones.** From Russia.

Tiffany Diamond. A yellow brilliant South African diamond, belonging to Tiffany & Co., N. Y. Weight 128.5 m.c.

Tiffany mine. A turquoise mine, seven miles from Los Cerillos, N. M., reputed to have produced large quantities of fine-quality gems previous to 1915.

Tiffany Queen Pearl. Same as the **Queen Pearl.**

tiger-eye. A yellow and yellowish-brown ornamental and gem variety of quartz. Pseudomorphous after **crocidolite.** Colored by limonite which by heating probably turns to hematite and produces a red and brownish-red tiger eye. Grey tiger eye is produced by an acid treatment. When cut with flat surface parallel to the fibers, the slightly differing colors produce a changeable silky **sheen** as the stone is moved. A popular stone for cameos and intaglios. When cut **cabochon** with base parallel to the fibers, produces a cat's-eye effect. Principal source Asbestos Mountains west of Griquatown, South Africa, Sometimes called tiger's-eye.

tigerite. Same as **tiger-eye.**

tiki (Maori). A figure carved from nephrite, worn as a neck ornament by Maori women; a symbol of fecundity.

"Timur Ruby". The largest known (361 m.c.) red **spinel**, famous for six centuries and thought to be a ruby for most of that time. Known as Khiraj-i-Alman (The Tribute of the World) it was seized by Timur in Delhi in 1398 (Smith). It continued to change hands usually in the same manner until it was presented to Queen Victoria by the East India Company in 1851. Now among British crown jewels, it is still uncut and bears inscriptions in Persian indicating six of its royal owners.

"tin cut." A misleading trade term sometimes applied to glass imitations of rock crystal beads which have been cut, as distinguished from moulded or cast beads. See **tin polished.**

tincture. Literally, a tint, but sometimes used to mean **foiling** or **foil back** or **lacquer back.**

tinge. A color designation. A faint trace of a hue which modifies another **hue** as, a blue with a tinge of green, i.e., blue tinged with green, or, stated differently, very slightly greenish-blue.

tin-lap. In gemology, a tin or tin-covered **lap.**

tin oxide. An abrasive usually used in the fashioning of all facetted **colored stones,** except possibly corundum or peridot to produce a high polish; not used on diamonds.

tin polished. A term correctly applied to gems which have been polished on tin laps. Also incorrectly used synonymously with the term **"tin cut."**

tin spar. Cassiterite.

tinstone. Cassiterite.

tint. An attribute of **color.** (1) Correctly, any light **tone** of hue. (2) Often loosely used to mean **tinge.** (3) In popular usage, *tint* is often used in error to mean **tone.**

Tintenbar opal. Opal from Tintenbar district in NE New South Wales which develops cracks on exposure and loses color.

Titania. See **rutile, synthetic.**

titanic schorl. Rutile.

titanite. (tye′ tan-ite). Same as **sphene.**

toad's-eye tin. Reddish cassiterite with concentric structure. Sometimes cut cabochon for collectors.

todai. Singhalese name for the water bailer or pearl fishing boat.

todo mundo stone. Brazilian term for dark-green tourmaline inclined to yellowish or brownish hue

"tokay lux sapphire." (1) Name for a brownish-black obsidian from Hungary,

"tokay lynx sapphire." Same as **"tokay lux sapphire."**

tola. An Indian measure of weight for pearls, 62 ratis or about ⅜ ounce.

toluene or **toluol.** A light hydrocarbon, related to benzine, with low surface tension. Used in place of water in accurate specific gravity determinations. Also used as a solvent to lower the S.G. or R.I. of methylene iodide.

tomb jade. Jade which has been buried, usually with the dead, conforming with a Chinese custom. Usually reddish or brownish. The Occident customarily confines the term tomb jade to such colors, although many other colors, all of which are due to oxidation, are recognized in China. Coloration may be reproduced artificially. See **Han Yü, mouth jade.**

tone. That attribute of a **color** which determines its position in a scale from light to dark. Thus white, and also light gray, are light tones, and dark gray the dark tone of the same color sensation; pink is a light tone of red, and maroon a dark tone. A light tone is usually known as a tint, a dark tone as a shade.

tongs. In gem cutting, a stand having at its upper end a vise-like arrangement by which to hold the cup in which a gem is cemented, so as to press the latter against the polishing wheel (Standard). See also **corn tongs; pearl tongs.**

tongue test. A test by which crystals or crystalline gemstones, all of which are genuine or synthetic, can be distinguished from glass which feels warmer in comparison, when held to the tongue.

"tooth turquoise." Odontolite.

top (of a stone). That portion above the girdle. See **crown.**

topacio (Span.). Topaz.

topaz. (1) A transparent mineral species, the best-known color varieties of which are brownish yellow, yellow-brown, and orangy brown (so-called **sherry** topaz); other colors in this range include reddish brown, yellow, orangy yellow, orange and orange-red. The majority of these vary in tone from very light to medium. Also popular are very light to light blue and very light to medium red to violetish red (the latter usually the result of heat treatment). Light yellowish green to greenish, light violet and colorless are seen less frequently. This gem mineral is sometimes called **precious topaz,** to distinguish it from **citrine,** or **topaz-quartz,** with which it has long been confused. Chemical composition, a fluosilicate of aluminum $Al_2(F,OH)_2SiO_4$; crystal system, orthorhombic; hardness, 8; specific gravity, 3.49 to 3.57; refractive index, 1.609-1.617 (colorless, blue and green) and 1.629-1.637 (yellow, brown and red); birefringence, .008; dispersion, .014. Sources: Brazil, Ceylon, Burma, Russia, Calif. and Madagascar. Topaz is one of the birthstones for November. (2) As an adjective, a color designation referring to the yellowish, brownish, orangy and reddish range in which this mineral occurs; e.g., topaz-quartz, topaz glass.

"topaz cat's-eye." Yellow girasol sapphire which theoretically can exhibit a more or less well-defined light line, or chatoyancy.

topaz glass. Topaz colored glass. Specific gravity may range as high as 4.98 and refractive indices up to 1.77.

topazolite. The transparent yellow, greenish-yellow to yellow-brown variety of **andradite garnet.** It occurs only in very small sizes. Sources: Colo., Germany, Norway, N.J. and Russia.

topographic agate. Agate with fine markings like lines on a topographic map. See **fortification agate.**

torsion balance. A sensitive weighing device which operates on the principal of the twisting (torsion) of a rod or bar of metal. A specially-designed balance of this type, known as the **Berman balance** is used for accurate specific gravity determination on small mineral fragments or gems.

tortoise shell. Mottled dark brown, light brown and yellow mottled shell of the hawk's-bill sea turtle *(Chelone imbricata)* Easily molded when hot; used for boxes, cigarette cases and fine toilet ware. Freely imitated in plastics in which the dark portions lack the swarms of spherical reddish particles seen under the microscope in the genuine (Anderson). S.G. 1.26-1.35; R.I. 1.55-1.56. From Celebes, New Guinea, China, India, Africa, and Australia.

tosa coral. Medium quality of Japanese coral.

total reflection. In gemology, total reflection occurs when a ray of light, after entering a gemstone, strikes any boundary of that gemstone at an angle *greater* than its **critical angle.** Total reflection may continue indefinitely within a stone, as the light striking any boundary is totally reflected until it strikes a boundary at an angle less than the critical angle, in which event it passes out of the stone.

total reflectometer. Another name for refractometer.

touchstone. Same as basanite.

toughness. The resistance a gemstone offers to *blows* and *breakage*, as distinguished from resistance to scratching, which is hardness. In practice, the word is also considered to include resistance to chipping and cracking. See **tenacity, cohesion.**

tourmaline (toor'-mah-leen). A transparent mineral species, the gem varieties of which occur in an unusually wide range of hues, tones and intensities. The most commonly encountered of these include light to dark red with purplish, violetish, brownish or orangy variations; light to dark green, varying from bluish green to yellowish green to brownish green; intense emerald green (chrome tourmaline); light to dark blue to greenish blue to violetish blue; yellowish brown to brownish yellow, greenish brown, orangy brown to brownish orange and greenish yellow; also colorless and opaque black. Particolored crystals (usually red and green) are seen frequently; when the central portion of a crystal is pink and the periphery green, the combination is referred to as "watermelon" tourmaline. Some chatoyant material (usually green) is encountered. Tourmaline with an attractive color change occurs rarely. Chemical composition, a very complex boron-aluminum silicate; crystal system, hexagonal; hardness, 7 to 7½; specific gravity, 3.00 to 3.15; refractive index, 1.624-1.644; birefringence, .020; dispersion, .017. Sources: Brazil, Calif., Russia, Ceylon, Burma, Malagasy Republic and Me. Tourmaline is one of the birthstones for October.

Trade Practice Rules. The United States Federal Trade Commission, at the request of representatives of an industry, undertakes to promulgate rules setting forth fair-trade practices, as agreed upon by groups speaking for the majority of the members of that trade. The first Trade Practices Rules for the jewelry trade were published in 1938 and revised in 1957.

translucency. State of being **translucent.**

translucent. Passing light imperfectly. A translucent material transmits light, but objects cannot be resolved through it. Translucent gem material is not suitable for brilliant cutting, but only for cabochon, beads, etc.

transmitted light. Light which has passed through an object as distinguished from **reflected light.** Gems are usually examined for **imperfections** by transmitted light.

transparent. Passing light perfectly. A transparent material transmits light, and objects can be seen clearly even through a considerable thickness.

"Transvaal emerald." Same as **"African emerald."**

Transvaal garnet. **Grossularite** garnet from near Pretoria, Transvaal, South Africa.

"Transvaal jade." A compact, fine-grained **grossularite garnet** (actually hydrogrossular). Light green in color. Specific gravity, 3.45 to 3.50; refractive index, 1.70-1.73. Often contains black inclusions of chromite and is used for ornamental objects. From near Pretoria, Transvaal, South Africa.

Transvaal tourmaline. A term applied to fine green tourmaline. Marketed through the Transvaal but probably from Southwest Africa.

trap brilliant. A trap or step cut stone, the girdle of which is approximately circular.

trap cut. Same as **step cut.**

trapeze cut. A fancy-shaped or **modern cut,** the girdle outline of which consists of four straight lines, the two larger ones being parallel but of unequal length; the shape of the trapezoid or truncated triangle.

Trapiche emerald. Emerald from Colombia that has the unusual crystal habit of six trapezohedral-shaped prisms extending outward from the six first-order prism faces of a central hexagonal prism. A colorless, fine-grained beryl separates the trapezohedral-shaped prisms from each other and from the central prism. Trapiche emeralds in cutting quality are characterized by echelons of white inclusions and a translucency, rather than full transparency. They have high refractive indices in the 1.583-1.590 range. See **emerald.**

trap rock. A dark, basic, heavy, igneous rock, fine-grained or dense in texture.

travertine (trav'-er-teen). Massive **calcite** (calcium carbonate), formed by deposition from underground or surface waters, especially by hot springs, and occurring as stalactites or stalagmites in caves or as the fillings of some veins and hot-springs conduits. When compact, parallel banded and capable of taking a good polish, it is the same as **onyx marble**; the softer, extremely porous material, with or without banding, is called **calcareous tufa**. Translucent to opaque, light colored and easily dyed, travertine is used to make small ornamental objects and as a decorative and architectural stone.

treated opal. Very dense white opal, and opal matrix almost entirely lacking in transparency, can be blackened and the play of color enhanced artificially. This is done by "cooking" the stone in a sugar solution for a prolonged period, often several days, and then giving it an acid treatment that carbonizes the sugar. The dark background shows off the near-surface color much better than a white background, and leaves an appearance deceptively like that of regular black opal. The characteristic appearance of this treatment is a very fragmented play of color and, under magnification, many tiny black spots. A second form of treatment is to impregnate very porous white opal that has a high degree of play of color with a black plastic. See **opal.**

treated stone. A heated stone, stained stone, coated stone or a stone which has been treated with X rays or radium, to improve or otherwise change its color. Also a stone which may have been treated to disguise flaws as are

doctored pearls, opals the cracks of which have been filled with oil, etc.

tree agate. See **mochastone.**

tree stone. Same as **tree agate.**

Tri. Abbr. used in this book for **triclinic system.**

triangle cut. A fancy shaped or **modern cut** of which the outline of girdle and table is a triangle.

triboluminescence. (trib"oe-lue-mi-nes'-ens) Luminescence produced by rubbing.

trichroic colors. (trye'-kroe-ik). The colors observable in a **trichroic stone.**

trichroic gem or **stone.** One possessing **trichroism.**

trichroism. The property of most doubly refractive, colored minerals of the orthorhombic, monoclinic, and triclinic systems, of transmitting three different colors in the three different directions which correspond with the three crystallographic axes. See **pleochroism, dichroism, dichroscope.**

triclinic mineral or **stone.** Mineral or stone of the **triclinic system.**

triclinic system. A system in crystallography based on three axes, no two of which are of equal length and no two of which are perpendicular to one another. The least symmetrical **crystal system.**

trilling. A symmetrical intergrowth of three crystals. The type of **twinning** such as the six-rayed twinned crystals, consisting of three individuals, which occur in chrysoberyl.

trimetric system. Same as **orthorhombic system.**

trimorphism (trye-mor' fism). The property of being **trimorphous.**

208

trimorphous. See **polymorphism.**

triphane. Same as **spodumene.**

triple pearl. A pearl formed of three distinct pearls united under a nacreous coating.

triplet. An **assembled stone** of two main portions bound together by a layer of cement or other thin substance which can be colored to reproduce the color of the stone which the triplet imitates. If it is of two portions of the species being imitated, plus a binding layer, it is a *genuine triplet*; if of one portion only, it is a *semigenuine triplet*; if it contains no portion of the species being imitated it is a *false triplet*; if no portion is a genuine mineral, it is an *imitation triplet.*

tripletine. A name for emerald-colored beryl triplet. See also "emerald triplet."

tripoli. A soft, friable siliceous rock (often diatomaceous) that is used in powdered form as a polishing agent. **Rottenstone** is similar, and in popular usage the two words are synonymous.

true amber. A term used by a few authorities for **succinite** only, especially those influenced by propaganda of the German government which has controlled the mining and manufacture of succinite. Most authorities include any fossil resin which contains succinic acid, among which are rumanite, simetite and burmite, although the presence of the acid in burmite is questioned. Still other authorities include other fossil resin such as **gedanite.**

true doublet. A genuine doublet. See **doublet.**

true pearl. Pearl unattached to the shell whose surface is formed from nacre, as distinguished from similar formations which are not nacreous or attached to shell. While a **cultured pearl** is scientifically classed as a true pearl, the popular description of it as such might be misinterpreted as meaning a genuine natural pearl and such description is considered by the F.T.C. as an unfair trade practice.

true star. Proprietary name for a patented star **triplet** made to imitate star sapphire. Composed of synthetic stones with polished top, cabochon cut, with a backing of unpolished plastic or stone, the two parts separated by foil upon which one or more systems of parallel lines have been inscribed. These lines produce a **star** in a somewhat similar manner as do inclusions in a natural **asteria.** See **star quartz.**

true topaz. Genuine topaz as distinguished especially from **citrine** or **topaz quartz.**

Tsao P'i Heng. Chinese name for date skin red jade.

Tschantabun ruby. Same as **Chantabun ruby.**

Tuamotu pearl. Pearl from the Tuamotu archipelago or Paomotu Islands, a French possession in the South Pacific, east of The Society Islands (also French), among which is Tahiti. Similar to **Tahiti pearl.**

tul. Ceylonese pearl trade term for seed pearls. The word means powder. Same as thool. See **chunam.**

tulip. A fancy-shaped or modern cut. The outline resembles the outline of a tulip, as seen from the side.

Tully refractometer. A large gemological refractometer designed for the laboratory. Employs a segment of a hemisphere of glass of high R.I. in a rotating hemisphere which expedites the rotation of a specimen for the purpose of obtaining **birefringence.** See **Rayner refractometer, Smith refractometer, Erb & Gray refractometer.**

tumbled stone. A piece of gem material that has been *tumble polished* without first having been preshaped; i.e., a polished gemstone with an irregular, or baroque, shape.

Tunisian coral. Coral from the coast of Tunis from around Sfax and around Tabarca. An Algerian coral.

turchese or **turchina** (Italian). Turquoise.

turcos (obsolete). Turquoise.

Turkestan jade. Nephrite from Chinese Turkestan.

Turkestan turquoise. Turquoise from several mines near Samarkand and Kuraminsk in Turkestan district of U.S.S.R.

turkey fat. Popular name for yellow **smithsonite** from Arkansas.

turkey stone. A misnomer for **turquoise.**

turkis (obsolete). Turquoise.

turkois. A rarely used spelling of **turquoise.**

turk's head. A name for Brazilian **tourmaline** crystal with a red termination or end.

turquesa (Span.) ; **turqueza** (Port.) Turquoise.

turquoise (tur'-koiz; tur'-kwoiz). A semitranslucent to opaque mineral species, the most important of the nontransparent gem materials. The most valuable color is intense medium-light to medium blue; less desirable are greenish blue, bluish green and yellowish green. Included black or brown matrix is common. Both powdered turquoise and various mixtures of chemicals producing the same color may be bonded in plastic to imitate the gem. Plastic, paraffin, wax, oil and other substances are often impregnated in turquoise to improve its color. Chemical composition, a complex hydrous copper-aluminum phosphate ($H_5(Al(OH)_2)_6Cu-OH(PO_4)_4$) ; crystal system, triclinic (cryptocrystalline aggregate ; the single world source of crystallized turquoise is in Campbell Co., Virginia, where it occurs as minute, pale-blue crystals in the form of thin druzy coatings on quartz breccia) ; hardness, 5 to 6; specific gravity, 2.61 to 2.84; refractive index, 1.61-1.65 (usually, one reading near 1.61). Sources: Iran, Sinai Peninsula, Ariz., N.M., Colo. and elsewhere.

turquoise matrix. Name for cabochon-cut mixtures of turquoise and its mother rock, which is usually brown, sometimes grey or almost black.

turritella agate. Agate containing silicified spiral shells of the marine gastropod, *Turritella*. A particularly fine black variety occurs in Wyoming; however, because of its highly opaque character, it should more correctly be called **turritella jasper.** See **agate.**

turtle back. (1) A name for **chlorastrolite**, especially the green variety with patches of color. (2)

Turquoise matrix or (3) variscite matrix. (4) A North American pearl fisher's term for an oblong domed-topped pearl. See **turtle-back pearl.**

turtle-back pearl. (1) American fresh-water pearl fisherman's name for a button pearl with a

low dome in contrast to **haystack pearl.** (2) A trade name for a pearl with irregular sur-

face more or less resembling the pattern of the depressions and elevations on a turtle's shell.

(3) A name rarely applied to round pearls from the variety of American clam known as the *turtle back.*

Tuticorin pearl. Pearl formerly fished near Tuticorin on coast of Madras Presidency, India, across the Gulf of Manaar from Ceylon. Similar to **Ceylon pearl.** See **Madras pearl.**

tuxtlite. A name for the mineral midway between the sodium and magnesium **pyroxenes.** From Tuxtla, Mexico. The principal constituent of **mayaite.** See also **diopside jadeite.**

tweezers. Small pincers used for picking up and holding gemstones.

twin. A term frequently employed to mean **twin crystal.**

twin crystal. The intergrowth of two or more individuals (crystals or parts of crystals) in such a way as to yield parallelism in the case of certain parts of the different individuals and at the same time other parts of the different individuals are in reverse position in respect to each other (Dana). A *contact twin* is one in which its two parts have grown side by side, in contact

with one another, but in reverse order, so that if one half of the twin crystal be rotated 180° on its joining plane, the form of the normal crystal will result. *An interpenetrant* or *penetration twin* is one in which the two crystals or parts have grown so they penetrate each other, often producing crosses or stars. *Polysynthetic* or *repeated twins* are composed of a great number of very small contact twins producing thin **laminae,** each twin crystal being arranged in reverse order to the next one. See **twinning.**

twinlones. Burmese mining term for any boring, pit or excavation sunk in alluvial deposits.

twinning. The process by which a twin crystal or crystals are produced. Caused by the reversal of the atomic position in the crystal lattice. *Polysynthetic* or *repeated twinning* is the production of **polysynthetic** or **repeated twins,** and frequently gives rise to characteristic fine parallel lines, called twinning striations, on the surface of a crystal

twinning laminae. The **laminae** or thin plates in repeated twins. See **twin.**

twinning striations. See **twinning.**

twin or **twinned pearl.** Same as **double pearl.**

twins. (1) The plural of **twin.** (2) A miner's abbreviation of **twinlones.**

twin stone. Staurolite.

two-color pearl or **two-colored pearl.** True pearl which exhibits two distinct colors. Undesirable for necklaces but satisfactory for rings or other jewels.

two-phase inclusions. An angular cavity in a gemstone consisting of a gas bubble in a liquid. The cavity may or may not coincide with a possible crystal form of the host mineral. Example: corundum.

U

uigite. (1) A white and yellow banded stone with a somewhat pearly sheen. Related to or classed as **prehnite**. From Uig on the Island of Skye, Scotland.

uintaite or uintahite. A variety of black, brilliant, lustrous asphalt which has many uses in the arts; from Utah; H. 2.-2.5, S.G. 1.065-1.070 (Dana). Has been used as a substitute for **jet**.

ultralite. Trade-marked name for a red-violet synthetic sapphire.

ultra-violet. The portion of the **spectrum** beyond visible violet. Ultra-violet light is of value in gemology as a means of exciting **fluorescence**.

ultraviolet lamp. A source of ultra-violet radiation used for exciting **fluorescence** in gemstones and other materials. The commonly used long-wave lamp has a peak wavelength emission at approximately 3660 Angstrom units (one Angstrom unit = one ten-millionth of a millimeter). The short-wave lamp has its principal emission peaks at 2537, 2553, 2650 and 2645 A.U., but, depending on the filter, may also emit long wave-lengths. The filter on the short-wave lamp is subject to deterioration and has an average effective life of approximately one year. The filter on the long-wave unit, on the other hand, is stable.

umina. Inca name for emerald.

unakite. A granitelike igneous rock composed of approximately equal proportions of light-green epidote and bright pink to red feldspar. It is a popular material among amateur lapidaries.

unctuous feel. Very smooth and slippery; greasy to the touch.

undurchsichtig (German). Opaque.

uneven fracture. Fracture producing an uneven or irregular surface.

uniaxial stone. One which has crystallized in the tetragonal or hexagonal system, and therefore has only one direction or axis of single refraction. See **biaxial stone**.

Unio Margaritifera (U'-ne-oh Mar"-gah-rih-tif'-er-ah). The genus of mussels (family *Unionidae*) that is the principal producer of **fresh-water pearls** in Europe and North America. It has an oblong shell, pearly within, and is covered with a greenish or blackish epidermis.

Unionidae. A very large family of fresh-water **bivalves** known as fresh-water mussels, certain genera of which, especially the genus **Unio**, yield **fresh-water pearls**.

univalve. A mollusc having a shell consisting of a single piece. A gastropod. See **bivalve**.

universal immersion stage. See **stage**.

universal or universal motion stage. See **stage**.

unripe amber. Gedanite.

unripe pearl. See **ripe pearl**.

"unripe ruby." Red **zircon**.

upala (Sanskrit). A precious stone. Opal is derived from the word.

uparatnani. The four lesser gems of the naoratna: jacinth, topaz, cat's-eye and coral. See **naoratna**.

Ural or **Uralian amethyst.** Same as **Siberian amethyst.**

Ural or **Uralian chrysoberyl.** Alexandrite.

"Ural" or **"Uralian chrysolite."** Demantoid garnet.

Ural or **Uralian emerald.** (1) Emerald from near Sverdlovsk, Siberia. Same as **Russian emerald.** (2) Incorrect term for **demantoid.**

"Ural or Uralian olivine." Demantoid garnet.

"Uralian sapphire." Blue tourmaline.

Uralian topaz. Mursinska topaz and also fine yellow topaz, and rose, violet and colorless topaz from Sanarka in the southern Urals.

Urals. The Ural Mts., a mountain system dividing European Russia from Siberia (Asiatic Russia). Many gemstones are found there; the more important ones on the Siberian side of the divide. See **Sverdlovsk.**

urea resin. A synthetic **plastic** that may be made to resemble closely any opaque to translucent gem material. It is highly resistant to shock and pressure. Luster, resinous; hardness, 2½; fracture, uneven; specific gravity, 1.48; refractive index, 1.54 to 1.60.

Uruguay or **Uruguayan agate.** Agate from same area as **Uruguay amethyst**; usually found in large masses of grayish color and before World War II, stained at Idar-Oberstein.

Uruguay or **Uruguayan amethyst.** A term which, when used to describe a trade grade or trade quality, usually refers to a deep violet, very transparent amethyst. A term also used to include all amethysts from an area along the border of Uruguay and Rio Grande do Sul, Brazil, which are mostly small and irregularly colored.

Utah jet. An inferior jet which came from Wayne Co., Utah.

utahlite. (1) Variscite found in nodular masses in Toole Co., Utah (Dana). Also (2) an alternate name for the species **variscite.**

utahlite matrix. An alternate name for **amatrice.**

"Utah turquoise." Misnomer for **variscite.**

uvarovite (oo-vah'rof-it or yuh-var'oe-vite). An uncommon almost emerald-green, chromium-colored species of **garnet**, which has occurred in sizes too small for gem use, excepting, perhaps the larger crystals mentioned by Spencer in 1936 as having been found in Finland. Iso. $Ca_3Cr_2(SiO_4)_3$; H. 7.5; S.G. 3.4-3.5; R.I. 1.84-1.85; (1.83-1.87 Winchell) From Urals, Transvaal, Calif., and elsewhere.

uwarowit. Same as **uvarovite.**

V

vabanite. A brown-red jasper with yellow flecks. From California.

vadivu. (1) A Ceylonese trade grade of pearl. Small, irregular in shape and of good luster. Larger than seed pearl and especially favored in the Orient (Kunz). (2) The term (which means *beautiful*) is also used by the Ceylonese for a·broader classification of pearls which include the medium grades, **machchakai,** vadivu, and **madanku** (Kunz) See **chevvu; kuruval.**

valence or **valency.** (1) The property possessed by elements of combining with or replacing other elements in definite and constant proportion. (2) Also the degree of this property—a degree which varies with different elements, oxygen having a valence of two, carbon a valence of four, etc.

valencianite. A name for **adularia** from the silver mine at Valencia, Mexico.

valuation. The act of comparing the desirability of anything such as a gemstone, in comparison with other things, not necessarily in terms of money, as in gemology to compare the value of one ruby with another, or of rubies with garnets. However, in the trade it is often used as a synonym of appraisal. See **appraisal; evaluation.**

value. The comparative desirability or worth of a thing, not necessarily in money. Not synonymous with price unless expressed in terms of money.

valve. In conchology, one of the parts or pieces of a mollusc's shell.

variegated agate. A kind of agate in which moss inclusions and coloring are distributed without pattern. See **agate.**

variegated jasper. A term for jasper in which the markings and colors are variegated. It is distributed widely on the California beaches and elsewhere. See **jasper.**

variety. In gemology, a division of a species, or of a genus, based on color, type of optical phenomenon or other distinguishing characteristic of appearance, as **emerald** and **aquamarine** are each a variety of beryl, and **alexandrite** and **cymophane** are each a variety of chrysoberyl; in addition, sometimes based on source, as **Brazilian aquamarine** and **Madagascar aquamarine,** or **Thursday Island pearl** or **Broome pearl.** In mineralogy, the variety may be based upon a minor variation in chemical composition.

variscite (var'is-cite). An **ornamental** or **curio stone;** yellow-green to blue-green; translucent to opaque. Ortho. $AlPO_4 2H_2O$. H. 4-5; S.G. 2.5; mean R.I. about 1.56-1.57. From Utah, Saxony and elsewhere. See also **amatrice, lucinite, peganite.**

variscite-matrix. A mixture of variscite and other mineral or rock, especially **amatrice.**

vashegyite. A mineral somewhat like **variscite** in appearance. A variety from Nevada has yielded some ornamental stones or gemstones for collectors. H. 2-3; S.G. 1.96; n 1.50,

vegetable ivory. See **ivory (vegetable).**

vein. A crack, crevice, or fissure,

215

filled, or practically filled, with mineral matter.

veinstone. Any mineral other than metal which occurs in a vein. See **gangue.**

Venezuela pearl. (1) A pearl from the waters of the western Caribbean, especially off the coasts of South America and lower Central America. From the *Pinctada Radiata* mollusc. It is softer and much whiter than Ceylon pearl and more yellowish than Persian Gulf pearl. (2) Bronze pearl from the hammer oyster, *Malleus*, and synonymous with La Paz and Panama pearl. See **Pinctada.**

venturina (Span.). Aventurine quartz.

Venus hair stone. Crystalline quartz containing inclusions of reddish brown or yellow **rutile** fibers which may be tangled. See **hair stone, Thetis hair stone. sagenitic quartz.**

verd-antique. Opaque green **serpentine** with veins of lighter colored calcite or other minerals of the calcite group. It is used extensively as a building decoration, and is also called **serpentine marble.**

verde de Corsica (Fr.). Same as **Corsican green.**

verdite. A beautiful green rock composed of **fuchsite** and clay. Rarely substituted for jade. From Transvaal.

vermeil or **vermeille.** (Fr. meaning vermillion). A word used usually to mean **vermeille garnet** but also to mean orangy-red spinel or zircon.

vermeil ruby. Orangy red to red-brown corundum.

vermeille garnet. A trade term for any orangy-red garnet; same as guarnaccine garnet (Kunz). A term also sometimes applied to any brownish-red garnet.

Verneuil process. A method announced in 1902 by Aguste Victor Louis Verneuil (1856-1913), a French chemist, for manufacturing **synthetic corundum.** It consists essentially of melting aluminum oxide in an oxyhydrogen blowpipe flamé. In addition, the process is used today to produce **synthetic spinel, synthetic rutile** and **strontium titanate.** There is good evidence that the method was used 15 or 20 years before its announcement.

vernier. A small movable auxiliary scale for obtaining fractional parts of the subdivisions of a fixed scale, as on various instruments of precision.

vesicle. A small cavity in a mineral or rock, in many cases produced by the liberation of vapor in the molten mass.

vesicular. Having steam or gas bubble cavities, as in certain igneous rocks.

"Vesuvian garnet." An early name for **leucite,** an isometric mineral of no gem value or interest, except that its crysals resemble garnet crystals in form.

"vesuvianite jade." Same as **californite.**

"Vesuvian jade." The californite variety of **vesuvianite.**

vesuvianite. Same as **idocrase.**

"Vienna turquoise." An amorphous imitation of turquoise formerly manufactured in Vienna, Czechoslovakia, France and England. More difficult to detect than the various blue stained minerals which have replaced it as a turquoise substitute, it has approximately the same chemical composition, hardness, specific gravity and fracture.

vigorite. Bakelite.

viluite. Same as **wiluite.**

vindharas. Skilled workmen who pierce and drill pearls in Bombay.

vinegar spinel (obsolete). Same as **rubicelle**

violan or **violane** (vye'oe-lane). A translucent massive bluish violet variety of diopside. H. 6; S.G. 3.23; R.I. about 1.69.

violet coral. A variety of **akori.**

violetish. Possessing the hue violet as a violetish blue color, a violetish ruby, etc., A coined word used in **color nomenclature system** of North American gemology.

violet stone. Cordierite.

violite. Trade-marked name for a purple synthetic sapphire.

Virgin Valley opal. Opal from Virgin Valley, Humbolt Co., Nevada. This source produces both black and white types, but stones usually have more internal fractures than Australian material, and have a decided tendency to crack after exposure to the air. Some outstanding opals have been found in Virgin Valley, including the 355.19-carat *Roebling Black Opal*, on display at the Smithsonian Institution, Washington, D.C. See **opal.**

viridine (manganoandalusite). A grass-green manganese-bearing variety of andalusite. Strongly dichroic. R.I. 1.66-1.69.

"viscoloid." A variety of celluloid.

visible light. The light of the **visible spectrum.** See also **invisible light.**

visible spectrum. That portion of the **electromagnetic** spectrum, the waves which normally produce, upon the human eye, color sensations of red, orange, yellow, green, blue, violet or their intermediate hues, or of white light if the rays are combined. Distinguished from radio, **infrared, ultra-violet,** gamma and X rays.

vitreous luster. A type of luster possessed by the majority of gemstones. It is the luster of broken glass. See also **subvitreous.**

vitrification. The act or process of becoming vitrified, i.e. converted into glass, as **crystalline quartz** is sometimes converted into **quartz glass.**

vitreo (Span.). Vitreous.

"volcanic chrysolite." Vesuvianite.

volcanic glass. Obsidian.

vorobievite or **vorobyevite.** Colorless or rose-colored beryl (**morganite**). From Urals and Madagascar.

vulcanite. Crude rubber heat-treated with sulphur. S.G. 1.15-1.20 (R. Webster). See **ebonite.**

W

walrus ivory. Ivory, usually yellowish cream in color, from the tusks of the walrus, or morse *(Odobaenus Rosmarus)*. It is less dense and somewhat coarser than that from the elephant or hippopotamus. This kind of ivory was popular in Persia and other Oriental countries for sword handles. The Scandanavians have used it extensively for chessmen and caskets. Hardness, 2½ to 3½; specific gravity, 1.90 to 2.00; refractive index, 1.55 to 1.57. Source: the Arctic seas and the colder parts of the north temperate zone.

Walton filter. An **emerald glass** or beryloscope mounted to resemble **a hand loupe** and called an emerald loupe in Europe. Observed through it the filament of an electric lamp appears reddish yellow, light from this filament passing through most genuine emerald appears the same color; through a Brazilian emerald from Minas Geraes, green; through an epidote, red; a dioptase, green, etc.

wardite. A mineral of gemological interest only for its occurrence in **amatrice** or as inclusions in **variscite,** where it resembles eyes because of its concretionary form. A hydrous aluminum phosphate. H. 5; S.G. 2.5; R.I. 1.59/1.60 (Dana). From Utah.

warrior. Trade term for cameos or intaglios carved with the figure of a warrior of ancient Greece or other ancient nation.

wart agate. Variety of carnelian of mammillary or small spherical growths. Often found as covering colored agate.

wart-hog ivory. A coarse kind of ivory, resembling bone more than elephant ivory, from the wart hog (the swine genus *Phacochoerus*). It is used occasionally for small carved objects. Hardness, 2¾; specific gravity, 1.90 to 2.00; refractive index, 1.55 to 1.57. Source: Africa.

wart pearls. German name for baroque pearls.

warty. Having small rounded protuberances, like warts.

warty-back pearl. Any fresh-water pearl from the Mississippi Valley mussel *Quadrula pustulosa* popularly known as the warty-back clam.

Washington Sapphire. A bust of George Washington carved from a dark-blue, 1997-carat sapphire found at Anakie, Queensland, Australia. The finished carving weighs 1056 carats and measures 2⁹⁄₁₆ inches high, 2¹⁄₁₆ inches wide, and 1¾ inches deep. The sculptor was Harry B. Derian and the technical advisor, Lincoln Borglum. This carving, together with those of Presidents Lincoln, Eisenhower and Jefferson and the *Black Star of Queensland,* were presented as a gift to the American people by the Kazanjian Foundation of Pasadena, California, a charitable, nonprofit organization founded by Kazanjian Bros., Los Angeles gem dealers. The *Washington Sapphire* is presently on display at the Smithsonian Institution, Washington, D.C.

wash opal. Alluvial opal, or floaters, found in dry stream beds, where they have been washed down by rain. See **opal.**

water. Term occasionally used in some countries, principally British, as a comparative quality designation for color and transparency of diamonds, rubies, and other stones which are described as rubies of second water, or diamonds of first water, etc.

water agate. Same as **enhydros.**

"water chrysolite." Moldavite.

water drop quartz. Rock crystal containing inclusions of water and air. A **curio stone.** Similar to **enhydros.**

watermelon tourmaline. A term applied to tourmaline, the center of which is pink and the edges green. Often seen in crystals but not in cut stones. See also **bocco de fogo.**

water opal. (1) Same as **hyalite**, or (2) any transparent precious opal similar to **Mexican water opal,** or (3) a misnomer for **moonstone.**

water sapphire. (1) Light-colored blue sapphire (Schlossmacher). (2) Misnomer for iolite. (3) A term which has been applied to water-worn pebbles of topaz, quartz, etc., from Ceylon, which usage is also misleading except when applied to sapphire pebbles.

water stone. (1) Moonstone. (2) Hyalite. (3) Enhydros. (4) A Chinese name for jade.

waterworn stones. Gem minerals, especially crystals, rounded by action of water rolling them against rocks or gravel in beds of rivers, lakes or ocean.

wave length. The length of a wave (of light, water, sound, etc.) measured from a given point on one wave to the same point on the following or preceding wave.

wave-length spectrometer. See **spectrometer.**

wax agate. Yellow or yellowish red chalcedony with a pronounced waxy luster. Similar to yellow **carnelian.**

wax-filled pearl. Imitation pearl made of a hollow glass sphere coated with **essence d'orient** and filled with wax. Same as **Roman pearl.**

wax opal. Yellow opal with a waxy luster.

waxy luster. Similar to **vitreous luster** but lacking its bright reflection.

weathering. Disintegration and decomposition of rocks or minerals by elements of the atmosphere, especially by the action of frost and ice which, forming in cracks, splits rocks.

wedding-anniversary list. The materials designated in the United States as being particularly appropriate for wedding-anniversary gifts are to be found in the following list. In 1948, the list was sponsored by the Jewelry Industry Council and approved by the National Wholesale Jewelers' Association, American National Retail Jewelers' Association and the National Jewelers' Association (the latter two organizations merged in 1957 to form the Retail Jewelers of America, Inc.): (1) clocks, (2) china, (3) crystal and glass, (4) electrical appliances, (5) silverware, (6) wood, (7) desk sets and pen-and-pencil sets, (8) linen and laces, (9) leather, (10) diamond jewelry, (11) silver, gold, gold-filled and gold-plated fashion jewelry and accessories, (12) pearls or colored stones, (13) textiles or furs, (14) gold jewelry,

(15) watches, (16) silver hollo-
ware (sterling or plate), (17) fur-
niture, (18) porcelain, (19) bronze,
(20) platinum, (25) sterling-silver
jubilee, (30) diamond, (35) jade,
(40) ruby, (45) sapphire, (50) golden
jubilee, (55) emerald, (60) diamond
jubilee.

Wedgwood. A well known make of
porcelain and semiporcelain, the
latter including **jasper ware** in
which the *Wedgwood cameo* is
moulded and set in jewelry.

well. A trade term for the dark
nonreflecting spot often seen in
the center of a fashioned stone,
especially in a colorless stone.

Weltauge (German). Same as **oculus mundi.**

wernerite. A species of the **scapolite** group. See **scapolite.**

Westphal's balance. A balance for
determining S.G. of **heavy
liquids;** employs a weight and a
sinker.

West's solution. A liquid consisting of eight parts of white phos-
phorous and eight parts of sulphur to one part of metheylene
iodide. Useful in obtaining R.I.
by the **Becke method.** R.I. 2.05.

Whitby jet. Jet from the coal mines
of Yorkshire, near Whitby, England. Was considered to be the
most desirable quality of jet
when jet was in vogue.

white agate. A term sometimes applied to white or whitish chalcedony.

"white beryl," "white zircon," etc.
A term often incorrectly but popularly applied to transparent
stones which are in fact colorless. For example, white quartz
is chalcedony and not rock crys-
stal. The latter, being transparent, is colorless.

white carnelian. A term which has
been used for white **chalcedony**
with faint tint of carnelian col-
or or spots or splashes of that
color. Also has been used even
less accurately for white or milky-white chalcedony.

White Cliffs opal. Opal from White
Cliffs, 60 miles north of Wil-
cannia, New South Wales, Australia; an opal-bearing area. See
light opal. Usually possesses a
milky to white body color.

"white emerald." Caesium **beryl.**

white garnet. A translucent variety
of **grossularite** which sometimes
resembles **white jade** in appearance.

"white iron pyrites." Same as **marcasite.**

white jade. (1) White jadeite or
nephrite. (2) Misnomer for
white translucent **grossularite**
garnet from California.

white moss agate. Agate containing large areas of white inclusions.

white opal. A trade term for precious opal with any light body
color as distinguished from **black
opal.**

white pearl. (1) Trade term for
fine **pearl** with white or very
nearly white body color, and
with no particular **overtone** or
orient except a very pale bluish
one. Does not include **light rosé
pearl.** (2) A trade term sometimes used to distinguish any
pearl with white or cream body
color from **black pearl, colored
pearl** or **two color pearl.**

"white sapphire." See **white beryl,**
etc.

"white schorl." A confusing and
undesirable name for **albite.**

white silk stone. Same as **satin spar.**

"white stone diamonds." Genuine or imitation colorless stones of various kinds.

"white topaz." Colorless topaz.

whorl. A turn as of a spiral shell.

wild pearl. Term sometimes used by scientists for a pearl whose growth began naturally as contrasted to a **cultured pearl.**

willemite. A mineral often strongly fluorescent, and sometimes fashioned as gemstone for collectors, especially if transparent. Transparent to opaque, white, greenish, yellow, yellowish-green, reddish and brown (Dana). Also more rarely blue, black, white and colorless (Kraus). Hex. Zn_2SiO_4; H. 5-6; S.G. 3.9-4.3; R.I. 1.69/1.72. Bi. 0.029 (Kraus). From New Jersey, and less important sources.

williamsite. A variety of massive yellowish green **precious serpentine** which has been represented as jade. From Chester Co., Pa. Also from near Baltimore, Md. (Dana). See **baltimorite.**

wilsonite. (1) Purplish-red scapolite (Merrill). (2) The name of a mineral that is also classed as **pinite** (Dana). Of no gem interest.

wiluite. (1) A greenish variety of **vesuvianite** from Yakutsk, Sibberia. Also (2) a name sometimes used for green **grossularite** garnet of the same region, probably because the first wiluite discovered there was grossularite in part. The name is of no other gemological interest.

winchellite. An alternate name for **lintonite.**

wine jade. A descriptive term applied by Chinese to a particular color of jade.

wing pearls. Pearls that are elongated or irregular, resembling a wing or part of a wing.

Wisconsin pearl. Formerly a term applied to the better quality of **fresh-water pearl** found in the Mississippi Valley; whether or not from the state of Wisconsin. Also a name more or less synonymous with fresh-water pearls, as a large quantity of them were marketed through Milwaukee, Wisconsin.

wisps. Whitish wisp-like fractures resembling thin wind - blown clouds. Occur in some synthetic emerald but never in the genuine.

wolf's-eye. (1) Same as moonstone (feldspar) or (2) Same as **wolf's-eye stone.**

wolf's-eye stone. A rarely used name for **tiger eye** especially that which is partly silicified and therefore intermediate between **tiger eye** and **hawk's-eye.**

wollastonite. A mineral, of gemological interest only as a constituent of so-called **rose garnet.** White, inclining to grey, yellow, red or brown. $CaSiO_3$. Mono. 4.5-5; S.G. 2.8-2.9; R.I. 1.62-1.63; Bi. 0.015

wonderstone. Rhyolite (a very fine-grained **igneous** rock, often porous, composed principally of cemented grains of orthoclase and quartz) banded in light tones of brown, yellow, red, orange and cream. It is used primarily as a decorative stone; only occasional specimens are suitable for cabochons. Sources: Madison Co., Montana; Elko, White Pine, Churchill and

Mineral Counties, Nevada; Sierra Co., New Mexico; and San Diego Co., California. The New Mexico locality produces a type called **elixirite,** which is harder, more compact and takes a much better polish.

wood agate. Agatized wood.

wood opal. Same as **opalized wood,** but not applied to precious opal pseudomorphous after wood.

Wood's filter. A very dark glass which absorbs almost all the **visible spectrum,** but transmits ultra-violet rays.

wood stone. An alternate name for petrified wood. See **Holzstein.**

world eye or **world's-eye.** A name for **hydrophane.**

Württemberg jet. Jet from Schombérg, Boll and many other places in Swabian Alps (Bauer-Schlossmacher). See **German jet.**

Wyoming jade. Nephrite from Wyoming. Jadeite also reported from Wyoming in 1944, was later proven to be nephrite.

"Wyse ruby." An alternate and obsolete name for **"Geneva ruby."**

X

xaga. California Indian name for **obsidian.**

xalostocite. Same as **landerite.**

xanthite. A name for yellowish to yellowish brown **vesuvianite** from Amity, N. Y., with no particularly different characteristics from other vesuvianite.

xilopalo (Span.). Wood opal.

Xiuitl (Mex.). Turquoise found by the Aztecs near the City of Mexico.

X-ray powder pattern. A characteristic pattern produced on photographic film when an X-ray beam strikes grains of a powdered material and is reflected by planes of atoms within the substance. Each reflection causes a spot on the film and the random orientation of the many grains of powder results in the spots coalescing into lines. The spacing of the lines is directly dependent on the manner in which the atoms within the crystal are arranged in space.

X-rays. Electromagnetic radiation with a wavelength range from about 0.1 A.U. to about 50 A.U. The ability of X-rays to penetrate objects opaque to visible light, and also to delineate the structure of crystalline materials by reflecting from planes of atoms, is very useful in identification. **X-radiography** (i.e., using X-rays as the source of energy to expose photographic film after passing through pearls) enables a pearl tester to distinguish between cultured and natural pearls. Cultured pearls usually fluoresce under X-radiation, whereas salt-water pearls usually do not. X-ray photographs of single crystals yield patterns of spots that are characteristic of the structure of atoms of the material, and powdered crystalline material rotated before a collimated X-ray beam yields lines that are reflections from planes of atoms in patterns that characterize that substance.

xylonite. A trade name for a celluloid.

xylopal. A name for **opalized wood.**

Y

YAG (yttrium aluminum garnet). A man-made material grown chiefly by flux methods and the Czochralski technique. Although its chemical composition, $Y_3Al_5O_{12}$, an aluminate, does not resemble naturally occurring garnets (a group of silicates), it is termed "garnet" because it has the same atomic structure. YAG is grown in various colors particularly for use in lasers, and the colorless form is used principally for the simulation of diamond. Colorless YAG is near 4.55 in specific gravity, has a 1.833 refractive index, and a hardness of 8¼.

Yahalom. The sixth stone in the Breastplate of the High Priest. Kunz believes the stone to have been onyx; Cooper believes it rock crystal. Some scholars argue that in the original Hebrew **Yashpheh** was the sixth stone in place of Yahalom. Engraved with name of Zebulom.

yakhont. Ancient Russian word for, or term denoting semiprecious stones, amethyst, sapphire, hyacinth, ruby, etc.

yanolite. (1) A name for violet **axinite.** (2) Same as axinite

Yarkand jade. Nephrite from the jade market and cutting center of Yarkand, Russian Turkestan, of inferior qualities as best qualities are usually sold to cutters in China.

Yashpheh. Twelfth stone in Breastplate of the High Priest. Ancient versions translate as jasper, probably a green jasper, though there is reason to believe that the stone may have been nephrite or jadeite, the Chinese **Yü** stone. Engraved with the name of Assher.

yellow-brown. In **color nomenclature system** of North American gemology, the color approximately midway between vivid yellow and the **tone** and **intensity** of brown which is almost black. Same as brown-yellow.

yellow-green. In **color nomenclature system** of North American gemology the **hue** midway between yellow and green. Same as green-yellow.

yellowish brown. In North American gemology a color between yellow-brown and the tone and intensity of brown which is almost black.

yellowish green. In North American gemology a **hue,** approximately midway between green and **yellow-green.** Therefore more green than yellow.

yellowish orange. In North American gemology, a **hue** approximately midway between orange and yellow orange, and therefore more orange than yellow.

yellow-orange. Same as orange-yellow.

yeso (Span.). Gypsum.

Yogo sapphire. Montana sapphire from Yogo Gulch, Montana, or mined by Yogo American Sapphire Syndicate.

youstone. An old English term for jade.

yowah nut. A term which has been used for a subvariety of boulder opal which occurs in the form of tiny boulders. Usually of walnut or almond size. The center of some of these is opal, at other times ironstone covered with a thin band of opal. They are less often hollow. From near Yowah station in West Queensland.

Yü (yue). Chinese word for jade, or for any very precious stone.

Yuh. Same as **yü.**

yustone. Jade.

zafirina (Span.). Misnomer for blue spinel or blue chalcedony.

zafiro (Span.). Sapphire. The name is sometimes also incorrectly applied to lapis lazuli.

zanzibar pearl. Same as **African pearl.**

zeasite. (1) Wood opal. (2) An old name for a variety of **fire opal.**

Zeberged. The island in the Red Sea where peridot was first discovered and from which the finest qualities have come. Also known as St. John's Island, Seberget, Sebirget and Zebirget.

zebra jasper. Dark brown jasper with lighter brown streaks. From India.

"zebra jasper." Same as **"zebra stone."**

"zebra stone." Brown limonite with lighter brown layers of ancient shell material.

"Zenithite." A trademarked name for **strontium titanate.**

zeuxite. A name for green Brazilian tourmaline.

zeylanite. Same as ceylonite.

zigzag agate. A brecciated **fortification** agate in which the bands have become broken and cemented together again by percolating silica-bearing waters. See **agate.**

Zimtstein (German). Hessonite.

zincblende. A name for **sphalerite.**

zincite (zink'-ite). A transparent to translucent, dark-red or occasionally, orange-yellow mineral species. Although zincite is too soft for jewelry use, its high refractive index, high luster and attractive color make it a collector's item of great desirability. Chemical composition, zinc oxide, (ZnO); crystal system, hexagonal (crystals rare; usually compact, granular or foliated masses); hardness, 4 to $4\frac{1}{2}$; specific gravity, 5.43 to 5.70; refractive index, 2.013-2.029; birefringence, .012. This mineral is found in rare gem quality only at Franklin Furnace, Sussex Co., N.J.

zinc spar. An early name for **smithsonite.**

zinc spinel. Same as **gahnite.**

zinni pearl. Pearl from the zinni variety of the *Pinctada Vulgaris* mollusc of the Persian Gulf. It is often yellowish in color.

zircolite. A copyrighted trade name for colorless synthetic spinel.

zircon (zur'kon). One of the most important gemstones, occurring naturally in transparent colorless, red, orange, brown, yellow and green varieties. The non-gemstone varieties are translucent to opaque brownish or greyish and certain of these, when heated, may change to transparent colors of the natural gemstone varieties, or frequently to blue, a color which never occurs in nature except perhaps such a pale blue that it is almost colorless. *As a species* zircon is unusual in its great range of S.G. and R.I. Tetr.; $ZrSiO_4$; H. 7.5; S.G. 4.0-4.8; R.I. 1.92/1.95 - 1.96/2.02; Bi. 0.060. The S.G. and R.I. vary because of variations in the crystal structure consisting of partial to complete breakdown of the crystal lattice; the lower properties occurring in the zircon indicate that the lattice is entirely broken down and the zircon therefore amorphous. This amorphous zircon is usually green and from Ceylon, with properties approaching H. 6.; S.G. 3.95; R.I. (singly refractive) 1.79. Often designated mineralogically as **gamma zircon**. It is rarely seen in the gem trade. The normal type of fully crystallized zircon is transparent and of the various gem colors. It is found naturally in all these colors, except blue, in Burma, Ceylon, Australia, Russia and elsewhere. This is the type almost always seen in the gem trade and has about S.G. 4.7; R.I. 1.92/1.98; Bi. 0.059. It is often designated mineralogically as **alpha zircon**. In all other zircon the S.G. and R.I. are intermediate between the normal crystal type and the amorphous type which is partly amorphous and partly crystalline. Most authorities include in this classification only greenish zircon from Ceylon. Mineralogically such stones· are often classed as **beta zircon**. No detailed reports cover the properties of the smoky brown zircon usually found in Indo-China, most of which is heat treated in Bangkok, Siam, to transparent gem qualities of all colors. After heat treatment these stones have properties of the normal (or alpha) zircon, but fracture more easily and often revert toward their original color when exposed to direct sunlight. See **jacinth; hyacinth; Siam zircon.**

zircon halo. Included zircon crystal in some gemstones, surrounded by black or dark-brown haloes of fractures. They are thought to be caused either by radioactive disin-

tegration of the zircon, or by unequal thermal expansion of the zircon and the host mineral. Another theory proposes that the expansion is caused by an increase in size of the included crystal, which has disintegrated to the **metamict** type. Zircon haloes are typical of much corundum. See **zircon.**

zirconite. A name for brown **zircon.**

zircon rose. European term for rose-cut zircon.

"zircon spinel." Synthetic blue spinel.

Zirctone. A trademarked name for **bluish-green synthetic sapphire.**

Zn. Abbr. for zinc.

zodiacal or **astral stones.** Gems believed to be peculiarly and mystically related to the zodiacal signs. These are: Aquarius (Jan. 21-Feb. 21) **garnet**; Pisces (Feb. 21-March21) **amethyst**; Aries (March 21-April 20) **bloodstone**; Taurus (April 20-May 21) **sapphire**; Gemini (May 21-June 21) **agate**; Cancer (June 21-July 22) **emerald**; Leo (July 22-August 22) **onyx**; Virgo (Aug. 22-Sept. 22) **carnelian**; Libra (Sept. 22-Oct. 23) **chrysolite**; Scorpio (Oct. 23-Nov. 21) **beryl**; Sagittarius (Nov. 21-Dec. 21) **topaz**; Capricorn (Dec. 21-Jan. 21) **ruby.**

zoisite (zo'-iss-site). A transparent to opaque mineral species, a member of the epidote group. Its principal varieties are a transparent, highly trichroic blue; a massive, semitransparent to semitranslucent light red to purplish red, often mottled with gray or white **(thulite)**; and massive white to grayish green to yellowish green (**saussurite**). Highly attractive and desirable faceted stones are fashioned from the transparent blue material, which is sold under the trade name **Tanzanite**. Thulite is used for cabochons and sometimes for cameos and intaglios. **Saussurite** finds occasional use as a jade substitute. Chemical composition, a calcium-aluminum silicate ($Ca_2Al_3Si_3O_{13}$); crystal system, orthorhombic; hardness, 6 to 6½ (transparent blue, 6½ to 7); specific gravity, 3.25 to 3.27 (transparent blue, 3.35 to 3.55); refractive index, 1.700-1.706 (transparent blue, 1.691-1.704); birefringence, .013. Sources: Tanzania (transparent blue material discovered in 1967); Sau-Alp, Carinthia; Salsburg, Austria; Zillerthal, Austrian Tyrol; Trentino, Italy; Zermat, Switzerland; Gefrees, Bavaria; Ross-shire, Scotland; Baja California, Mexico; Hampshire and Franklin Counties, Massachusetts; Chester Co., Pennsylvania; and Ducktown, Tennessee.

zoning. Straight growth lines of bands with definite angles often seen in crystals. If present in gemstones, this is an indication that the stone is of natural origin.

zonite. A name which has been used in Arizona for locally occurring jasper or chert of various colors.

zonochlorite (zo-no-klor'ite). A green banded pebble found in Lake Superior region. **Prehnite** similar to **chlorastrolite**.

Zr. Abbr. for zirconium.

zylonite. Same as **xylonite**.

THE GEMOLOGICAL INSTITUTE OF AMERICA

The Gemological Institute of America, known to most jewelers as GIA or "the Institute," is the educational, research and testing center of the jewelry industry. The purpose of this endowed nonprofit organization is to provide professional training and other services for jewelers and other gem enthusiasts. GIA was founded in 1931 by Robert M. Shipley. When he retired in 1952, Richard T. Liddicoat, Jr., became Executive Director.

GIA offers a number of technical services other than education. These services include publishing, laboratory services, and the development of diamond, gem-testing and sales instruments for the jewelry profession.

GIA Educational Activities

The Gemological Institute's training is provided on a home-study or correspondence basis; by classroom instruction; or partially by correspondence and partially in residence. Courses are offered on diamonds, colored stones, gem identification, pearls, jewelry retailing, creative jewelry display, and jewelry designing. After successful completion of the Diamond Course, the *Diamond Certificate* is awarded, or if the Colored Stone and Gem-Identification Courses are completed, the *Colored-Stone Certificate* is awarded. When all three are completed successfully by home study, the *Gemologist Diploma* is conferred. The *Graduate Gemologist Diploma* by home study is awarded to students who have completed the requirements for the Gemologist Diploma including two one-week resident classes in Diamond Appraising and Gem Identification. The GIA *Graduate Gemologist Diploma in Residence* is awarded after successful completion of the full-time Resident Training Program, a 26-week, 780-hour intensive course consisting of the Diamond Program and the Colored-Stone and Gem-Identification Program. A Jewelry Arts Program of equal length was started in 1978.

One-week classes in Diamond Grading, Gem Identification, Jewelry Design, and two-week classes in Wax Carving and Modeling as well as Diamond Setting and Jewelry Repair are conducted in major cities throughout the United States; some one-week classes are given abroad.

GIA Gem Trade Laboratory

The GIA Gem Trade Laboratories in New York, Santa Monica, and Los Angeles provide complete testing and grading facilities for jewelers and the public. In addition to routine testing, grading, and determination of extent and cause of damage, the laboratories develop identification methods for new gemstone substitutes or artificial enhancement of natural stones. Services are performed for many organizations, including the U.S. Customs, the FBI, Better Business Bureaus, the Jewelers' Vigilance Committee, Chambers of Commerce, and insurance companies.

Special Instruments
A third function of the Institute is the design and manufacture of professional gem-testing and gem-merchandising instruments. These are manufactured and marketed by a wholly owned subsidiary, Gem Instruments, Inc. Among the equipment manufactured by GEM familiar to most jewelers are the Deluxe Mark V Gemolite, Custom Mark V Gemolite, Gem Detector, Diamond Grader, Illuminator Polariscope, Duplex Refractometer, DiamondLite Spectroscope Unit, DiamondLux, ProportionScope, Dichroscope, Mini-Lab and Diamond Pen.

Publishing
A fourth important service is publishing reference works and *Gems & Gemology*, a professional quarterly in the field of gems and related subjects that has been published since 1934. A number of books and pamphlets also have been published. In addition to this book, some of the titles include: *The Jewelers' Manual, Diamond Dictionary, Handbook of Gem Identification*, and *Diamonds ... Famous, Notable and Unique*.

Technical and Teaching Staff
The technical and teaching staff of the Institute consists of specialists who are trained and experienced in one or more of the fields of jewelry marketing, the sciences, education, and designing. Its policy-setting body is its Board of Governors, elected annually from the Sustaining Membership, plus scientists, educators and other specialists. The administrative head since 1952, is the President, Richard T. Liddicoat, Jr., who directs the organization from its Santa Monica headquarters. The Board of Governors and other officers, except for the President and Ray Ouderkirk, the Assistant Secretary, serve without compensation. Many GIA staff members are widely known gemologists and other scientists. Vice Presidents Robert Crowningshield and Bertram Krashes direct GIA's two New York Gem Trade Laboratories. Paul Holt directs educational activities. Eunice Miles is Student Counsellor. Laboratory assistants and instructors include John Dible, David Fowler, David Hargett, Ingrid Nolte, Margaret Nowak, Richard Robinson, Robert Saling, Tom Yonelunas. Among a staff of over 100 at the Santa Monica Headquarters are Gemology Resident Course Supervisor, Robert A. Earnest; Gem Trade Laboratory Supervisor, Charles Fryer, who is assisted by Karin

Hurwit and James Sweaney; Home Study Course Supervisor, Dennis Foltz; Research Scientist, Dr. Vincent Manson; A. Richard Shalberg, Supervisor of the Jewelry Arts Training Program; J. Michael Allbritton, Supervisor of the one-week traveling class program, plus instructors Jan Arnold, William Boyajian, Archie Curtis, Mark Ebert, Douglas Hucker, Loren Leong, William Levine, James Lucey, Janice Mack, Raymond Page, Betsy Schuster, Rick Shaw and Sharon Thompson. Others in Santa Monica include Jackie Becker, Wax Carving & Modeling and Jewelry Display Instructor; Jill Fisher, Pearl Instructor and J. Burton Streeter, Jewelry Retailing Instructor. Walter Brueggeman is Building Manager; Michael Waitzman is Operations Coordinator and T. J. Barrows is Education Administrator. Margaret Orozco handles the GIA Bookstore, printing and shipping departments and Ray Ouderkirk is the comptroller and head of the Accounting Department. The downtown Los Angeles Gem Trade Laboratory is supervised by Sally Ehmke, who is assisted by Gary Roskin and Sheryl Stewart.

The policy-setting body of the Institute is the Board of Governors, elected annually. The present Chairman is Arthur F. Gleim; George Kaplan, Vice Chairman; Stanley E. Church, Secretary-Treasurer. Other members of the Board include Arnold Bockstruck; Carleton G. Broer, Jr.; John Penn Fix; Kurt Nassau, Ph.D.; Henry B. Platt; James Rudder; Harold Seburn; George J. Sloan; Robert E. Spratford and Edward B. Tiffany.

Facilities

GIA, Gem Instruments and GIA's Gem Trade Laboratories combined have six locations. Its new modern 50,000-square foot headquarters building on 3½ acres is located at 1660 Stewart Street, Santa Monica, California 90404. A new building at 1735 Stewart Street houses Education Administration, Accounting, the Registrar's Office, Personnel, Printing, Shipping, Purchasing, Gem Instruments Sales, a bookstore and the student and faculty cafeteria in 34,000 square feet. Gem Instrument Manufacturing occupies 25,000 square feet around the corner on Colorado Boulevard. The home-study courses are conducted from the headquarters. The Eastern Division, including two Gem Trade Laboratories, maintains offices and classrooms at 580 Fifth Avenue, New York, New York 10036. Instructors from both facilities conduct classes throughout the nation and elsewhere. Full-time resident classes are given in Santa Monica and New York. A fourth Gem Trade Laboratory is located at 606 South Olive Street, Suite 910, Los Angeles, California 90014.